GLOBAL HISTORY OF THE PRESENT
**Series editor | Nicholas Guyatt**

In the Global History of the Present series, historians address the upheavals in world history since 1989, as we have lurched from the Cold War to the War on Terror. Each book considers the unique story of an individual country or region, refuting grandiose claims of 'the end of history', and linking local narratives to international developments.

Lively and accessible, these books are ideal introductions to the contemporary politics and history of a diverse range of countries.

By bringing a historical perspective to recent debates and events, from democracy and terrorism to nationalism and globalization, the series challenges assumptions about the past and the present.

**Published**

Nicholas Guyatt is assistant professor University in Canada.

D1410177

**About the author**

Kerem Öktem is research fellow at the European Studies Centre, St Antony's College, and teaches the politics of the Middle East at the Oriental Institute. He read modern Middle Eastern studies at Oxford, where he also completed his DPhil thesis at the School of Geography in 2006. In the thesis, he explored the destruction of imperial space in the Ottoman Empire and the subsequent construction of an exclusively Turkish national territory. His research interests range from the history of nationalism, ethno-politics and minority rights in Turkey to debates on history, memory and trauma, and to Turkey's conflicted relations with Armenia and Greece. More recently, he has started a research project on the emergence of Islam as a central discursive category in European public debates.

# Turkey since 1989: Angry Nation

Kerem Öktem

Fernwood Publishing
HALIFAX | WINNIPEG

Zed Books
LONDON | NEW YORK

*Turkey since 1989: Angry Nation* was first published in 2011

Published in Canada by Fernwood Publishing Ltd, 32 Oceanvista Lane, Black Point, Nova Scotia B0J 1B0 <www.fernwoodpublishing.ca>

Published in the rest of the world by Zed Books Ltd, 7 Cynthia Street, London N1 9JF, UK and Room 400, 175 Fifth Avenue, New York, NY 10010, USA <www.zedbooks.co.uk>

FSC
www.fsc.org
MIX
Paper from
responsible sources
FSC® C013604

Set in OurType Arnhem and Futura Bold by Ewan Smith, London
Cover designed by Andrew Corbett
Index: <ed.emery@thefreeuniversity.net>
Printed and bound in Great Britain by Antony Rowe, Chippenham and Eastbourne

Distributed in the USA exclusively by Palgrave Macmillan, a division of St Martin's Press, LLC, 175 Fifth Avenue, New York, NY 10010.

A catalogue record for this book is available from the British Library.
US CIP data are available from the Library of Congress.

Library and Archives Canada Cataloguing in Publication:
Öktem, Kerem, 1969-
    Angry nation: Turkey since 1989 / Kerem Oktem.
(Global history of the present)
Includes bibliographical references.
ISBN 978-1-55266-426-1
    1. Turkey--History--1960-. 2. Turkey--Politics and government--1980-.
I. Title. II. Series: Global history of the present
DR603.O37 2011    956.103'9    C2010-908052-1

ISBN  978 1 84813 210 8  hb (Zed Books)
ISBN  978 1 84813 211 5  pb (Zed Books)
ISBN  978 1 84813 212 2  eb (Zed Books)
ISBN  978 1 55266 426 1  (Fernwood Publishing)

# Contents

# Acknowledgements

Many friends and colleagues have supported me in the rather daunting effort to make sense of Turkey's contemporary history. Ayşe Kadıoğlu (Istanbul) and Dimitar Bechev (Sofia) have been intellectual soulmates and meticulous readers of the final draft. Harun Yılmaz (Oxford), Ipek Yosmaoğlu (Chicago), Nora Fisher Onar, Deniz Yazgan and Sevin Turan (all Istanbul) have commented on various drafts of the book. May Dabbagh (Dubai), Rahul Rao (London), Gustaf Arrhenius (Stockholm) and Leila Vignal (Rennes), were all in Oxford at various stages of writing the book, and their input and criticism were crucial in every sense. Ceren Zeynep Ak, Karabekir Akkoyunlu (London) and Adam Becker (New York) have helped me greatly with the final touches.

Ece Temelkuran (Istanbul) was a true inspiration for courageous investigative journalism, Osman Can (Ankara) an indispensable intellectual companion, especially in the critical discussion of Turkey's judiciary, and Abdullah Demirbaş, district mayor in Diyarbakır, an impressive role model for Kurdish–Turkish friendship in times of war and peace. To Thierry Fabre (Marseille) I owe a couple of last-minute but crucial suggestions on the issues of fear, anger and rage. The Maison Française in Oxford, and its former director Alexis Tadié, provided me with an intellectually challenging environment. My housemates Deniz Bostancı and Dimitris Antoniou gave me much-needed friendship and respite from writing, Justin Smith was an indispensable anchor, while my sister Ayşe Öktem and my aunt Fatma Sayman supported me in exploring the intersections between our family history and the history of contemporary Turkey.

Many colleagues and friends at the University of Oxford helped me to develop the argument for this book. I am particularly grateful to Kalypso Nicolaidis and to Othon Anastasakis from the South East European Studies Programme (SEESOX) of St Antony's College, with whom I have discussed all matters Turkish throughout much of the last six years, and to Mehmet Karlı for his indefatigable criticism. Celia Kerslake and

Philip Robins of the Oriental Institute introduced me to different aspects of Turkey's engagement with modernity, while Reem Abou-el Fadl reminded me of the importance of comparative analysis and alerted me to the evils of an isolated study of Turkey's politics. The administrators of SEESOX and the European Studies Centre (ESC), Julie Adams and Anne-Laure Guillermain, were always ready to help when time and temper were running short. Thanks to my mentor Timothy Garton Ash of the ESC, I already had a sense of what a history of contemporary Turkey could look like, when Nicholas Guyatt and Ken Barlow of Zed Books first approached me. They proved to be wonderful editors indeed, and they continued to bear with me through the often erratic process of writing a 'history of the present', as this very history stubbornly kept unfolding, defying any end point.

Yet more friends and colleagues helped me during my research in Turkey and its many diasporas. Gökhan Yücel opened many doors for me in the long corridors of Ankara's state bureaucracy. Susan Pattie and Levon Chilingirian (London) generously helped me pass through numerous boundaries separating Armenians and Turks, both politically and emotionally. My Cypriot friends Olga Demetriou, Murat Erdal and Sossie Kasbarian ensured that the 'forgotten revolution' of the Turkish Cypriots in 2003 did not go unnoticed, at least not in this book, and Filiz Çelik (Swansea) introduced me to the mountains of Dersim, their mournful past and their remarkable residents. Baskın and Feyhan Oran (Ankara and Bodrum) were loving and critical, encouraging and forceful, and their friendship helped me to go beyond the fears and restrictions that have shaped so much of the scholarship within Turkish studies.

And finally, I would like to thank the men and women, Turks, Kurds and Armenians, Alevis and Sunnis, Muslims and Christians, Islamists, social democrats and socialists, scholars, politicians, activists and writers, who gave me generous insights into their political and private lives and shared with me their intimate knowledge of what the film director Nuri Bilge Ceylan called 'my beautiful and lonely country, which I love passionately'. It is their unadulterated frankness and determination to make their country a better and less lonely place which have made this book possible. The responsibility for all omissions, ambiguities and mistakes rests, of course, solely with the author.

# Overview of political parties in Turkey

| | Political tradition | Party name in Turkish | Party name in English | Established | Closed down | |
|---|---|---|---|---|---|---|
| ITC | Proto-Kemalist | İttihat ve Terakki Cemiyeti | Committee of Union and Progress (CUP) | 1906 | 1920 | Court martial |
| **CHP** | Kemalist | Cumhuriyet Halk Partisi | Republican People's Party (RPP) | 1923 | [1981] | 1980 military coup Relaunched in 1992 |
| HP | Kemalist | Halkçı Parti | Popular Party | 1983 | 1985 | Merged with SODEP |
| SODEP | Social democrat | Sosyal Demokrasi Partisi | Social Democracy Party | 1983 | 1985 | Merged with HP |
| **SHP** | Social democrat | Sosyal Demokrat Halkçı Parti | Social Democrat Popular Party | 1985 | — | |
| **DSP** | Social democrat | Demokrat Sol Parti | Democratic Left Party | 1985 | — | |
| **TKP** | Left/socialist | Türkiye Komünist Partisi | Communist Party of Turkey | 1920 | 1921 | Illegal since 1921 Re-established in 1987 |
| TIP | Left/socialist | Türkiye İşçi Partisi | Labour Party of Turkey | 1961 | 1971 | 1971 military coup |
| **ÖDP** | Left/socialist | Özgürlük ve Demokrasi Partisi | Freedom and Solidarity Party | 1993 | — | Split in 2009 |
| **DP** | Conservative | Demokrat Parti | Democrat Party | 1946 | 1960 | 1960 military coup Re-established in 2002 and 2007 |
| AP | Conservative | Adalet Partisi | Justice Party | 1961 | 1981 | 1980 military coup Relaunched in 1992 |
| DYP | Conservative | Doğru Yol Partisi | True Path Party (TPP) | 1983 | 2007 | Voluntary liquidation Re-established in 2007 |

| Abbr. | Ideology | Turkish name | English name | Founded | Closed | Fate |
|---|---|---|---|---|---|---|
| ANAP | Conservative | Anavatan Partisi | Motherland Party | 1983 | 2009 | Voluntary liquidation and merger with DP |
| MNP | Islamist/national view | Milli Nizam Partisi | National Order Party | 1970 | 1971 | 1971 military coup Constitutional Court |
| MSP | Islamist/nat. view | Milli Selamet Partisi | National Salvation Party | 1972 | 1981 | 1980 military coup |
| RP | Islamist/nat. view | Refah Partisi | Welfare Party | 1983 | 1998 | Constitutional Court |
| FP | Islamist/nat. view | Fazilet Partisi | Virtue Party | 1997 | 2001 | Constitutional Court |
| **SP** | Islamist/nat. view | Saadet Partisi | Felicity Party | 2001 | — | |
| **AKP** | Post-Islamist | Adalet ve Kalkınma Partisi | Justice and Development Party | 2001 | — | |
| CKMP | Nationalist | Cumhuriyet Köylü Millet Partisi | Republican Peasants Nation Party | 1958 | 1969 | Voluntary liquidation Becomes MHP |
| **MHP** | Nationalist | Milliyetçi Hareket Partisi | Nationalist Action Party | 1969 | [1981] | 1980 military coup Relaunched in 1993 |
| MDP | Nationalist | Milliyetçi Demokrasi Partisi | Nationalist Democracy Party | 1983 | 1986 | Pro-coup party Voluntary liquidation |
| MÇP | Nationalist | Miliyetçi Çalışma Partisi | Nationalist Working Party | 1983 | 1993 | Voluntary liquidation |
| **BBP** | Nationalist/ Islamist | Büyük Birlik Partisi | Great Unity Party | 1993 | — | |
| HEP | Pro-Kurdish | Halkın Emek Partisi | People's Labour Party | 1990 | 1993 | Constitutional Court |
| DEP | Pro-Kurdish | Demokrasi Partisi | Democracy Party | 1993 | 1994 | Constitutional Court |
| HADEP | Pro-Kurdish | Halkın Demokrasi Partisi | People's Democracy Party | 1994 | 2003 | Constitutional Court |
| DEHAP | Pro-Kurdish | Demokratik Halk Partisi | Democratic People's Party | 1997 | 2005 | Constitutional Court |
| DTP | Pro-Kurdish | Demokratik Toplum Partisi | Democratic Society Party | 2005 | 2009 | Constitutional Court |
| **BDP** | Pro-Kurdish | Barış ve Demokrasi Partisi | Peace and Democracy Party | 2009 | — | |

Currently active parties are shown in **bold**.

# Key moments in Turkey's history

## Turkey before 1980

1839  Announcement of the Tanzimat, the era of reorganization, i.e. military and legal reforms.

1875  Ottoman Empire defaults on its European creditors.

1876  First period of constitutional rule, soon aborted by Sultan Abdülhamit.

1878  The British Empire acquires Cyprus from the Ottomans.

1908  Constitutional revolution, Young Turks reinstate the constitution of 1876.

1912–13 and 1914  Balkan Wars end the presence of the Ottoman Empire in the Balkans ('Turkey in Europe'); 400,000 Muslims flee to the capital.

1914  Start of First World War.

1915  Gallipoli campaign, British and Commonwealth forces lose against the Ottoman army.

1915–16 Armenian genocide executed by parts of the Ottoman army and bureaucracy, under the direction of the Committee of Union and Progress.

15 May 1919  Occupation of Smyrna by Greek troops. The event sparks national feelings among Muslims and Turks and triggers the 'War of Independence'. Greek troops foray deep into Anatolian territory.

23 April 1920  The Turkish Grand National Assembly (Türkiye Büyük Millet Meclisi), the parliament of the nationalist movement, has its constitutive meeting in the future capital Ankara.

1 November 1922  Abolition of the Sultanate clears the way for the emerging Turkish Republic.

9 September 1922  Turkish troops march into Smyrna and terminate the Greek occupation. The great fire of Smyrna consumes the Greek, Armenian and central quarters of the city.

24 July 1923  The Treaty of Lausanne formalizes the conditions of Turkey's statehood and of the population exchange between Greece and Turkey.

29 October 1923  Establishment of the Turkish Republic. Mustafa Kemal becomes first president.

3 March 1924  The Turkish Grand National Assembly decides the

abolition of the Caliphate and thereby ends one of the most important institutions of Sunni Islam.

February 1925   A rebellion under Sheikh Sait Piran in Bingöl and Diyarbakır marks the first Kurdish uprising against the republican government.

1924–1930s   Period of top-down bureaucratic reforms and legal changes (also called Kemalist reforms or revolutions).

1931   Turkey officially becomes a one-party state with the Republican People's Party and Mustafa Kemal as 'eternal leader'.

18 July 1932   The Directorate of Religious Affairs (Diyanet) mandates the Arabic call to prayer (Ezan) to be delivered in the Turkish language.

October 1933   Mustafa Kemal delivers his 'Speech' (Nutuk), in which he gives a personal account of the history of the War of Independence.

25 December 1935   The 'Tunceli Law' prepares the legal framework for the destruction of Alevi tribesmen in the province of Dersim.

March 1937–December 1938   Ethnocide of Alevis in the eastern province of Dersim (later renamed Tunceli). The Turkish air force and Mustafa Kemal's adopted daughter, the female pilot Sabiha Gökçen, bombard towns and villages, while soldiers attack the villagers. Tens of thousands of men, women and children are tortured and killed.

15 November 1937   Seyit Rıza, the leader of the Dersim tribes, is executed together with his son, despite his old age. During the course of the year, all leading Dersim tribesmen are executed.

10 November 1938   Mustafa Kemal dies. He is succeeded by Ismet İnönü as second president of the republic.

September 1939   Start of Second World War. Turkey remains neutral until the end of the war.

November 1942   Wealth tax levied on all non-Muslim citizens. Many Armenians, Greeks and Jews, who fail to pay exorbitant tax dues, are deported to eastern Anatolia.

February 1945   Turkey joins Allied forces in a symbolic gesture and declares war on Germany.

21 July 1946   First multiparty elections take place with allegations of vote-rigging and heavy manipulation. The Republican People's Party remains in power.

12 March 1947   The USA declares the Truman Doctrine and supports Turkey and Greece as front-line states against Russia.

9 August 1949   Turkey becomes member of the Council of Europe.

14 May 1950   Election of the Democrat Party under Prime Minister Adnan Menderes brings to an end three decades of Kemalist rule.

16 June 1950   The Arabic call to prayer is reinstated by the Democrat government.

18 February 1952   Turkey enters NATO and officially becomes part of the 'West'.

6/7 September 1955   September Pogroms (Septemvriana) against non-Muslims devastate large parts of Istanbul and trigger a wave of emigration by Istanbul Greeks.

31 July 1959   Turkey applies for membership of the European Economic Community. The EEC initiates an interim association agreement before full membership.

27 May 1960   The first military coup after the introduction of democratic elections in 1946 goes hand in hand with the drafting of a new constitution that strengthens military control over politics.

19 August 1960   Cyprus becomes an independent republic, after almost a century of British colonial rule. Turkey and Greece are among the guarantors of the new republic.

16 September 1961   Former prime minister Adnan Menderes is executed on behest of the putschist generals, after a show trial and a hate campaign in the state media and newspapers.

31 October 1961   Turkey and Germany sign immigration treaty, marking the start of mass immigration from Turkey to western European countries.

12 September 1963   Turkey and the European Economic Community sign the Ankara Agreement, which sets out a time frame for Turkey's gradual integration into the EEC and the realization of a customs union. The goal of full membership is spelled out in the agreement.

1963   Conflicts between Greek Cypriot nationalists (EOKA) and Turkish nationalists lead to the establishment of Turkish safe zones and ethnic cantons. The capital (Levkosia or Nicosia) is divided into a Turkish part in the north and a Greek part in the south.

20 February 1965   Democracy is restored with the election of the Justice Party under Prime Minister Süleyman Demirel. The Labour Party of Turkey also enters parliament.

16 February 1969   Bloody Sunday; three student leaders killed in Istanbul's Beyazıt Square.

12 March 1971   With a military memorandum, the acting generals force Prime Minister Demirel to form a new cabinet.

30 March 1972   Massacre of the student leaders of the People's Liberation Army in Kızıldere.

6 May 1972   Deniz Gezmiş, leader of the socialist youth movement, is executed in Ankara, together with two of his companions.

14 October 1973   Elections produce unstable coalition governments, while political violence becomes normalized.

29 October 1973   The first Bosporus Bridge connecting Europe and Asia is inaugurated in Istanbul.

20 July 1974   Turkish forces invade Cyprus to protect the Turkish-Cypriot community. A second invasion results in the occupation of a third of the island by Turkish forces.

1 May 1977   Bloody May Day; thirty-four demonstrators are killed in Istanbul's Taksim Square by covert security agents acting on behalf of the state.

19 December 1978   Maraş massacres against Alevis. More than one hundred people are confirmed dead officially, while eyewitnesses speak of up to five hundred deaths.

27 December 1979   Memorandum of general staff warning the government to re-establish order and security.

## Turkey since 1980

24 January 1980   Important decisions on Turkey's economic future, also called the '24 January Decisions'.

9 July 1980   The military descends on the eastern Black Sea town of Fatsa in a show of strength against the socialist mayor and his local experiment of a socialist democracy.

6 September 1980   Massive protests against the declaration of Jerusalem as Israel's capital in the conservative city of Konya. Used by the generals as a pretext for the looming intervention.

12 September 1980   Military coup under the leadership of General Kenan Evren. Evren becomes president and signs a warrant for the torture of hundreds of thousands of citizens.

9 November 1982   Generals impose a new constitution that severely limits human rights after a tightly controlled referendum held under military law.

1980–83   Reign of the military. Hundreds of thousands are tortured and many executed extralegally as well as imprisoned. The terror of the armed forces and police is particularly grave in the Kurdish provinces.

6 November 1983   First post-coup elections lead to the victory of the Motherland Party, a choice not condoned by the generals. Turgut Özal becomes prime minister.

15 November 1983   Turkish Cypriot leaders declare the 'Turkish Republic of Northern Cyprus' with the support of Ankara.

1984   The Kurdistan Workers' Party (PKK) starts a guerrilla war against the Turkish Republic with the aim of establishing an independent Kurdistan. The state responds with heavy military campaigns.

17 July 1986   The Turkish Human Rights Association is established.

28 January 1987   The Turkish Grand National Assembly ratifies the rights of individuals to apply to the European Court of Human Rights.

14 April 1987   Turkey applies for membership of the European Community.

17 May 1987   Women's march in Kadıköy, Istanbul. First major public demonstration after the coup in western Turkey.

3 July 1988   Second Bosporus Bridge (named after Fatih Sultan Mehmet) is inaugurated by Prime Minister Turgut Özal.

October 1988   Turkey's first shopping mall, called Galleria, opens in the Istanbul suburb of Ataköy.

May 1989   Bulgarian Turks are allowed to leave Bulgaria after a five-year campaign of enforced assimilation. Around 300,000 rush to the Turkish border. The Zhivkov government euphemistically calls this flight the 'grand excursion'.

26 May 1989   First private Turkish TV channel, STAR 1, starts broadcasting from Germany despite a ban on private broadcasting in Turkey. Many other channels follow in the coming years.

9 November 1989   The fall of the wall in Berlin marks the end of communist rule in Europe. In Turkey, Turgut Özal is elected the first civilian president of the Turkish Republic. A period of proactive foreign policy begins.

20 December 1989   The European Commission postpones a decision on Turkey's membership application on the grounds of the political situation but reinstates the goal of full membership.

2 August 1990   President Turgut Özal supports US war efforts in the First Gulf War with an eye on increasing Turkey's role in the Middle East.

5 July 1991   The Kurdish activist and political leader Vedat Aydın is killed by counter-terrorism operatives in Diyarbakır. Dozens are killed during his funeral, when counter-terrorism forces open fire on the crowd.

25 June 1992   Establishment of the Black Sea Economic Corporation Council with its seat in Istanbul.

19 August 1992   A PKK unit attacks the Kurdish town of Şırnak. In response, army units raze the town.

24 January 1993   The investigative journalist Uğur Mumcu, who was researching allegations of the 'deep state' (see Preface), is assassinated.

17 February 1993   The commander of the Gendarmerie, General Eşref Bitlis, known for his efforts to find a solution to the Kurdish problem, is killed in a plane crash under suspicious circumstances.

17 April 1993   President Turgut Özal dies unexpectedly of heart failure,

sparking rumours that he might have been poisoned. He is succeeded by Süleyman Demirel.

25 June 1993    Tansu Çiller becomes Turkey's first female prime minister.

2 July 1993    The Sıvas Massacre results in the incineration of thirty-five mostly Alevi and leftist activists and intellectuals in the eastern Anatolian town of Sıvas after attacks by an angry Islamist mob.

27 March 1994    The Islamist Welfare Party wins the local elections in major cities like Istanbul and Ankara with around 20 per cent of the votes, after the two social democrat parties fail to act together.

3 November 1994    Tansu Çiller becomes the first Turkish prime minister to visit Israel. Start of a strategic military and security partnership between the two countries.

1995    The Kurdish provinces are effectively ruled by counter-terrorism officers and covert operatives. Thousands of activists are detained, tortured and killed.

12 March 1995    'Gazi events'; police attack and kill Alevi youth in Istanbul's Gazi neighbourhood.

26 December 1995    Sixteen teenagers are apprehended and tortured in the Aegean town of Manisa.

December 1995/January 1996    A dispute over the uninhabited islet of Imia/Kardak in the Aegean brings Turkey and Greece close to war.

1 January 1996    Turkey enters customs union with the European Community.

June 1996    The Manisa trials begin and expose the torture of innocent university students by regular policemen.

5 November 1996    The Susurluk incident exposes links between police, mafia and crime networks.

30 January 1997    'Jerusalem night' in the Ankara suburb of Sincan is seen as a provocation by the military.

1 February 1997    The citizens' initiative 'One minute of darkness for enduring light' takes on the character of a mass protest with several million participants all over the country, in part as reaction to Susurluk.

28 February 1997    Bloodless military intervention against 'Islamist' reaction and the Islamist government of Necmettin Erbakan, also called the 'Postmodern Coup'.

30 June 1997    Prime Minister Erbakan resigns after pressure from military and opposition.

12/13 December 1997    European Council in Luxembourg refuses to classify Turkey as candidate state.

16 January 1998    The Constitutional Court bans the Welfare Party of Necmettin Erbakan. The Virtue Party, established a year earlier, comes in its stead.

15 February 1999   The leader of the Kurdistan Workers' Party (PKK), Abdullah Öcalan, is captured in Kenya.

17 August 1999   During the Marmara earthquake east of Istanbul, at least 17,000 are killed. A large proportion of Turkey's industrial heartland is destroyed.

10 December 1999   European Council meeting in Helsinki declares Turkey a candidate for EU accession on equal footing with other candidate countries.

16 May 2000   Ahmet Necdet Sezer, chair of the Constitutional Court, is elected president by the Turkish parliament.

November 2000   First signs of a financial crisis; the Turkish lira is devalued by a third.

February 2001   A stand-off between President Sezer and Prime Minister Ecevit sparks a severe economic crisis, which leads to the collapse of the banking sector and the destruction of a million jobs.

3 March 2001   Prime Minister Ecevit appoints former World Bank vice-president as minister of economy.

22 June 2001   Constitutional Court bans Virtue Party. Virtue is succeeded by the Felicity (Saadet Partisi). Reformist members establish the Justice and Development Party (AKP).

11 September 2001   The 9/11 attacks on New York's World Trade Center.

1 January 2002   New Civil Code comes into force and introduces complete legal equality of men and women.

3 August 2002   The Turkish Grand National Assembly abolishes the death penalty in peacetime.

3 November 2002   Justice and Development Party (AKP) wins landslide victory.

11 November 2002   The United Nations announces a new plan for a comprehensive solution in Cyprus (also called the Annan Plan).

12 December 2002   European Council meeting in Copenhagen sets timetable for start of accession negotiations.

27 February 2003   February Uprising: close to 80,000 Turkish Cypriots march in Nicosia to demonstrate in favour of the Annan Plan, a united Republic of Cyprus made up of two constituent states, and against the Turkish Cypriot leader Rauf Denktash.

1 March 2003   Parliament refuses authorization for the use of Turkish territory and airspace by US troops for the invasion of Iraq.

9 March 2003   Recep Tayyip Erdoğan is elected in a by-election in Siirt province. Five days later he becomes prime minister.

23 April 2003   After massive protests in the north, the Turkish Cypriot leader Rauf Denktash opens the first border crossing between the Republic of Cyprus and the Turkish north.

15 and 20 November 2003   Istanbul attacks on British interests, banks and synagogues in Istanbul by a group with al-Qaeda contacts;

fifty-seven residents including the British consul general, Roger Short, are killed.

24 April 2004   Referendum on the unification of Cyprus. Turkish Cypriots vote for, Greek Cypriots against, reunification.

1 May 2004   Cyprus joins the European Union with eight eastern European countries and Malta.

December 2004   European Council agrees to open EU accession negotiations with Turkey in 2005.

1 January 2005   New Turkish lira is introduced with six zeros stripped from denominations.

3 October 2005   Turkey and the European Union begin membership negotiations. The first six chapters of the Aquis are opened.

9 November 2005   The Şemdinli affair; gendarmerie officers are caught in the act of committing a terrorist attack.

10 November 2005   In the case of Leyla Şahin v. Turkey, European Court of Human Rights decides that Turkey can exclude women with headscarves from university education.

5 February 2006   A sixteen-year-old high-school student kills the Italian Catholic Father Santoro of Trabzon.

17 May 2006   Alpaslan Aslan, member of an extreme nationalist-Islamist group, murders the prominent judge Mustafa Yücel Özbilgin, allegedly for his anti-headscarf rulings.

3 July 2006   Turkish parliament passes Anti-Terror Law that leads to the detention of hundreds of 'stone-throwing' Kurdish children.

11 December 2006   Foreign minister of the European Union freezes eight acquis chapters over Turkey's refusal to open its ports and airports to Cypriot vessels.

20 January 2007   Armenian-Turkish journalist and public intellectual Hrant Dink is assassinated by Ogün Samast in front of the offices of the Armenian *Agos* newspaper.

23 January 2007   100,000 mourners attend Hrant Dink's funeral, which turns into a statement of civil disobedience against the manipulations and murders of the deep state.

April 2007   Republican marches against the presidential candidacies of Erdoğan and Gül.

18 April 2007   Three Christian missionaries are tortured and murdered in the south-eastern city of Malatya.

24 April 2007   E-memorandum; the website of the Chief of the General Staff declares that the election of a non-secular president would be considered a reason to start a military intervention.

22 July 2007   AKP wins early parliamentary elections.

28 August 2007   Turkish parliament elects Abdullah Gül as president.

30 July 2008   Constitutional Court narrowly decides not to close down the AKP, Turkey's governing party.

October 2008   The effects of the global financial crisis reach Turkey. Over the course of the next twelve months, the economy contracts by a massive 12 per cent.

20 October 2008   First Ergenekon trial of retired generals, journalists and university rectors begins in the Silivri courthouse.

May 2009   The AKP government initiates a 'Kurdish Opening', whose content remains very vague. Opposition parties – Republican People's Party and National Action Party – accuse the AKP of splitting the country.

9 July 2009   Legal changes allow for serving officers to be tried in civilian courts in cases of organized crime and military interventions.

10 October 2009   Turkey and Armenia sign protocols on improving relations. Both parliaments, however, refuse to ratify the protocols.

January 2010   Investigations into and court case against the 'Sledgehammer', 'Blonde Girl' and 'Moonlight' conspiracies to overthrow the elected AKP government. Retired and serving officers are heard in a civilian court.

April 2010   Start of the constitutional reform debate in the Turkish Grand National Assembly.

31 May 2010   The ferry *Mavi Marmara*, laden with food and technical supplies for the Gaza Strip, is raided by Israeli Defence Forces. Israeli commandos kill nine activists of the 'Humanitarian Help Foundation' (IHH). Political relations between Turkey and Israel are severely disrupted.

June 2010   Turkey's economic growth accelerates to almost 12 per cent.

12 September 2010   The government's proposal for constitutional reform is accepted with a vote of 58 per cent in a nationwide referendum, after a divisive campaign. The changes open the way for the trial of the generals and torturers of the 1980 coup. Hundreds of court cases are opened.

15 September 2010   The European Court of Human Rights convicts Turkey for the murder of Hrant Dink and for failing to grant a fair trial. The government does not appeal against the decision.

19 September 2010   An Armenian apostolic mass is held on the Ahtamar island of Van in the reconstructed Surp Khach (Holy Cross) Church. The first such service since 1915, the event is visited by thousands, but also boycotted by some Armenian diaspora organizations, which believe this to be a publicity stunt on the part of the Turkish government.

October 2010   Cross-party talks on a new constitution begin.

# Note on orthography and pronunciation

This book uses the modern Turkish orthography based on Latin letters. The following letters differ from the English alphabet and are pronounced as shown below:

Ç, ç    'ch' as in 'China'

ğ      when at the end of a word, or before a consonant, lengthens the preceding vowel; when between two vowels, not pronounced

I, ı    the sound represented by 'a' in 'among'

Ö, ö   Umlauted 'ö' as in German 'Köln'

Ş, ş   'sh' as in 'ship'

Ü, ü   Umlauted 'ü' as in German 'München'

## Explanatory note

As I was writing *Turkey since 1989: Angry Nation*, Turkey was going through an unprecedented flurry of revelations about the workings of the 'guardian state', the network of 'deep state' actors, including the military and the judiciary, which has effectively run the country through much of the twentieth century. Some of the disclosed information – about the role of the police and the military in creating havoc, assassinating public personages and engaging in torture and murder – was spine-chilling. After years of failing to make sense of the unexpected twists and turns in Turkey's history, of the many instances of abrupt outbursts of mass violence and eruption of hatred between communities that had lived peacefully side by side for centuries, a new and clearer image of Turkey's recent history emerged.

However, some of the allegations, which were disclosed by leaks from investigations and court cases, have been shown to be based only on limited evidence. Prosecutors involved in the investigation of conspiracies and military plots have often worked with the same biased methodologies with which their counterparts in the high judiciary, one of the key actors of the guardian state, have whitewashed arbitrary state action throughout the decades. Nor has the AKP government been able to withstand the lure of power: it has not been acting as disinterested arbiter waiting for the final defeat of the 'guardian state', but has used these investigations to settle scores with its political enemies. All these interferences have hence complicated the already complex process of understanding the morass that is Turkey's recent history. The empirical material on which this book rests is hence provisional, but as accurate as it can be in a time of great ruptures and ongoing revelations about a parallel authoritarian regime based on 'state reason' rather than legitimate political process.

A second note is appropriate with regard to terminology. As in some of its neighbouring countries – think of Greece's staunch opposition to the very name of the Republic of Macedonia – many words in Turkey are contested. Even ostensibly innocent historical terms can take on high political meanings and occasionally lead to judicial inquiries and even convictions. The use of words like 'Kurdistan' and 'Armenia', when applied to the region of south-east Turkey, caused serious vexations in the recent past, and might do so today, even for academics. The Turkish sociologist Ismail Beşikçi, for instance, was incarcerated for a total of seventeen years on trumped-up charges for his pioneering work on Kurdish identity. And another sociologist and feminist, Pınar Selek, has been repeatedly subjected to court cases, prolonged detention and ill treatment for her remarkable studies on Turkish masculinities, transsexuals and Kurds. At times, even book titles containing regional assignations like 'Cilicia' were confiscated. Like everything else in the social world, however, all these terms are conventions that have taken on different meanings over time. Ottoman emperors, in line with the worldview of traditional universalist empires, were happy to have fuzzy borders, locally diverse administrative arrangements and multilingual place names. In the mid-nineteenth century, there was an Ottoman province of Kurdistan and the official name of the eastern Black Sea province of Rize until 1921 was Lazistan (Land of the Laz, a community related to the Georgians). In the mid-1930s, however, the usage of both names was forbidden by what was now the Turkish Republic, and a ban imposed on the importation of maps containing these terms. Even the word 'Turkey' had not been used within the Ottoman Empire before the twentieth century, and 'Turks' were considered, at least by the residents of the imperial capital Istanbul (or Constantinopolis!), to be the uncouth peasants of Anatolia, deprived of the trappings of Ottoman civilization.

When I use the term 'Turk', its meaning depends on the context. It can comprise all residents of Turkey regardless of their ethno-religious and linguistic community. This was the spirit which some tried to instil, if unsuccessfully, into the definition of citizenship in the Turkish Republic. Especially when I write about bilateral relations with other states, I use 'Turkish' as representing the government of the Republic of Turkey. When I contrast the term with 'Kurds', I mean the Turkish-speaking communities of Turkey, who self-identify as Turks.

The term 'Kurdistan' made a forceful comeback in the 1980s, with the emergence of the Kurdistan Workers' Party (PKK), which initially aspired to establish an independent state with the same name. In this book, Kurdistan is taken to comprise the geographical region of south-east Turkey which has a majority Kurdish population and has been, in the past and again since the 1980s, referred to as 'Kurdistan'. This region is largely congruent with another historical region, that of Armenia. The fact that these two historical regions overlap underlines the contested nature of both, as well as the futility of ethnogenetic claims on territory.

Another historical term has been a bone of contention for many and could lead to charges of 'denigration of Turkishness' according to the now reformulated Article 301 of the Turkish Penal Code: the term 'Armenian genocide', which I also use in this book. The term 'genocide' has many facets, above all legal, political and ethical. Debates on whether the destruction of Ottoman Armenians by the secretive Committee of Union and Progress and members of the state apparatus constituted genocide are often shaped by political rather than historical considerations. Whether one uses the term or not is supposed to signify on 'whose side' one stands. These debates, however, often only obfuscate the facts: anywhere up to a million (and probably more) men, women and children, most of them non-combatants, were forced from their ancestral homelands and most of them were killed under heart-rending circumstances, while many were forcibly or voluntarily converted to Islam. There is a wide range of terms which one can use to describe these events – crimes against humanity, the 'Great Catastrophe' or *Metz Yeghern*', eviction and destruction, and also genocide – and I use all of them interchangeably, without prioritizing one over the other, or implying legal consequences. I do, however, not use terms like 'relocation', 'resettlement' or 'evacuation', which are inaccurate and used by the deniers of the great calamity that was brought upon the Armenians of Asia Minor in 1915.

# Preface

This book is about Turkey and its turbulent recent history. It deals with political institutions and ideologies, with parties and political leaders, with civil society organizations and with individuals who have tried to negotiate a startlingly complex country. It seeks to elucidate the role of the state in the country's political history and the decisive impact of the non-elected 'guardians of the republic' – the military high command, the high judiciary and bureaucracy – that have been shaping Turkey's politics at least since the 1950s. Also referred to as the 'deep state', these actors and their 'behind-the-scenes' politics are defining characteristics of politics in Turkey. So are the chilling absence of humaneness and judiciousness in many court decisions and the high levels of political violence which have permeated much of the twentieth century and the decades under scrutiny in this book. *Turkey since 1989: Angry Nation* also looks into the spells of political reform and societal change and seeks to understand the ambiguous role of the European Union in the processes that have shaped Turkey in the last three decades.

The book is also about the many ruptures and interventions in the country's recent history, which have shaped the biographies of literally every citizen of Turkey. Members of my family and I have observed and experienced many of them personally. Take my parents. They were politically active as students in the 1950s, with my father leaning towards the Turkish Communist Party. After the coup of 1960, they quickly realized that incriminating literature with socialist themes, some of it published in communist Bulgaria, could put their lives at risk. Living in a modern flat in Istanbul's central Aksaray district, they burned the books in the bathtub, in a small and badly ventilated bathroom. Or my grandmother, Semiha Hanım. After the military intervention in 1971, my aunt was on the run as a socialist activist. Many of her books – Marx's *Capital*, Politzer's *Elementary Principles of Philosophy*, forbidden copies of the prose of communist poet Nazım Hikmet, the standard armament of a Turkish socialist at the time – were stored in a slowly crumbling mansion in Istanbul's Asian suburb, where the family used to gather for the summer months. One day in the summer of 1971, a military commander demanded to search the premises with his unit. Semiha Hanım was well aware that the books would cause great grief to the family if discovered. Herself the daughter of a general, and gifted with theatrical talent, she pulled off what was probably the performance of her lifetime: frequently invoking her deceased father and her status as 'daughter of a soldier', she invited the commander in to do whatever was necessary to serve the nation, even if this entailed the whole house being stormed or torn to pieces. Stunned by such militant fervour, the commander politely requested permission to leave after a superficial search. Nevertheless, my grandmother had the books carried into the basement and immured. My aunt was eventually caught, imprisoned and, like so many other politically active youths of the time, tortured.

I grew up with the letters my aunt sent us from prison. They were adorned with colourful drawings of vast landscapes, open skies, blue seas, kites and birds. But it was in high school during the years after the military coup of 1980 that I discovered the prison atmosphere myself. For a student in Turkey in the mid-1980s, only what was not explicitly forbidden was allowed, and this was not a lot. There were no Kurds, no Armenians, no Greeks and no Alevis in this grim post-coup world, or so I thought. My school was an elite institution, the German School of Istanbul (Deutsche Schule Istanbul), and there we were all Turkish, mostly Sunni Muslims, secular in our outlook and ready to defend any criticism levelled against the country by outsiders. Ironically, I did have quite a number of fellow pupils of Jewish and Armenian background at this school, but I did not think much about it. Freethinking was not encouraged anyway, and as is possible only in authoritarian regimes, I believed that Turkey was a tolerant place, where everybody lived together in peace, even though I knew that in fact people were being tortured in every bit of the country and being a non-Muslim was almost as bad as being a 'terrorist'. Our school week began and ended with the obligatory flag ceremony and the chanting of the national hymn, and we were subjected to weekly lectures on 'National Security', in which we had to learn by heart the different ranks of the army and the external and internal enemies of Turkey, who were many. The lecture was delivered by a retired general, and strangely, I remember him as one of the more humane teachers we had.

All theatre plays performed in schools, all books read in literature classes, had to be approved by educational commissions, which ensured that no subversive idea and no incitement to insubordination would enter the classrooms. There was little space for socialization outside the family circle, with restaurants and nightclubs reserved for the very rich, the very intellectual or the underworld. Unfortunately, one could say, I came of age at a sorry time for Turkey. But then, and as you will see in this book, Turkey's recent history has been dominated by such sorry times and the anger it has created among its people. Importantly, however, these dark patches alternated with hopeful phases of political stabilization and rapid economic development, with short bursts of artistic and intellectual genius and significant leaps forward in terms of personal and group rights. These 'light spells' were underpinned by longer-term processes of societal change – unexpected when looking only at the erratic nature of the political sphere – that triggered the emergence of a large middle class and significantly increased wealth and educational levels in society as a whole in the three decades since 1980.

This book is hence about the transformation from an inward-looking, conflict-ridden country in the 1980s to the vibrant economy and differentiated yet still-contested society of the twenty-first century. Turkey today is a country that holds great promise: the expanding economy, Turkey's growing regional and international weight as a political actor, and the globalization of Istanbul, which has become a major cultural and economic centre of the Balkans, the Caucasus, the Middle East and beyond, are powerful indicators. Yet conflict remains the defining experience of contemporary Turkey – conflicts over history, identity, over poverty and gender discrimination, and over Europe and the country's position in the world. The roots of these conflicts, as well as their impact on Turkey's people, are the story I have tried to capture in *Turkey since 1989: Angry Nation*.

*Kerem Öktem*
*Oxford, December 2010*

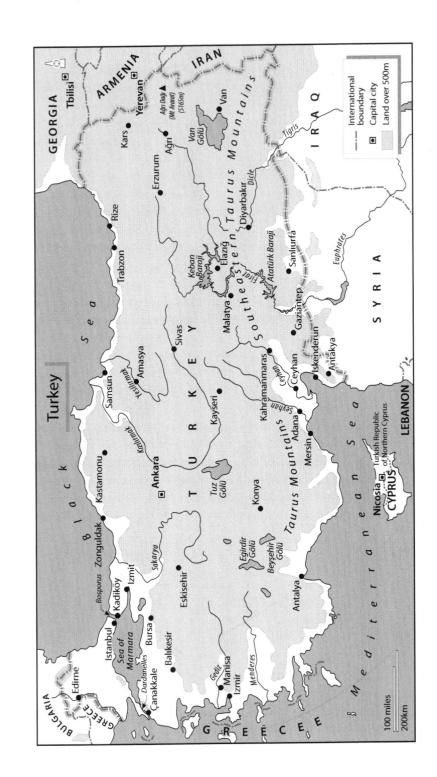

# Introduction

**Imagine** a country that is known more for the metaphors with which it is described than for its rather complex politics, society and history – a country that is unfailingly described as a 'Bridge between East and West', a passageway which links Europe and Asia, combines tradition and modernity, and raises hopes for the coexistence of Islam and democracy. This country is, of course, Turkey, the modern state on the Asia Minor landmass, which stretches out into the Aegean Sea and also includes a small part of Europe in its Thracian west. This is a country that has a mostly Muslim population, shares borders with some of the most feared dictatorships of the Middle East as well as with the European Union, and an economy with one of the fastest growth rates in the world. Few places are so often alluded to in world historical debates on the 'clash of civilizations' or the 'future of Europe', and few countries are so frequently misread and misunderstood. The metaphors of bridges and passages are often but euphemisms that seem to obfuscate conflicts between the binaries that the metaphors celebrate: conflicts between East and West, between Europe and Asia, between Islam and secularism. And yet again, these simple binaries are inappropriate if we want to understand the startlingly complex, but also intriguingly dynamic, country which Turkey is today, and the historical processes that have brought it about. This book proposes a framework that seeks to make sense of the complexities and counter-intuitive conflicts in Turkey's recent past and its political life today.

Unlike the other books in the 'Global History of the Present' series, *Turkey since 1989: Angry Nation* begins in 1980 rather than 1989, and it has an introductory chapter on the country's emergence as a modern nation-state since the nineteenth century. The main story of this book has hence two starting points: the year 1980 constitutes the key traumatic rupture, while 1989 marks a new context for Turkey's future engagement with the world. Many of the momentous changes that are often ascribed to the 1989 revolutions in eastern Europe – the abrupt end of authoritarian regimes and socialism, the ostensible victory of liberal democracy and free enterprise – in short Fukuyama's premature fantasy of the 'end of history' – were anticipated in Turkey in the 1980s. The military intervention of 12 September 1980 was ruthlessly brutal: it led to the imprisonment and torture by the armed forces and police of more than half a million citizens, the proscription of trade unions and the next-to-complete elimination of the country's associational life. This massively destructive act, however, also created a *tabula rasa* for the swift transition from an inward-looking corporatist economy based on import substitution to a firmly globalized and export-oriented economy, whose self-confident capitalists would eventually defy gagging attempts by the state. The September Coup, together with a programme of neoliberal restructuring announced on 24 January 1980, hence constitutes the zero hour in Turkey's recent history. It has unleashed the forces of market liberalization, anticipating comparable transformative processes in eastern Europe. Despite the bloody nature of its birth, the September Coup also opened the gateways for the generation of new social classes, rising levels of wealth, a more liberal political culture and the emergence of new social and identity-based politics.

The second key moment was 1989, when a significant historical turning point in Turkey coincided with the ruptures in eastern Europe: on the day the Berlin Wall fell, on 9 November 1989, the Grand National Assembly, Turkey's parliament, elected Turgut Özal as president of the republic. Taking over office from the commander of the 1980 *coup d'état*, General Kenan Evren, Özal became the symbol of the return of civilian government and the military's reluctant and incomplete retreat to the barracks. He also stood for the emergence of a new entrepreneurial class that was brash and profit-oriented and laid the foundations for a new market-oriented spirit. It fuelled the expansion of the economy and the commodification of everyday life well beyond the established industrial centres in western Turkey. On the home front, competing camps of secularists and Islamists replaced the preceding divide between socialists and conservatives, while the war between the security services and the Kurdish guerrillas escalated.

The year 1989 created a myriad of new opportunities in Turkey's immediate neighbourhood, which Özal artfully seized upon: the collapse of the Soviet Union opened the route to the 'Turkic' republics of Central Asia, the end of communism in the Balkans cleared the roads to Turkey's immediate neighbourhood, and US interventionism in Iraq promised to pave the way for a more prominent regional role. It was in the same context that Özal applied for full membership of the European Community, as the European Union was called back then, but was eventually forestalled. Most of the major domestic and international issues which determined Turkey's politics in the last three decades can hence be traced back to Özal's brief role as prime minister and president, and most of the achievements and failures of the country's political and economic trajectory can be measured against the backdrop of this period.

Another aspect of the eastern European transformations of 1989 was the onerous process of facing up to the multiple societal traumas of cynical dictatorships and to histories falsified by nationalist and communist regimes. The seeds of a reckoning with its authoritarian past were sown in Turkey in these years, but they only began to bloom in the 2000s, when critical intellectuals and activists began to reject the ethno-racist ideology of Turkey's founding fathers and challenged the official historiography. From the forced 'population exchange' with Greece in the 1920s and the genocide of Ottoman Armenians in 1915, to the policies of denial and assimilation towards Kurds and Alevis, the debate on what constitutes Turkey and what a Turk has transcended the narrow confines of what used to be a tightly ethno-religiously defined and ostensibly homogeneous polity.

There was a third key moment, in which world historical ruptures and domestic shifts coincided, if with a time lag. The September 11th attacks in New York significantly reshaped the context for Turkey's interaction with the world: George Bush's 'global war on terror', the assault on Iraq on Turkey's doorstep, the ensuing discursive polarization between 'Islam' and the 'West' and an increasingly security-based policy outlook in most European Union governments contributed to a growing sense of European essentialism and EU fundamentalism. The reformist zeal and pro-European excitement that unfolded in Turkey in the early 2000s was soon countered by a growing anti-Muslim and anti-Turkish sentiment in Europe. Wary of further enlargement, fearful of more immigration, unsympathetic to cultural differences and increasingly less convinced by the virtues of democracy and human rights, European publics shifted to the right, while the prospect of Turkey's EU membership turned into a memento of Europe's immanent 'Islamic conquest'. The erratic process of Turkey's relations with the

European Union in the 2000s hence had an ambiguous effect, which may have prepared what many see as Turkey's 'shift of axis' to the East. In fact, this was not much more than a course correction that responded to the European Union's increasing internal conflicts and to the inability to engage meaningfully with the shift of global economic and political power to centres outside the Euro-Atlantic world.

If we take 1980, 1989 and 11 September 2001 as the key historic moments when world historical events interacted with domestic processes, and the year 2010 as the temporary end point of this history of the present, we see two ostensibly contradictory phenomena: rapid change and development in economy and society as opposed to stagnation and violent conflict in politics. From globalization and Europeanization to rapid economic development, migration and urbanization, even individualization, Turkey has changed radically and at breakneck speed. Within three decades, the peoples living within the borders of the Turkish Republic have experienced their country's transition from an inward-looking agrarian economy dominated by a parochial and often neurotic worldview to a major regional power and, in 2010, the sixteenth-largest economy in the world. In the same period, Turkey has shifted from being a travel destination for backpackers and culturally interested individuals into the world's eighth-largest tourism market.

This story of relative economic and international success, however, has been overshadowed by institutional weakness, recurring political crises, religious conflict, ethno-national strife, mass violence and political manipulation. From the 1978 film *Midnight Express*, which illustrated in rather unsympathetic terms the conditions and experiences of torture in a Turkish jail, to the reports of international human rights organizations, Turkey has been depicted as a country of police brutality and arbitrary rule, and rightly so. Many of the images that accompanied news coverage of Turkey since the 1980s contained angry faces: members of Turkey's most significant religious minority, the Alevis, remembering community members killed in large-scale massacres, followers of the extreme right protesting against the critical reappraisal of Turkey's past, secularists screaming against the ruling Justice and Development (AKP) party, soldiers attacking the positions of the Kurdistan Workers' Party (PKK), and Kurds demonstrating against state repression. Violence also spilled over into the daily lives of anxious ordinary citizens in the form of intra-family violence, mounting criminality and hate crimes against members of sexual and ethnic minorities. This mounting violence was further aggravated by the country's abysmal 'gender gap', according to which Turkey is ranked 121 among 128 countries with regard to the economic participation, the educational achievements and political empowerment of women.

Much of the violence may be a function of the rising insecurity in the wake of a fast-changing society. But there are more immediate reasons. Tens of thousands of tortured men and women were eventually released into freedom and had to make do in a society that had become foreign to them after a decade or two in prison. Many soldiers who returned from the Kurdish war in the 1990s with deep scars in their psyches in turn began to traumatize their social environments. More than a dozen transsexual sex workers have been killed in Istanbul alone every year for many years now, indicating a new level of brutalization of the everyday world. And the anger has not been confined to Turkish territory: especially during the 1990s, when the military campaign against the guerrilla war of the PKK was at its height, supporters of the party blocked motorways in Germany and attacked Turkish embassies all over Europe. When the PKK's now imprisoned leader Abdullah Öcalan was captured in a Greek embassy in Kenya in 1999, outraged Kurdish nationalists attacked Greek missions from Moscow to Berlin.

Yet, as Slavoj Žižek reminds us in his reflections on violence published in 2008, violence is never only limited to the subjective violence performed by a clearly identifiable agent, who is visible to the outside observer. It is shaped by the 'symbolic violence' of language and ideology and by the 'systemic violence' of economic and political systems. In this book, I seek to explain why Turkey in the 2000s became such an 'angry nation' and explore, as far as possible in the confines of a concise account, the symbolic and systemic spheres where this anger has been created. In addition to a consideration of the violent politics of today, this necessitates reaching farther back into the history than 1980 and 1989. On the political level, much of the anger can be traced back to the underpinnings of Turkey's dominant ideology of nationalist modernization, in its early form of 'Unionism' (*Ittihatçılık*), and, after the foundation of the Turkish Republic in 1923, Kemalism (after the state founder, Mustafa Kemal). Based on an unlikely amalgam of ruthlessly modernizing policies, the authoritarian state forms of 1920s and 1930s Europe, the ethno-national ideology of Turkism and a restrictive form of state Islam, Kemalism has had a lasting effect on the country's institutions and mindsets. It was in three fields especially that the founding ideology of the republic paved the way for the tensions in today's Turkey: the definition of citizenship, the relationship between religion and society (laicism or *laiklik*) and, finally, the incomplete separation of powers between elected governments and non-elected actors like the military, the bureaucracy and the judiciary.

The Kemalist modernization project paid lip-service to civic notions of Turkish identity, yet in practice, and much as in the neighbouring Balkans and Greece, created groups of 'others', who were denied full citizenship rights. Kurds, Alevis and non-Muslim minorities were the most marginalized, if in different ways. Kurds and Alevis could be assimilated into the body politic when they denied their ethnic and religious origins, while non-Muslims were generally seen as a potential security risk and deemed unfit for full citizenship. All of them, however, had to suffer degrees of social exclusion and state repression. Even though they are minorities, taken together Kurds and Alevis probably make up more than a third of Turkey's population today, which is a substantial group in a country with more than seventy million inhabitants. Yet even conservative Muslims, who rejected the state-sanctioned Kemalist version of Islam and chose different readings of their religion, were pushed to the margins of the political system, and sometimes also to the margins of society. From the 1950s to the 1980s and until the end of the Cold War, communists and socialists, despite their growing significance in the political and cultural life of the country, were prosecuted and had their rights curtailed too. In this exclusionary mindset, 'full citizenship' was extended only to those Turkish Sunni Muslims of the Hanefi sect who subscribed to the secularist policies of the Kemalist regime, while members of all other groups experienced exclusion on different levels in public life. The political scientist and public intellectual Baskın Oran captured this idealized notion of a Turkish citizen with the derisory acronym LAHASÜMÜT (Laik, Hanefi, Sünni, Müslüman, Türk), the Turkish equivalent of the US WASP (White Anglo-Saxon Protestant).

*Laiklik*, the Turkish derivative of the French term *laicité*, was regarded as one of the founding principles of the republic and is still often presented as the separation of the public and religious spheres, which at least in France it was. However, in Turkey, *laiklik* came to mean the control and imposition of a certain reading of Islam, the Kemalist one, by the state, financed by public monies. This led to irresolvable contradictions whereby state-employed imams of the Directorate of Religious Affairs (Diyanet) would endorse the wearing of the headscarf in their sermons, while state universities barred scarf-wearing students from entering university campuses, as happened after the 1997 military intervention. Likewise, state monopolies produced and promoted the consumption of raki and wine, while imams warned their flock never to give in to the temptations of alcohol. This was a schizophrenic world only possible in authoritarian regimes.

The political system, which emerged from this contradictory trajectory of modernization, especially since its shift to competitive politics in the late 1940s, has been another source of constant tension: a dual structure emerged, with a 'guardian state' of an all-powerful coalition of the judiciary, the bureaucracy and the military on the one side, and elected, yet often insecure, governments on the other. The guardian state was a reincarnation of the Kemalist one-party state and a result of the country's incomplete transformation to democracy. In 1946, the Republican People's Party did introduce elections, but never fully renounced its role as the party of the state and of Mustafa Kemal's reforms. It remained part of a coalition of the military high command, the high judiciary and bureaucracy, whose leaders continued to consider themselves the rightful owners of the state, which they felt obliged to defend against whoever they believed were internal and external challengers to its hegemony.

## The workings of the guardian state

Let us discuss in more detail the workings of this body, which we will frequently come across throughout the book, with different names and in different disguises: the guardian state is an amorphous power structure within the state hierarchy, which is upheld by interpersonal contacts at the highest levels. It extends into all walks of life and can easily be prompted into action if state preservation so requires. The guardian state uses the methods and acts in accordance with the state preservation of the one-party era from which it emerged. Its worldview is also shaped by the clandestine nationalist movements of the nineteenth century, which have paved the way for the key ideological and political movement of Turkey's twentieth century, Turkish nationalist modernization, and by the necessity to cover up the dark moments in the emergence of the republic, such as the Armenian genocide or the extermination of Dersim Alevis in the 1930s.

The core method of guardian state governance is prescribed by the notions of divide and rule – a nod to the Ottoman imperial tradition of governance – and by manipulation and deceit. The distinguishing feature of the guardian state is the importance attached to state preservation as opposed to legitimate political processes. Governance is achieved by creating enmity and conflict between different groups, by exploiting religious or linguistic difference, as in the case of Alevis and Kurds, and by nudging political groups into radicalization. All these conflicts then eventually escalate – sometimes beyond the expectations of the guardians – and become justifications for overt military intervention. This was the case in the coups of 1960, 1971, 1980 and 1997, and in the modified form of 'electronic memoranda' by the Chief of the General Staff in the 2000s. In all these interventions, as well as in the civilian periods between them, the guardians act with a rationality of purpose to sustain power. From manipulation of the public sphere to the deceit of individuals, from incitement of mass violence to widespread torture by proxies and security services, all possible methods are permitted as long as they are justified by the ends of 'saving the state', which is often just a euphemism for the perpetuation of power.

There are different names for this coalition of guardians, ranging from 'deep state', 'security state' and the 'guardians of the republic' to the notion of the 'praetorian state'. They have clandestine and overt agencies, which carry out the dirty business of political manipulation: in the course of the twentieth century, the Special Organization (*Teşkilat-ı mahsusa*) of the Committee of Union and Progress, the Special War Office (*Özel Harp Dairesi*), the Village Guards (*Köy Korucuları*) and the Gendarmerie Counter-Terrorism Unit JITEM (*Jandarma Istıhbarat ve Terörle Mücadele Grup Komutanlığı*) have all committed crimes and killed thousands in the name of defending the state against its perceived enemies. For much of the time covered in this book, the 'guardians' were able to keep key social groups – parts of the intelligentsia, the middle classes and the Istanbul-based industrial bourgeoisie – within a republican hegemonic bloc, which was, however, challenged repeatedly during phases of strong civilian politics.

On the other side, and ever since the transition to democracy in the late 1940s, there are governments formed after competitive and almost always fair elections. They coexist, uneasily, with the guardian state. At key historical moments these governments not only represent a large segment of popular will, but they also integrate emerging social groups and their demands into the political system. This was the case with the election of the Democrat Party and Menderes in 1950, the brief left-wing interlude of the Republican People's Party under Ecevit in the 1970s, Turgut Özal's election to prime minister in 1983 and the election victory of the Justice and Development Party in 2002.

At their best, these governments are powerful enough to challenge the guardians and to keep the military, the judiciary and the bureaucracy at bay. Sometimes, they also succeed in manning state institutions with their own cadres. These moments also tend to coincide with major periods of economic growth and with a proactive regional and international policy, as was the case with Menderes and Özal and is still the case with Prime Minister Erdoğan. Eventually, however, these governments lose their electoral support. This may happen owing to an increasingly authoritarian turn in the style of government, which closely resembles that of the guardian state, to economic crises, to the creeping return of guardian meddling, or to a combination of all three of these factors. When political parties fail to garner the support of significant parts of the electorate and fall short of representing popular will, weak coalition governments emerge, which are easily pushed into giving in to the demands of the guardian state and helping rebuild its hegemonic position. The coalition governments of the 1960s and 1970s, as well as the 1990s, are a case in point.

The distinction between the guardian state and the actual government is never as clear cut as some recent critics would suggest. First of all, there are ample connections between the two spheres, and in times of relative stability, the guardian state may retreat and the military and judiciary may act according to their constitutional obligations. It is in times of crises, and particularly during military interventions, that the duality of the system becomes most apparent, if only for a short period of time. These are the moments when the military singles out groups and individuals, who are tortured, tried and convicted by the police and the courts, while the torturers and putschists are shielded from prosecution. Criminals walk free while the courts often target innocents and almost never mete out justice to victims. Second, elected governments may eventually emulate the guardian state in both method and discourse, thereby blurring the differences between the two, as was the case in Tansu Çiller's term as prime minister in the late 1990s with its extremely violent anti-Kurdish policy. Finally, individuals and groups may end up being enlisted by the guardians or their middlemen without even realizing their role in the larger scheme of things. The exploitation of left-wing students in the 1940s to the 1960s against the right, the instrumentalization of the extreme right and the guardian cajoling of the Islamists to move against the socialist movements in the 1960s and 1970s, as well as the enrolment of Alevis, secularists and social democrats in the fight against the Justice and Development Party in the 2000s, are examples of this guardian state practice of governance.

To call the guardian state to account for most of the episodes of violence and destruction in Turkey's contemporary history does not entail absolving from responsibility the elected political leaders, who have often found ways of accommodation within the dual power structure. It is, however, necessary for analytical reasons to focus on the guardian state, as only an understanding of its manipulative capacity begins to explain the counter-intuitive twists and turns in Turkey's history which have consistently forced neighbours and friends to become enemies, often to the surprise of the very same people, especially in retrospect. It is this counter-intuitive element in Turkey's politics which lies at the root of its angry and torn politics, but which has nevertheless failed to stop Turkish society advancing economically and culturally.

**Life-world transformations**

An Istanbulite, let's say a socialist activist, who fled the country after the military coup of 1980 – as many tens of thousands did – would probably not recognize her former city if she returned today. Gone is the grey and dusty melancholy of a self-interested bourgeoisie, which Orhan Pamuk described so succinctly in his biographic essay *Istanbul: memories of a city* (2005). Gone also is the sense of isolation from the world and from the imperial Ottoman past. The nation-builders of the early republican years had made a point of creating a new nation in a new city. Ankara, despite its significant, yet more easily destructible, Armenian and Jewish heritage, appeared untainted by the cosmopolitan diversity of Istanbul, and the republic channelled its limited resources into the construction of this new capital. Istanbul was neglected, and even with the start of massive industrialization in the 1960s, the metropolis remained demoted to the status of a secondary city. All this has changed now, and Istanbul has once again become a cosmopolitan hub, busily reconnecting to the world and to its past: the Ottoman Empire has become a positive reference; a faux neo-Ottoman style adorns hotels, restaurants and bars in the old town. Even in everyday fashion, the empire's stamp is increasingly visible: young religious women experiment with the kaftans and headscarf arrangements of Ottoman princesses, or rather with the models that European orientalist painters of the nineteenth century believed to be Ottoman. Head coverings have increased in numbers, but so have the women on the streets, which used to be mostly male domains. A desecularization of the public sphere and a secularization of society have been happening at the same time.

Istanbul welcomes more than seven million visitors a year and is acknowledged as a cultural capital in its own right, serving as a meeting place for artists from the Middle East, the Caucasus, the Balkans and the rest of the world. Even if its Europeanness is contested by smaller minds on the continent, the city proudly celebrated it status as 'European Capital of Culture' in 2010 and the signifiers of its manifold connections with its Western neighbours: from the city's most important Byzantine monument, the Haghia Sophia (the Church of the Holy Wisdom) to the 'Belgrade Forest', the 'Polish Village' (*Polonezköy*) and 'New Bosnia' (*Yenibosna*), Istanbul's toponymy marks its deeply European identity, while the Baghdad Road in the former suburb of Kadıköy hints at its more distant Arab connections. Motorways, new metro lines, fast ferries, social housing blocks, luxury villa compounds, business parks and shopping malls, new airports, even a 'Trump tower' – they all are testimony to the rapid modernization and globalization of the Turkish economy and the city's climb in the global hierarchy. Processes of gentrification, the often violent expulsion of 'unwanted' social groups such as Roma, transvestite sex workers, African immigrants and squatters from inner-city areas, and conflicts between old and new residents are the darker aspects of this rapid commodification of urban space in times of 'high globalization' and rent-obsessed local governments.

This massive developmental drive has not been limited to Turkey's traditionally more advanced western provinces. The entire country has been changing along the same lines, if not always in equal measure. Medium-sized cities of around half a million inhabitants have turned into centres of industrial production and have generated unexpected wealth. Denizli, Manisa, Kayseri, Konya, Gaziantep, Kahramanmaraş and other cities are hence referred to as 'Anatolian tigers', cities where within two generations artisanal work and handicrafts were transformed into global industrial production. More recently, Kurdish cities like Van and Diyarbakır have witnessed the rise of a growing Kurdish middle class, which seems to agree only partially with the maximalist demands of the Kurdish nationalist movement. With more than a hundred universities – both state and private – a gross domestic product of around US$13,000 per capita and an upwardly mobile society, Turkey is probably more economically dynamic than all of its neighbours. The transition from a low-income country to a developed economy appears imminent. The counter-intuitive mismatch between this rapid modernization on the one hand and the inability of the political system to overcome its ethno-national and illiberal foundations on the other accounts for much of the anger. This book explores the tensions and conflicts emanating from this mismatch, and the conditions under which it emerged.

There is no question that the world historic events of 1989 and the rupture of 9/11, together with Turkey's own key moment in 1980, have changed the country profoundly. Turkey is a different place and little has remained of the prison atmosphere of the September Coup. Owing to this rupture, Turkey has entered the era of neoliberal restructuring and globalization. Thanks to 1989, Turkey was reunited with its historical neighbourhood, from which it had been cut off throughout much of the Cold War. And with 9/11, the country was catapulted to the front lines of the 'clash of civilizations' and the war between 'Islam and the West', and then – with a time lag of a few years – directed to the antechamber of the European Union. The European Union itself, troubled by the aftershocks of the 2008/09 economic crisis and by growing populism and xenophobia, has lost much of its appeal as a beacon of democracy and prosperity. In 2010, Turkey remains a country where ethnic conflict, political tensions, authoritarian modes of governance and ongoing 'behind-the-scenes' manipulation by the guardians still muddy the waters. Yet the country is infinitely richer, more democratic, more humane and more civilized than in 1980. The perpetrators of the 1980 coup may soon have to defend themselves in court. The guardians are losing their omnipotence. The Kemalist Republic is obsolescent, but whether the anger may be about to subside or will be incited yet again remains to be seen. Turkey is emerging as an important new actor in its Eurasian neighbourhood, stretching from the European

Union to the Middle East, and from the Black Sea and the Caucasus to Central Asia, but the prime question remains to be answered: can a religiously inspired party with roots in political Islam Europeanize and modernize a society, tolerate its deepening secularization and accept non- and anti-religious life choices? In short, are political Islam and liberal democracy reconcilable, or is this coexistence doomed to be a half-hearted marriage of convenience? Will Turkey continue its erratic but progressive democratic consolidation, which began in the late 1940s, or will the Muslim democracy of Justice and Development prove to be a dead-end scenario for politics in Turkey? The following chapters might not give a definitive answer, but they will provide the reader with a wide range of historical connections that will help clarify the opaque storyline of Turkey's most recent history.

# 1 | Empire and nation before 1980: the late Ottoman state and the Turkish Republic

Turkey is a country with a surplus of history, and hence even a contemporary history of the last three decades will need to take a step back and make sense of the key legacies that have shaped its present. As I seek to show in this chapter and the following, much of the violence and anger that have marked Turkey since the 1980s stem from a particular trajectory of top-down modernization by the state, often acting against its very own people, and by a political culture dominated by a 'guardian' or 'deep' state operating through manipulation and deceit. In order to understand the period 1980–2010, therefore, a brief appraisal of three foundational moments, which have prepared the conditions for the political, ideological and institutional infrastructure of modern Turkey, is in order. The first is the late Ottoman experience of military, legal and administrative reform in the context of territorial loss to European powers and episodes of war and ethnic cleansing. It was in this period between the late eighteenth and early twentieth centuries that the institutions of the modern state emerged together with the ideology and cadres that governed it. The second is the period of the Kemalist one-party state, with the Turkish Republic emerging from the conflicted Westernization efforts of the nineteenth century. These efforts were conflicted because Europe was both an enemy intent on destroying the empire as well as a civilizational benchmark to aspire to, if only to be accepted as an equal rather than as the 'sick man of Europe'. Lasting from 1923 until the shift to multiparty politics at the end of the 1940s, this was the period in which the idea of an ethnically and religiously homogeneous nation-state was put into practice through a highly ideological and authoritarian one-party state. The third period, which led up to the military coup of 1980 and hence to the immediate antecedents of Turkey's present history, was that of 'guardian state in action', characterized by incomplete democratic transition, political manipulation, weak party politics, and power struggles between elected governments and non-elected actors such as the military, the bureaucracy and the judiciary, as well as by growing political polarization and mass violence.

Many of the major themes that dominate the conflicts in Turkey's contemporary everyday life crystallized in these successive periods: the questions of who a Turk is, and related to that who Kurds, Alevis and non-Muslims are and what their social and political status is, i.e. the issue of citizenship; the wars and violent events leading up to the dissolution of the empire and the consolidation of the republic; the exclusive nature of nationalism and nation-building, but also Turkey's place in the international order of the twentieth century and its relationship with Europe, the United States and its immediate neighbourhood. Above all, however, there is one question that seems to weave all of the above together in a complex web: were the elected governments of the 1950s to the 1970s really in power, or were they merely responding to the conspiracies plotted by the non-elected guardians of the state, i.e. the military, the judiciary and the bureaucracy? How was it possible that the guardians, when stepping out of their constitutional roles, were immediately absolved by the judiciary and protected by the bureaucracy? Were the 'progressive' students of the 1950s aware that it was the 'Special War Office' which had galvanized them into taking to the streets? Were socialists and fascists, Islamists and the communists fighting their own battles when they attacked each other in the 1960s and 1970s, or had they become puppets in a cynical game staged to maintain control over a society that was spiralling out of control?

## Reform and imperial dissolution

For almost five centuries before the demise of the empire in the 1920s, the Ottoman sultans ruled Asia Minor, the Balkans and much of the Arab world from their capital in Constantinople. At the height of Ottoman military, political and economic power in the sixteenth century, the empire stretched from Austria and Hungary to Romania and the Crimea in Europe, and to Algeria in the southern Mediterranean, incorporating all the lands and people in between. By the eighteenth century, however, this power was past its prime. Its waning military technology could not withstand the more advanced European armies, and its agrarian economic base failed to compete with the industriousness of early European capitalist expansion. With Sultan Selim III, and coterminous with the French Revolution, the age of reform and the vocabulary of modernity entered Ottoman lands. From now on, and well into the twentieth century, Ottoman and Turkish history would be dominated by three interlinked processes: the erosion of sovereignty, processes of administrative reform and centralization, and the search for a new ideology that could legitimize Ottoman and later Turkish rule. Military defeats and the ensuing loss of territory and sovereignty to European powers necessitated wide-ranging changes, which came in the form of top-down military and administrative reform aimed at 'saving the state'. They failed, however, in countering rising nationalism and inter-ethnic strife, both among Christian subject nationalities such as Greeks and Armenians and the Turkish-Muslim population majority.

Many of the fears of modern political discourse in Turkey go back to this period: a concern over territorial integrity and the fear that the country might one day be divided by foreign powers, the suspicion towards non-Muslim residents as potential fifth columns of European states, the contested relationship with modernity and moderniza-tion as a state-led, top-down effort with a strong military overtone, the uneasy interaction between Islam and the state, and finally the machinations of clandestine power centres that act on behalf of the state. All these are built into the country's political DNA, and even an occasional follower of Turkish politics will recognize them instantly as key themes in today's political debate.

*Loss of sovereignty* Throughout the late nineteenth and early twentieth centuries, military defeat and territorial loss shaped the Ottoman world. The Islamic yet multicultural empire was out of tune with the great political and economic leap experienced in some European countries and helpless with regard to the aggressive expansionism of emerging colonial powers. The empire was experiencing a loss of sovereignty on multiple levels: France and the British Empire extracted favourable trading terms within the Ottoman lands, which not only resulted in a breakdown of local economic structures and in the influx of cheap, industrially produced goods in what was a backward agrarian economy, but also led to an asymmetric relation of economic dependency. A vicious cycle of borrowing and debt ensued: in order to finance administrative reform and modern infrastructure from roads to railways and ports, and to fund ongoing military campaigns, Ottoman governments took to borrowing increasingly fantastic sums from European lenders. What began as an ostensibly straightforward way to pay for the army's equipment for the Crimean War with Russia (1853–56) ended with the empire's default on its debt only two decades later in 1875. As a result, the country came to be governed effectively by a body of European creditors (*Düyun-ı umumiye*).

The loss of sovereignty, however, was not limited to the growing influence of European interests in Ottoman government and economy. Simultaneously, provinces with Christian majority populations saw the ascent of nationalist cultural elites, who would soon galvanize peasants into the fight for independent nation-states. Throughout the nineteenth and early twentieth centuries, Ottoman statesmen were compelled to organize the gradual retreat from the Balkans, or 'Turkey in Europe' as it was called, and hence from provinces that had been under Ottoman sovereignty for centuries. These provinces would eventually become the nation-states of Greece, Serbia, Romania, Bulgaria, Macedonia and Albania. With every new state or interim principality, another wave of Muslim refugees – unwelcome in the emerging, Christian majority states – would be pushed towards the Ottoman capital. The worst such instance of territorial contraction and refugee movements arguably came with the First Balkan War in 1912/13, when a coalition of the newly independent Balkan countries attacked the remaining Ottoman enclave in the Balkans, the region of Rumelia (*Rumeli*), stretching from today's Albania, Macedonia and northern Greece to eastern Bulgaria. This war and the Treaty of London signed on 30 May 1913 ended Ottoman rule in all but a small remnant of Turkey in Europe, only a few kilometres west of the municipal boundaries of Istanbul. No fewer than 400,000 Muslims of different ethnic and linguistic origins fled their homes and joined the retreating Ottoman army on their way to the remaining territories under the Sultan's control. Mosques and barracks in Istanbul became their first dwellings.

Every such wave of Muslim refugees in the capital suggested that the futures of Muslim and Christian nations, intertwined throughout centuries of albeit unequal coexistence in the empire, would eventually part ways. Muslim political thinkers of the day came to hold the view that the Christian subjects of the Sultan would ultimately side with the Christian European powers, and hence constitute a threat to the political aspirations of the empire's Muslims. The Ottoman retreat from the Balkans and the waves of Muslim refugees also prepared the ground for new episodes of ethnic cleansing and genocide in the empire's final days: the destruction of Ottoman Armenians in 1915, as well as the Greek–Turkish population exchange stipulated in the Lausanne Treaty in 1923, was but an amplified sequel to the destruction of Muslim communities in the Balkans.

Ottoman statesmen were appalled to see their power waning even in the majority Muslim territories of the Arab world, where the Sultan's sovereignty became at best nominal: Egypt was invaded by France in 1798, and then elevated to a monarchy with the Albanian Otto-man statesman Mehmet Ali Paşa of Kavala (Muhammed Ali) crowned viceroy in 1805. By the middle of the nineteenth century, Egypt was largely independent, if under effective British control. In a similar fashion, the North African provinces of Tunis and Algeria came under French protection in the first half of the nineteenth century, and only the Arab territories in the Levant and Mesopotamia remained under control of the 'Porte', the seat of the Ottoman government.

If the sovereignty of the Ottoman sultan was receding throughout the nineteenth century, it was seriously undermined and then effec-tively ended by the beginning of the twentieth: the Sultan and his government's decision to enter the First World War on the side of Germany resulted in a complete Ottoman defeat and ignited the final destruction of the empire. Amid the carnage of war, the Armenian genocide and Franco-British partition plans, which marked most of the remaining territories for imperial domination by European powers, the Ottoman Empire turned into an empty shell under European control. In the summer of 1920, there was no Ottoman sovereignty left to speak of, but a European plan to divide what was left of the empire. The Sèvres Peace Treaty proposed an Ottoman rump state in central Anatolia, internationalized Istanbul and the Straits, and apportioned Smyrna and parts of western Anatolia to Greece. The plan also had provisions for a future Armenian and possibly also a Kurdish state in the east and opened the Mediterranean shores and Arab provinces to Italian, French and British colonial domination. The Sèvres Treaty was never implemented, yet it became a powerful symbol of the near-annihilation of the empire's Muslims and Turks. It took on a new role in Turkish political discourse in the 1990s as an argument against granting rights to Kurds and other minority groups.

The certitude in Turkish political discourse that Europe is, first and foremost, a Christian entity, as well as the deep suspicion directed not only towards Christians, even if they are citizens of Turkey, but also towards Arabs, can be traced back to this historical experience.

*Reform to save the state* Continuing loss of sovereignty and growing European interventionism necessitated reform. Muslim Ottoman intellectuals were aware of a shift of fortunes as early as in the eighteenth century. As military defeats multiplied, and ever since the premature introduction of a modern army by Sultan Selim III in the late eighteenth century, statesmen internalized the imperative for reform as the precondition for the survival of the Ottoman state. Not surprisingly, this reform began in the military domain: territorial loss was seen above all as a failure of military planning, discipline and apparel. Throughout the nineteenth century, the state established modern military schools for the education of a military and administrative elite that would be able to build and run a strong modern state and stave off efforts at European domination. Ironically, though, the schools were manned mostly by European instructors in the first place and did not always live up to the mission that the sultans devised for them. The young military cadres and administrators who graduated from the imperial schools gained access to political treatises of French and English provenance and soon became eager recipients of revolutionary ideas, such as constitutionalism and the equality of all subjects. Founded as bastions against European encroachment, the new schools hence became hotbeds for clandestine groups with radical ideas: the 'Young Ottomans', and later the 'Young Turks', initially emerged as secret societies, which developed their own visions of a future Ottoman state.

State-led and largely domestically driven reform efforts were complemented by another trajectory of reform, which was partly externally devised: European countries gradually took on the role as protecting powers of the empire's Christian peoples and pressured Ottoman governments into ensuring their safety and legal equality. Especially Armenian communities in the Kurdish-dominated eastern provinces were at risk, and Russia soon became an active participant in the politics of the region. France supported the Maronites of Lebanon and Syria and used them as a pretext to meddle in the affairs of Mount Lebanon. Measures ostensibly introduced for the protection of Christian people against the despotism of Ottoman local governors resulted in a gradual colonization of parts of the empire's territory and undermined the reformist efforts of the Porte.

Even though the idea of equality of Muslim and non-Muslim ran contrary to the founding ideology of what was ultimately a Muslim empire where non-Muslims were only 'protected', the successive reform edicts of the nineteenth century, beginning with the 'Noble Edict of Gülhane' and inaugurating the era of 'Reorganization' (*Tanzimat*) in 1839, did recognize the idea of full legal equality of all subjects of the Sultan, irrespective of their faith. With the edicts, Ottoman governments sought to pave the way for a more effective and more centralized administration that would be able to establish control over local strongmen and hence stand up to European interference. While 'rational' government ushered in an era of more effective local administration and helped the emergence of new urban trading elites, however, centralization and modernization also had unintended side effects.

In the cities, a growing Christian and Jewish middle class benefited from the rising European economic presence and appeared to surpass the established Muslim merchant families and administrators in wealth and sophistication. In peripheral areas, delicate power balances between Muslim and non-Muslim communities were upset too. Largely autonomous throughout imperial history, Kurdish feudal leaders were now forced to accept the sovereignty of the Ottoman central state and abandon their military and administrative rights. The first Kurdish uprising in 1830 came as a response to increased government control in the fiefdom of Bedirxan Bey of Botan and triggered a series of revolts that would continue well into the 1990s. The unsettled power structure in Kurdistan would also leave the Armenians of the east in a vulnerable position and increase competition over scarce resources. This Kurdish–Armenian conflict created the local conditions for massive Kurdish involvement in the Armenian genocide, further strengthened by the foundation of Kurdish irregular troops in the second half of the nineteenth century by Sultan Abdülhamit II.

Whether shaped by domestic concerns over the future of the empire or by European interests, however, towards the end of the nineteenth century the quest for reform and modernization had became internalized as an Ottoman affair, its political agenda represented by the clandestine movement of the 'Young Ottomans': the vocabulary of European political thought had entered the empire in earnest, including the idea of constitutional government, of parliament and the curtailment of the powers of the Sultan. A brief constitutional revolution in 1876 was soon aborted and followed by the restoration of absolutist government under Sultan Abdülhamit II, yet the modernist agenda of the Young Ottomans would shape much of the political debate in the empire and beyond. As the eminent political scientist Şerif Mardin remarked: '[T]here is hardly a single area of modernization in Turkey today, from the simplification of the written language to the idea of fundamental civil liberties that does not take its roots in the pioneering work of the Young Ottomans' (Mardin 2000 [1962]: 3f.)

Abdülhamit succeeded in dispersing the followers of constitutional government and the Young Ottomans, yet failed to prevent the emergence of a new group of modernizers, later called the 'Young Turks', who continued this trajectory of European modernization. In both groups, members of the officers' corps were prominent, underlining the central role of the army in Ottoman and Turkish engagement with modernity. The continuous reform efforts of the nineteenth and early twentieth centuries failed in achieving their ultimate goal, i.e. to enable a strong Ottoman state to stand up to European interference, guarantee safety and prosperity for all its subjects and survive as the sole Muslim empire in a world of colonial empires and emerging Christian nation-states. They not only failed in preserving the Ottoman Empire, but they fuelled the very process of its demise by necessitating ever higher spending and debt and by undermining the delicate balances of power, which had kept Muslim and non-Muslim subjects at peace. Yet even though the reforms failed in preserving the state, they laid the foundations of the modern Turkish Republic.

A century and a half of Ottoman reform and interaction with the European powers created many of the cornerstones of Turkey's current political structure: a conflicted relationship with a Europe that is both the principal enemy intent on destroying the country and the foremost place to emulate and be accepted by; the fear that any liberalization on minority issues will bring eventual partition and territorial disintegration; the special role that the army plays in the politics of the country, but also the understanding that Turkey can survive only by bringing itself up to the standard of the times, and that change is necessary for survival, even though preferably administered by the state.

*Ideological experiment and nationalist nadir* The third area in which the experiences of the late Ottoman Empire shaped the Turkish Republic was that of ideology and political culture: most ideologies that have dominated contemporary politics in Turkey, as well as much of the political culture of the state elites, have their origins in the nineteenth and early twentieth centuries. In earlier centuries, the Islamic character of the empire was indisputable, manifested by the Sultan's role as Caliph, as well as protector of the non-Muslim subjects of the empire. The latter lacked equal rights but could count on protection by the authorities as well as on a degree of autonomy in legal and administrative matters. This system was often called the *millet* system, translated as community or nation. This asymmetric deal became dysfunctional with the emergence of independence movements among Christian communities, first in the Balkans, and later in Anatolia, i.e. in what is now modern Turkey. In the nineteenth century, the Ottoman Empire had to address two contradictory processes: on the one hand, the foundation of mostly Christian nation-states in the Balkans led to the loss of large Christian populations, while on the other the influx of hundreds of thousands of Muslim refugees to the Ottoman heartlands increased the proportion of Muslims in the remaining territories. As the empire's demography was becoming predominantly Muslim, the empire itself was impelled by European powers, non-Muslim subjects of the empire as well as Muslim modernizers to move beyond the imperial Islamic character, and transform itself into a 'modern' nation of all of its communities.

In this search for a new imperial contract, many political ideologies emerged and disappeared as quickly, yet the overall move was towards increasingly exclusive notions of identity and citizenship: Ottomanism tried to provide a secular, inclusive notion of Ottoman citizenship based on the 'Unity of [ethnic] elements' (*Ittihad-ı anasır*) and reached its climax during the brief constitutional period of 1876. It had a late and ephemeral resurgence during the revolution of 1908, when Armenians, Greeks and Turks celebrated the idea of a common Ottoman state once again and for the last time. As territorial loss in the Balkans continued unabated, however, ideologues and statesmen hardened and the notion of coexistence with non-Muslims seemed to become increasingly undesirable for a future Turkish Muslim state. Liberal movements such as Prince Sabahaddin's party for individual enterprise and decentralization, and the pro-British, economically and politically liberal Ottoman Liberal Party (*Osmanlı Ahrar Fırkası*) were soon displaced by the aggressive nationalism of the Young Turks. Especially after the Balkan Wars of 1912–14, nationalism became the dominant ideology both among Ottoman Muslim political elites and in the two most important non-Muslim communities in the empire, the Greek Orthodox and the Armenian *millets*. The order of the day was that of homogeneous nation-states, i.e. states where territorial and ethno-religious borders coincided. The Turkish, Greek and Armenian nation-state projects, however, were competing over the same territories.

It was the Muslim-Turkish nationalism of the 'Young Turks' and the Darwinist outlook of the leaders of the Committee of Union and Progress (*Ittihat ve Terakki Cemiyeti*) which set the parameters of Turkish nationalism at the turn of the century. It also forced the empire into the Great War, a war which it would not survive. In government, the Committee managed to man three key ministries with their men: War Minister Enver, Interior Minister Talat and Minister of the Navy Cemal. In power, they hoped to put their modernizing policies – nationalization of the economy, creation of a national Muslim bourgeoisie, secularizing the legal foundations of the empire and addressing the unequal status of women – into practice. Amid the carnage of the First World War, however, these programmes were overshadowed by the aim to create a territory for the empire's Muslim Turks. In the summer of 1915, the Committee unleashed a series of genocidal episodes that aimed at the ethnic cleansing of all eastern and many western provinces of their Armenian inhabitants. The preparations were carried out by a secret organization of the War Department under Enver Paşa, which acted as an extension of the Committee of Union and Progress. Called the special organization (*Teşkilat-ı mahsusa*), it would also play a role in the organization of the national struggle a decade later. The special organization was an early harbinger of the many secret organizations that would come to play a role in the politics of modern Turkey. Much is contested about the events of 1915, but it is next to certain that somewhere between 600,000 and over a million Armenian men, women and children – a large majority of them non-combatants – were killed by hunger, disease and neglect, during death marches, massacres and mass executions. The killings were organized by the Committee at a time when it had taken over the state, making partial use of the army and state agencies, as well as of provincial organizations of the Committee and of Kurdish irregular forces.

It is this single most ignominious moment in the demise of the Ottoman Empire and the Darwinist-racist underpinnings of the Young Turks' reformist modernism which has shaped the dark core of Turkish nationalism and elevated it to the hegemonic position it enjoyed well into the 2000s. In fact, Philip Gourevitch's stark aphorism that genocide is an 'exercise in community-building' (1998) comes disturbingly close to capturing the role of 1915 for the formation of modern Turkish identity. Much of the state ideology of the early republic and the period after the military coup of 1980 comes from the political heritage of the Committee of Union and Progress and its roots in manipulative 'behind-the-scenes' politics: a political mindset made up of the binary extremes of survival or annihilation, of independence or slavery, a fetishization of the state as a precondition for the survival of Muslim Turks, the denial of Kurdish and Armenian identities, an exaggerated sense of Turkishness and an exclusive sense of citizenship, which sees only Turkish Sunni Muslims as the state's rightful owners. Even though the empire perished, these sensibilities and attitudes shaped the emerging Turkish Republic as well as modern-day political debates.

## The Kemalist one-party state (1920s–1946)

The three decades between the demise of the empire and the end of the first republic in 1946 began with an unexpected series of military victories in a territory that European governments had devised for colonial land grab. It saw the emergence of the Turkish Republic in 1923 under the leadership of Mustafa Kemal (Atatürk, 'Father of the Turks'), which soon turned into a one-party state with an authoritarian but impressive modernization agenda that compares only to the Sovietization campaigns of Central Asia under Stalin or Enver Hoxha's cultural revolution in Albania. The republic aimed to consolidate its grip over the territories inherited from the defeated empire and ensure ethno-religious homogeneity within its borders by creating what Arjun Appadurai (2006) calls the 'national ethnos'. The republic was built by Ottoman cadres and continued many of their modernizing policies. Despite Kemalist historiographies that see a big rupture and a completely new beginning in the republic, there was much more continuity than rupture. The republic took over from the empire a functioning state machinery, its administrative infrastructure, the prevailing ideologies of the day – nationalism and secularism – the army and much of the political culture. The republic's partial demise came in 1946 with an incomplete shift to democratic policies. The conflicts that arise from the ideology of the republic and its notions of citizenship and belonging, as well as the institutional set-up of modern Turkey, crystallized in this period.

To understand the historical backdrop to the emergence of the republic, I will briefly explore the allied efforts to divide the Ottoman Empire and apportion large chunks of Asia Minor to European powers. Then I will examine the ideological and institutional foundations of the republic and its citizenship policies, which clarified who would count as Turk and who would be excluded.

*Imperialist designs and nationalist resistance* By the spring of 1920, French and British forces had occupied the capital. Sultan Vahdettin became a prisoner of the victorious powers and was ready to sign off the terms for capitulation. Yet before the partition plan of the Treaty of Sèvres could be implemented, national forces (*Kuvva-i Milliye*) under the leadership of the officer Mustafa Kemal and other commanders of the Ottoman army had established themselves as a de facto Turkish government and declared the Sultan powerless. Based on defence leagues that had sprung up throughout Anatolia in opposition to the Greek occupation of Smyrna in May 1919, the nationalist government gradually became a sovereign body of regional committees and congresses that soon were enjoined into a national parliament. The Turkish Grand National Assembly (*Türkiye Büyük Millet Meclisi*) convened for the first time in April 1920 in Ankara. This government had an army made up of units whose commanders defied the orders of the Sultan and who joined the war against the Greek armies in the Aegean, the French and British armies in the south-east and the Russians in the east. This was quite a remarkable turn of events: a country ravaged by decades of war and ethnic cleansing, with a sultan under Allied observation and European designs of partition, returned to world politics in a different guise and through the military success of an initially clandestine nationalist movement.

Most of the fighting occurred in western and central Anatolia with the Greek army, which entered deep into Anatolian territory in 1919, only to be beaten into a humiliating retreat three years later. This last episode of the First World War brought havoc and destruction to Greeks and Turks alike. Once again, hundreds of thousands were on the run, Orthodox Greeks fleeing with the retreating Greek armies, Turks returning to their destroyed villages. If the Turkish War of Independence had begun in earnest with the Greek occupation of Smyrna/Izmir in May 1919, the entry of the nationalist forces into the Aegean port town on 9 September 1922 marked its victorious, if bloody, end. Tens of thousands of Greeks and Armenians died in the Great Fire that consumed much of central Smyrna. Mustafa Kemal, who was witnessing the fire, reportedly said: 'Let the fires burn. We will all rebuild it, and we will rebuild it more beautifully' (translated from Ipek Çalışlar 2006).

Rebuilding the remains of an empire destroyed by more than two decades of war and violence would indeed be the major task of the early republic. Yet the rebuilding was also a reinvention, which saw the full-scale implementation of the modernizing agenda of the Committee of Union and Progress, from which most cadres of the republic hailed. The modernizing authoritarianism of this era, its ideological underpinnings and the traumatic experience of what the political scientist Baskın Oran called an administrative 'revolution from above', have contributed significantly to the political structures and ideological fault lines of modern Turkey. In the first three decades of the republic, in all but name a dictatorship under the 'eternal leader' Mustafa Kemal, the new state created its own ideology and culture – later called Kemalism – and defined what its 'ideal citizens' would be like: according to the letter of law, the republic was secular and civic, but in practice, and as was the case in neighbouring Greece, only the dominant ethno-religious group had full citizenship rights. Only Turkish-speaking Sunni Muslims were considered as Turks, while all other groups faced different levels of exclusion. Non-Turkish groups such as Kurds or Laz, an ancient people living on the eastern Black Sea coast, had at least theoretically the potential to be 'Turkified', i.e. assimilated as Muslims. Non-Muslims were categorically excluded from the circle of full citizenship rights, as they were deemed unfit for full integration into the Turkish polity.

Foreign policy was not at the heart of the Kemalist republic, which dissociated itself from almost all claims on imperial possessions in the Balkans and the Arab world. All former Arab provinces were under British or French mandate rule, and hence there were no governments to engage with and no regional policy to be made in the east. The only foreign policy initiative in which Turkey was actively involved was the

Balkan Entente, which was signed in 1934 to lay aside mutual territorial claims and prevent conflict between the signatories. Apart from that, Mustafa Kemal and later Inönü followed a moderately isolationist policy and a politics of pragmatic regional and international balance. During the Second World War, Turkey refrained from declaring war on Germany until its defeat was ensured. The nation-builders' foremost goal was to concentrate on the consolidation of the territory under their control into modern 'Turkey' and its diverse communities into 'Turks'. They could build on the extraordinary military success with which they had thwarted European domination and which was the primary source of their popular legitimacy. Hence the key importance of the military in the national psyche, which went back to the days of the national struggle, if not to the times of empire. The 'myth of the military nation' (Altinay 2005) therefore formed part of the foundations of the republic and was sustained by the system of general conscription, which continues to the present day.

*Ideology and revolution: the discourse of the republic* The victors of the national liberation war declared the Turkish Republic on 29 October 1923 and elevated Ankara to the seat of government. Mustafa Kemal and his associates established the Republican People's Party (*Cumhuriyet Halk Partisi*, CHP) and created a state that would gradually take on all the trappings of a corporatist one-party regime. In March 1924, the Grand National Assembly abrogated the Caliphate, the symbolic institution of the world's Sunni Muslims, very much to the shock of Muslim people living under foreign domination. The nationalist government thereby cut the last remaining official link to the Ottoman Empire, yet it also removed the most important emotive bond with its non-Turkish Muslim citizens, and especially the Kurds. What followed has often been described as a revolution. Yet most of the reforms that President Mustafa Kemal decreed and the Turkish Grand National Assembly – controlled by the Republican People's Party – duly signed off were an admittedly radical implementation of earlier reform policies of the Young Ottomans and the Committee of Union and Progress.

The legal reform acts were shrouded in a modernist language and set out the goal of 'reaching the level of contemporary civilization'. Some were concerned with the highly symbolic issues of appearance. A case for the latter was the Hat Law of 1925. It proscribed the wearing of the fez, which had been introduced only in the nineteenth century with the reforms of Mahmud II, ironically as a symbol of the modern bureaucracy and military. Even more effectual were the many laws that came into force in the mid-1920s and sought to reshape the everyday life-world of citizens along the lines of a modern secular society. In March 1924, all religious schools were closed down and replaced by a unified and secular state education system, which, however, reached only a fraction of society. A year later, all religious convents, Sufi brotherhoods and dervish lodges, the cornerstones of a specifically Ottoman Islamic tradition and the repositories of Ottoman religious culture, were closed down. Both moves displaced thousands of religious scholars (*ulema*) and Islamic judges, who lost their livelihoods, and left myriad followers of the convents without spiritual guidance. Most brotherhoods went underground and struggled to continue their religious practice in secret until they re-emerged in the more liberal climate of the late 1940s. With the discontinuation of religious schools and lodges, all centres of Kurdish teaching and learning were also closed down, at least on the surface.

The Weekend Act and the introduction of the international time and calendar system abolished the Islamic holiday on Friday and replaced it with the Christian day of rest, Sunday. The Islamic calendar was substituted for the Gregorian calendar, and the time regime based on prayer times, also called 'Turkish time' (*Alaturka saat*), was superseded by European time. In symbolic terms, the time regime of Islam was now a thing of the past. In 1928, the most visible articulation of the Islamic cultural heritage, the use of the Ottoman-Arabic script, was prohibited amid Mustafa Kemal's well-publicized tours through Anatolia, during which he inducted the masses to the new 'Turkish', i.e. Latin, alphabet. Owing to very low levels of literacy, few people outside the cities may have been directly affected, but many people in Turkey nevertheless remember their grandmothers and grandfathers using the Ottoman-Arabic script as shorthand when taking notes. They also come across journals from the first republican years, which were printed in an ostensibly foreign language, which they do not understand. For the generations educated in the new alphabet and without access to the 'old script' (*eski yazı*), as it was called, primary sources of the Ottoman past, including the many inscriptions in mosques, the books, newspapers and journals published before 1928, would become inaccessible. The republic's children were raised to become illiterate with regard to their Ottoman past.

Major legal innovations were the adaptation of obligation and commercial laws, as well as of Italy's – in fact Mussolini's – penal code and the Swiss civil code, translated by the ardent nationalist and Turkish supremacist justice minister Mahmut Esat Bozkurt. Rather than building on already secularized Ottoman law traditions and ongoing codification efforts, which would have allowed for a thorough transformation of the law of the land, Bozkurt succeeded in convincing Mustafa Kemal that only a radical break with tradition would allow society to be refashioned in the image of the new republic. The civil code (*Medenî Kanun*) indeed significantly improved the legal situation of women in society and transferred family matters from the realm of religion to the jurisdiction of the state. Polygamy, religious divorce and other provisions of Islamic law were dropped. Many of these practices were, however, continued in conservative circles and in the countryside. As with other legal changes of the time, the civil code did not reflect society's norms and conventions but was devised as an instrument to create a new society rather than provide the normative basis for justice. Much of the dismay with which republican elites would treat common people up to the present day rests on this particular normative worldview and civilizational narrative, which completely disregarded everything that had been considered Muslim and Turkish until then.

In the next few years, women would gradually gain rights to vote and to stand for office, first in mayoral elections, then in rural polls and finally, in 1934, in general elections. While the Republican People's Party provided almost equal rights for women, however, it also forbade the associations that represented what had been a vocal Ottoman women's movement. Nevertheless, many contemporary observers thought they were witnessing the unravelling of a cultural revolution that carried a theocratic state and a backward people into modernity. This assumption was, however, doubly false: the Ottoman Empire in its last centuries was not theocratic and nor was society an undifferentiated mass of peasants. Critical scholars today see the Kemalist legal reforms as building blocks of a project of authoritarian modernization and 'social engineering' of the masses by an educated elite, and by the subtle ways of adaptation, negotiation and subversion with which society responded. Few of the reforms initially penetrated into society, and if their impact was felt more in the western provinces and urban centres, the east, where resistance to the project of secularization and Turkification was deeper, remained a closed conflict zone well into the 1960s.

Yet looking from the new capital Ankara, these extensive legal changes, together with yet another symbolic change – the introduction of family names and the abolition of titles and deferential forms of address, which represented the complex social relations of the empire – laid the foundations for the republic's social and cultural orientation towards secular modernity. A new generation of secular-minded Turks was educated in schools and village institutes (*köy enstitüleri*) and the republican ideology was disseminated in 'People's Houses' (*Halkevleri*). Indeed, since 1931, the Republican People's Party had included the principle of '*laiklik*' in its party programme. Unlike France, however, where it signified the disestablishment of religion and state, '*laiklik*' referred to the state-led generation and dissemination of a religious practice that would suit the needs of the new republic. In 1924, after the abolition of the office of the Sheykh-ul Islam (the *Meshihat*), the Assembly established the Presidency of Religious Affairs (*Diyanet İşleri Riyaseti*, later *Diyanet İşleri Başkanlığı*), which was to organize the religious life of all Muslims and render a Turkified form of Sunni Islam hegemonic. Alevis, members of a heterodox Muslim community with a distant relationship to Shiite Islam, were also subjected to this particular reading of Sunni Islam. In 1932, the Diyanet mandated the call to prayers (*ezan*) to be performed in Turkish rather than Arabic. This made Turkey the only country at any point in history where the call to prayer was delivered in any language other than Arabic. A Turkish translation or *tafsir* of the Qur'an was published in 1938. The republican state shunned the institutions of the Ottoman Empire and visible manifestations of public piety well into the late 1940s. Yet disestablishment of religion from the state never occurred. In fact, the state remained intertwined with Islam in a way that was not very different from the set-up of the late Ottoman Empire, save for the dominance of secular civil law over Islamic personal status law and for the suppression of religious brotherhoods. What the enforced practice of *laiklik* did, however, was to block processes of secularization that had been going on in the empire for many decades.

Particularly important for the ideological consolidation of the republic, at least in the eyes of Mustafa Kemal, was the rewriting of history and the creation of a new language: the establishment, on Kemal's personal directive, of the Turkish History Society (*Türk Tarihi*

*Tetkik Heyeti,* later *Türk Tarih Kurumu*) in 1931 and of the Turkish Language Society (*Türk Dil Kurumu*) a year later would serve precisely this aim. The new Turkish history was written by a very small group of people around the young historian Afet Inan. Inan, an adopted daughter and protégée of Kemal, had studied at the University of Geneva with the anthropologist-historian Eugene Pittard, who believed that world history was a contest between superior and inferior races. Many of Pittard's racialist views entered the 'Turkish History Thesis', which soon became the official doctrine of the republican education system. It suggested that the Turkish race had been displaced from Central Asia owing to climatic changes and the loss of agricultural lands and, hence, migrated into different corners of the world, in the process establishing all major civilizations of history. Arguably defeating arguments that Turks belonged to a lesser race, the thesis established, in the eyes of its creators, racial equality with Europe. The thesis also helped to square the circle between the postulate that the Turks' homeland was in Central Asia and the republican claim on the territory of modern Turkey: Inan turned the Hittites, an ancient people of the second millennium BC, into one of the Turkish tribes that had emigrated to Anatolia, and thereby established Turkish ownership of the Asia Minor landmass that pre-dated Greek and Armenian claims.

The Turkish Language Society developed a similar theory: all languages had emerged from a Central Asian Turkish idiom. Using the image of the rays of the sun enlightening the world, the 'Sun-Language' theory also made its way into the school books of the republic. Much more influential than this Turkish version of the racial and language histories in vogue in Europe at the time, however, were the Society's efforts to create a new Turkish language: the new Turkish would not only be written in Latin script but would also be purged of its crucial Arabic and Persian components. Mustafa Kemal took a particular interest in this experiment. Every week, newspapers published lists of Arabic and Persian words and encouraged readers to send in suggestions for Turkish equivalents. Before long, the 'Turkish Language Reform' took on a life of its own: the bureaucrats of the Turkish Language Society not only actively opposed the usage of 'old' words, which they deemed reminiscent of the Ottoman Empire, they also eagerly invented ever stranger words based on other Turkic languages, translated them from Western languages or simply made them up. The doyen of Turkish studies at Oxford, the late Geoffrey Lewis, called the reform a 'catastrophic success' (Lewis 1999), because Turkish emerged from this period of purges greatly impoverished, lacking the depth and wealth of Ottoman Turkish. The vocabulary has changed so significantly that even a well-educated university student today cannot fully understand a Turkish newspaper article written in the 1920s.

Republican efforts to create a new language and a new history were aggravated by the zeal of local party and municipal administrations in purging non-Turkish village and street names and excising all reminders of non-Turkish and non-Muslim communities in the country's toponymy. The Thracian town of Kırkkilise (Forty Churches, an already Turkified form of the Greek *Seranda Ekklesies*), for instance, was renamed Kırklareli (Land of the Forties). Even the renaming of Ankara was considered at some point, but the effort to change it to Gaziyuva (the Gazi's nest, Gazi being another title of Mustafa Kemal) was ineffective. All these purges and name changes contributed to a deep sense of historical displacement and cultural rupture. The opening sentence of L. P. Hartley's novel *The Go Between* could not be more appropriate to describe the *zeitgeist* of the early republic: 'The past is a foreign country: they do things differently there' (Hartley 1985).

Nowhere was this sense of displacement better reflected than in the foremost monument to the Kemalist revolution: the new capital, Ankara. Initially an important provincial town at the crossroads of central Anatolia, the city had had vibrant Armenian and Jewish, as well as Muslim populations, yet suffered significantly during the deportations and murders of 1915. Chosen as a base by the nationalist government during the War of Independence for its easy accessibility, the city developed as a showcase of the republic, first in a rather anarchic fashion, and then along the lines of the urban development plan of the German architect Hermann Jansen. German, Swiss and German Jewish architects and academics began to arrive in Turkey in the late 1920s, reinforced by those fleeing prosecution in Hitler's Germany in the 1930s. Many of them took an active part in the foundation of state institutions and university faculties. Architects designed the representative buildings of the republic – from the parliament building to the General Staff Headquarters, from ministries to the Faculty for Languages, History and Geography – in the style of continental European radical modernity.

The official journal *La Turquie Kemaliste* included a regular feature on the building progress in a section called '*Ankara Construit*' (Ankara constructed) and presented Ankara as a modern capital in the steppes, whose new monuments were proudly competing with the architectural gems of Nazi Germany and Fascist Italy. By the mid-1930s, Ankara had indeed taken on the air of a modern if modest town with straight-lined boulevards, national monuments and progressive residential architecture, as well as public parks and theatres where men and women would go out for evening walks and drinks. The heart of Ankara clinging to the hills around the castle, however, remained untouched by the new city developing in the valley below. The metaphor of Ankara's partial modernization captured the situation in the country as a whole: the administrative and legal reforms of the 1920s sought to decree a new Turkey, which reflected the political projects of a homogenized ethno-national state and the norms and rituals of the Europe of dictators. They did not revolutionize society so much as they created a layer of modernity and Western mores and architecture, which obfuscated the poverty and underdevelopment and the many ethnic and religious tensions it failed to resolve. The abyss between republican civilizational discourse and reality on the ground fuelled the contempt with which republican elites treated the common man and the common woman.

*Citizenship, ethnicity, religion: the 'others' of the republic* The most obvious contradiction of the Turkish Republic was the failure of its leaders to accommodate peacefully the ethnic, linguistic and religious diversity, which had survived the wars, the episodes of population exchange, ethnic cleansing and the Armenian genocide. Instead, they tried to impose their restrictive notion of Turkishness by force, and they expelled communities deemed unfit for assimilation. Turkish supremacy was the order of the day: on the tenth anniversary of the republic, in October 1933, Mustafa Kemal recounted his version of the Turkish War of Independence in a five-day marathon address to the Turkish Grand National Assembly. Called *Nutuk* (Speech), it became the foundation of 'Kemalist' historiography after his death. His speech was addressed to the 'Great Turkish nation', and ended with the words that would come to symbolize the Turkish Republic, inscribed into the minds of its citizens and into mountains and hillsides all over the country: 'Happy is he who calls himself a Turk' (*Ne mutlu Türküm Diyene*).

Citizenship in the early republic, as in much of continental Europe, was based on an amalgam of ethnic, religious and civic properties:

the only ethno-national identity that was accepted in public was Turkishness (Sunni-secular Muslim), but in theory non-Turkish citizens could benefit from citizenship rights by denouncing their ancestral roots. Most communities complied in public and found ways of nurturing their traditions at home and through marriage within the group. Non-Turkish Muslim communities in the Black Sea region (Laz, Hemşin Armenians, Pontic Greeks and Georgians), as well as Muslim refugees from the Balkans (Slavs from Macedonia, Bulgaria and Bosnia, Albanians, Vlahs) and the Caucasus (Circassians, Abkhaz, Georgians), belonged to this category. Many of these communities went through some form of cultural and linguistic assimilation, as their members sought to conceal their ethnic origins outside family and community circles. Alevis, a religious minority amounting to anywhere between 15 and 20 per cent of Turkey's population, had a particularly ambiguous position in the Kemalist mindset: as followers of a heterodox religious tradition that has its roots in Shia Islam as well as in pre-Islamic customs, many Alevis supported the Turkish Republic owing to its ostensibly secular character. Even though this support was welcome in Ankara, the state never really trusted the mostly rural Alevis and used a set of policies from benign neglect to enforced assimilation into Sunni Islam to control them. Mostly Turkish speakers, Alevis were curtailed in their religious practices, but could use their Turkishness as a way to power within the republican state.

Yet for non-Muslim as well as for the largest non-Turkish group in the republic, the Kurds (both Sunni and Alevi), Turkification was not a feasible option. The Christians were by now a small minority, making up less than 10 per cent of the population. Greek Orthodox and Armenians had been reduced to small pockets in Istanbul and Izmir and a community of followers of the Syriac Orthodox Church in the south-east, while significant, if invisible, communities of, and scores of individual, Armenian and Syriac converts lived in secrecy in the eastern provinces. Jews remained dispersed throughout the country and were particularly visible in the cities and villages of the Turkish part of Thrace. Campaigns were organized to pressure them into speaking only Turkish, and especially in the 1930s, and amid growing anti-Semitic propaganda by Germany, pogroms occurred where significant Jewish communities resided. By the mid-1930s, most Jewish communities of Thrace had been forced out of their homes. A 'Wealth Tax' at the height of the Second World War in 1942 targeted all non-

Muslim groups, and effectively destroyed their economic base while transferring their capital to the newly nurtured Muslim bourgeoisie. For the non-Muslim communities, the republican era was one of marginalization and gradual squeezing out.

In Kurdistan, the majority population now consisted of tribes which identified as Kurmanch or Zaza. For these tribes, who had fought for the Sultan and for the Ankara government during the War of Independence, the abolition of the Sultanate and Caliphate terminated the bond between Turkish overlords and Kurdish clients. With the closure of religious schools, Kurdish-Muslim madrasas were outlawed and any reference to Kurdish identity and language, let alone to the bygone Ottoman province of Kurdistan, became a punishable offence. The first uprising in the east came in February 1925, when the religious leader Sheikh Said Piran mustered an army of around 15,000 Zaza and took over much of Diyarbakır and adjacent provinces. The largest Kurdish group, the Kurmanchs, however, did not join this first uprising. It was contained by the military in March with the help of massive air bombardment. Sheikh Said and his followers were hanged and many tribes that had been implicated in the rebellion were deported to western Anatolia. The readers of Turkish newspapers were told that a group of primitive religious zealots had been put down, because they had attempted to destroy the republic, yet Sheikh Said soon became a symbol of Kurdish resistance against Turkish oppressors.

The uprisings continued, and a pattern commenced of revolt, seizure of towns, followed by heavy military engagement, execution of the leaders and deportation of the rebelling tribes throughout the late 1920s and 1930s. The level of violence and the number of casualties were rising with every new engagement and further radicalized the responses of the Ankara government under Prime Minister Ismet İnönü. The Settlement Law of 1934 provided the legal framework for a more comprehensive policy of pacification. It stipulated that Kurdish areas causing unrest would be depopulated (and repopulated with Turks) and their residents dispersed to western Turkey, where they would be encouraged to assimilate into the Turkish majority. The law was never implemented systematically, but an increasing number of Kurds would be deported to non-Kurdish territories as the uprisings continued.

*The genocide in Dersim* The rebellion in Dersim proved to be the end point of this pattern of recurring revolts and reprisals. In the mid-

1930s, the mountainous province of Dersim was the last territory that defied full government control. A fiercely independent tribal society of not more than 70,000 Alevi and mostly Zazaki-speaking clansmen, Dersim was poor, marred by internecine conflict, and had never been subject to central government control in the Ottoman Empire. In the first decade of the republic, the government tried to establish its grip by cooperating with some tribal leaders and pitting them against the others. By 1935, however, the republican state had decided to use Dersim as an example for its strategy of 'civilizing' the 'others' of the republic through annihilation and enforced assimilation. The Tunceli Law of December 1935 planned the deportation of most tribes from their homelands and their transfer to Turkish majority areas. The province was placed under military administration, which indeed brought brigandage and infighting between the tribes to an end. According to recently disclosed state documents, and contrary to the republican version of events, the security situation in the province was satisfactory by 1937, and no threat of a serious uprising was imminent. That the massive assault on Dersim took place nevertheless suggests that it was planned independently from the security situation on the ground and with the intention of destroying any opposition to the republic.

When the tribe of Seyid (Sey) Rıza caused a minor incident in March 1937, the commander general and governor, Abdullah Alpdoğan, launched a campaign that went well beyond retaliation. Throughout the summer, the military attacked all tribes, whether they were supportive of the government or not, and executed their members indiscriminately, whether combatant or civilian. Thousands, if not tens of thousands, of *Dersimli* (residents of Dersim) were killed in the campaign that saw the incineration of women and children as well as the use of massive air attacks. Testimonies of survivors refer to the common practice of rape by soldiers and the suicide of women to escape them. Seyid (Sey) Rıza was executed despite his advanced age of almost eighty, together with his son, in November 1937. Before his execution, and with reference to the seventh-century battle of Karbala, in which members of the Shia group were slain, he is reported to have said: 'We are the children of Karbala, this is a shame, this is injustice, this is a murder.'

The symbol of this republican war on the Alevi Zaza of Dersim was Sabiha Gökçen, Mustafa Kemal's adoptive daughter and the world's first female fighter pilot, probably herself an orphaned survivor of the Armenian genocide. She became a role model for the 'modern Turkish woman', highlighting the genocidal foundations of modern Turkish identity. Another one was Abdullah Alpdoğan, the commander general of Dersim, who was responsible for the destruction of the province and its people. Alpdoğan was honoured for his work, when the General Staff named the barracks next to Elazığ airport, from where the operations had been launched, after him. The name still remains, and since the early 2000s Istanbul's second airport has been named after Sabiha Gökçen, underlining the cynical continuity of state memory when it comes to punishing insubordination not only with violence but also with names.

The campaign was concluded in August 1938, when all its leaders had been executed and survivors deported to western Anatolia. The historical name of Dersim was excised from maps and replaced with the Turkish Tunceli (Land of Copper). The Turkish public was led to believe that yet another uprising of feudal tribes had been suppressed in the name of 'civilizing the country', and few in the outside world heard about the massacres at all – which is not surprising considering that the Second World War was just about to break out in Europe. Today, however, the massacre of Dersim is classified as 'ethnocide', while some speak of a veritable genocide that led to the destruction of close to half of the population of the province. The survivors use the Zazaki term *'Tertele Dersim'*. With the Dersim campaign, the government had sent out a clear signal: resistance would result in annihilation. Kurdish tribal leaders and nationalists understood the message and muffled their claims for identity and territory. Until the 1980s, Kurdistan was pacified. Sey Rıza's last words, however, would be anathema for the decades to come.

*Fault lines: the contradictions of the republic* The 'revolutions' of the Kemalist regime managed to create a discourse of nationalist modernity that permeates debates in Turkey even today, if increasingly less so. Yet the reforms initially created only a very thin layer of modernity that was confined mostly to the urban middle classes in western Turkey and expressed in the authoritarian aesthetics of the dictatorships of the time. Despite new civil codes and legal equality, family law remained under the spell of Islamic legal norms, and beneath the ostensibly modern layer, feudal structures and religious conservatism continued to govern rural life. Religious structures and institutions had been destroyed, and with religious schools and institutions closed down, much of the fabric of pre-republican Ottoman society had gone underground. The Kurds were pacified, albeit at the heavy price of relentless violence against civilians and ethnic cleansing of defiers. It is this confusing mismatch between the modernist discourse of the republic and the experiences on the ground which has complicated the appraisal of the early republican years and the evaluation of their impact on modern Turkey. For three decades, state discourse was infused with notions of secularism, republicanism and industrial development, while in reality state action was directed at keeping a still diverse society on a tight leash: the state continued to marginalize non-Muslims legally and economically by expropriating their properties, and forcefully assimilated the Muslim communities. The Alevis of Dersim, however, faced near-annihilation in a campaign of destruction that called to mind the 1915 genocide.

The result of the one-party state was a stagnating society, with the state dominating all sectors from economy and culture to politics, from the army and the bureaucracy to the legislative and the executive. All were working towards the same goal of 'achieving contemporary civilization', but in fact were engaging in the exertion of complete societal control within a dictatorship in order to create a society in line with European fashions. Surely, it is important to remember that Turkey's one-party dictatorship, authoritarian and preposterous as it may have been, was consolidated at a time when literally anywhere in Europe, Nazi occupiers and Fascist leaders were implementing racial policies that made Turkey appear a rather benign place. This was certainly true of Mustafa Kemal and slightly less so of his successor Ismet Inönü, who took over as president and leader of the Republican People's Party in 1938.

Inönü was under significant pressure to join the war from both the Allies and the Axis powers, but he struggled – successfully – to keep his country out of the war. It was only in February 1945 that Turkey joined the Allies in a symbolic gesture, and hence was able to become one of the founding members of the United Nations and an ally of the 'West'. Wary of Stalin's demands regarding control of the Straits and an increasingly aggressive Soviet foreign policy, Inönü opted for the United States and western Europe. As a consequence of both internal and American pressures, he was compelled to allow for the registration of opposition parties and introduce elections. He did comply with this request, first reluctantly, with the rigged elections of 1946. In 1947, US president Harry Truman introduced a policy of active containment against the Soviet Union, which resulted in generous military and development aid for Turkey and Greece, the two southern flank countries, both at risk – at least in the eyes of the US administration – of falling under communist rule (also called the Truman Doctrine). Turkey was included in the Marshall Plan for the reconstruction of post-war Europe in 1948 and joined the Council of Europe in 1949. Free and fair elections were first carried out in 1950: after almost three decades of rule by an inward-looking state-party dictatorship, İnönü handed over power to the incumbent Democrat Party and its leader Adnan Menderes. In 1952, Turkey was admitted to the North Atlantic Treaty Organization (NATO), completing the country's institutional integration into 'Western' security structures.

In the three foundational decades of the republic, Kemalist nation-builders laid the foundations of modern Turkey, even though civilizational discourse and reality on the ground were two different things. Kemalism, an amalgam of nationalism, statism and authoritarian modernizing policies, became state doctrine, disseminated by a one-party state with all powers brought into line. The country remained poor, held back by state capitalism, lack of a bourgeoisie (after the destruction of the non-Muslim middle classes) and a backward agrarian sector. Key contradictions emerged in these years, between secular modernizing elites and religious conservatives in the smaller towns, between a Turkish-dominated state and a Kurdish-dominated Kurdistan, between the poor masses and the republican elites, as well as between the hegemonic state bloc – the judiciary, the military, the bureaucracy and the party – and new social classes which were denied political representation. If the civilizational narrative and the Kemalist project of modernity were imposed on the people with often brutal force in the 1920s and 1930s, the Second World War facilitated an even higher level of authoritarian control under Mustafa Kemal's successor Ismet İnönü. By the end of the war, however, the discourse of Turkishness and 'contemporary civilization' had lost its appeal, and both internal demand for change and the new geopolitical conditions of the Cold War made a continuation of the one-party state impossible.

## The guardian state's incomplete democracy (1946–80)

If the three decades of republican consolidation witnessed the emergence of a highly ideological modernist and authoritarian one-party state, the following three decades saw the incomplete transformation of this system of governance into a weak multiparty system. One-party rule was abolished, and free and fair elections in 1950 allowed for the legislature and executive to change hands. Yet the remaining branches of government, the judiciary, the army and the bureaucracy, defied the democratic shift and continued to reproduce a one-party state ideology under the virtual leadership of the Republican People's Party. It was in this period that Turkey's incomplete and conflict-ridden democracy emerged with a resilient authoritarian parallel state at its core which would regularly intervene in order to keep elected governments in line, to get rid of them if need be and to manipulate society to sustain its power. During the 1950s and 1960s, the partner of choice of the 'guardians' of the republic was the Republican People's Party. In the 1970s, during the RPP's temporary democratic turn under Bülent Ecevit, right-wing parties came to be wooed. This parallel 'republican guardian state', since the 2000s also referred to as the 'deep state', survived throughout this period, strengthened by repeated military interventions, when the 'deep' and the visible state coincided, and weakened only temporarily when elected governments accrued sufficient power to challenge the guardians of the republic.

The politics of this era were murky and impossible to untangle at the time, as many of the events can be understood only with the benefit of hindsight and the manipulations of the guardian state in mind, whether in the case of the pogroms against non-Muslims in 1955 or the extreme political polarization and mass violence in the 1970s. This guardian state and its cynical behind-the-scenes politics emerged with the first election in 1950 and have continued ever since. Throughout this period, Turkey remained a staunch ally of the Atlantic Alliance, and the USA especially tolerated and often actively supported guardian interventions that ensured Turkey's geostrategic role as the southern flank of NATO. Three important themes dominated these decades, which are crucial for the understanding of Turkey's politics of the present: the emergence of conservative democracy, the manipulation of politics by the guardians through military interventions and fabricated mass violence, and the challenges from a radicalized socialist left and extreme right to both conservative democracy and the guardian state.

*The emergence of conservative democracy: cadres and policies* The win-
ner of the 1950 elections was the Democrat Party (DP) and its leader
Adnan Menderes, a former member of parliament of the Republican
People's Party and large landowner from the Aegean town of Aydın.
The DP created an alliance of social classes that would form the
backbone of Turkey's succession of conservative democratic parties,
from the Justice Party, which came into power in 1965, to the Party
of the True Path, from Turgut Özal's Motherland to Recep Tayyip
Erdoğan's Justice and Development of the 2000s. It was made up of
two unlikely bedfellows: a growing bourgeoisie that wished for more
autonomy from the state – which had created the Muslim industrialists
in the first place – and the conservative, mostly rural population of
Anatolia, which wanted to maintain a degree of autonomy from state
intervention and attain better material conditions. As a consequence,
the DP's policies, whether in the field of economic planning or political
reform, would be an opportunistic mix of class-based interest policies
for industrialists and large landowners on the one hand, and populist
and paternalist policies for the rural poor on the other. These were
permeated, however, by a discourse promoting individual achievement
and wealth, development and equality as well as religious piety and
social conservatism.

   One of the DP government's first actions, for instance, was the
highly symbolic revocation of the Turkish call to prayer. The return of
the Arabic *ezan* to the public space – audible everywhere in the country
five times a day – was a relief for the large majority of Muslims, and
reinstated the country's hitherto tightly regulated Islamic identity.
This move also led to instant resentment within the army and the
Republican People's Party, which saw a counter-revolution against
the Kemalist Republic in the making. Yet for the time being, the
power of the people appeared too tangible for the generals to take
action. Struggling with the unfamiliar word '*Demokrat*', ordinary men
and women transformed it into the Turkish '*Demir Kır At*' ('Iron Grey
Horse') and made it something of their own. In popular parlance, the
Iron Grey Horse would gallop through Turkey's contemporary history,
occasionally thrown off course by military interventions. Soon, the
Democrat Party incorporated the symbol of the galloping horse into
its own emblem. Subsequently, democratic politics in Turkey were
dominated by conservative and centrist actors, whereas the socialist
left and the republicans would look to the military for a revolution

from above. With the military intervention in 1971, however, the left would realize that the guardian state did not feel any moral obligations towards its one-time collaborators.

On the economic front, rapid development and institution-building alternated with reluctant economic policies. Four universities established in this era – the Middle East Technical University in Ankara, the Black Sea Technical University in Trabzon, the Atatürk University in Erzurum and the Aegean University in Izmir – introduced a strong US orientation into the hitherto mostly continental European academic tradition. Meanwhile, the Marshall Plan fuelled the industrialization of agriculture and increased the output of cash crops for the growing markets of post-Second World War western Europe. Opposed to any notion of national planning, which Menderes and his successor Demirel associated with the Soviet-style five-year plans of the early republic, the governments of the time shied away from macroeconomic planning and failed to develop coherent development strategies. Revitalized by US aid and foreign borrowing, the Turkish economy took on many key characteristics, which would remain for a long time to come: cyclical financial crises, devaluation of the lira, foreign debt and dependence on international agencies such as the IMF and World Bank. The economically liberal outlook was soon watered down with a policy of import substitution and protective measures, predominantly to please the representatives of the entrepreneurial classes. Despite the free market rhetoric of the Democrat and later the Justice Party, the Turkish economy remained a mixed economy with an important share of 'public sector enterprises' (*Kamu Iktisadi Teşekküller*).

While the industrialization of the agricultural sector improved the economic situation of small and large landholders (with the exception of farm labourers in the semi-feudal landholdings in the Kurdish provinces), it also resulted in a redundant workforce. Emigration to the large cities began in earnest, and by the mid-1950s, makeshift houses began to spring up on the peripheries of Istanbul and Ankara, called *gecekondu* ('built overnight'). Leaving the provision of affordable housing to the semi-formal market, the Menderes administration pursued a number of urban projects in Istanbul, which had been wilfully neglected under earlier republican governments. Concentrating on the creation of large squares and boulevards, especially in the old town, Menderes brought a rather brutal form of modernity to Istanbul: the emblematic boulevards 'Nation' and 'Fatherland' (*Millet* and *Vatan*

*Caddeleri*) pierced Istanbul's historic peninsula with much modernist fervour and little interest in the city's intricate urban structures. Road construction was also an absolute priority of the Directorate of Highways, which was established in 1950 and inspired by US advisers, who anticipated Eisenhower's Federal Highway Act of 1956 in Turkey. The new roads decreased transport costs and connected parts of the country that had remained isolated in economic and cultural terms. At the cost of the state railways, which were now seen as relics of statism, a road and petrol-dependent infrastructure and private transportation system emerged that would soon criss-cross the entire country. In the 1970s, the Keban Dam in Elazığ and the first Bosporus Bridge in Istanbul, as well as the continued modernization of the road network and the electrification of villages, became part of the Justice Party and Süleyman Demirel's developmental project for a 'Great Turkey'.

Despite these projects for a 'Great Turkey', however, Turkey's foreign policy in those years was rather 'small', and largely dictated by its front-state status and alliance with the United States. In addition to the Cyprus issue – violence between Turkish and Greek Cypriots escalated after the institutional provisions of the republic of 1960 collapsed – two developments stood out. One was Turkey's largely ineffective involvement in the US-led Central Treaty Organization (CENTO, also called the Baghdad Pact), established in 1955 by Iran, Iraq, Pakistan and the United Kingdom to encircle the Soviet Union with a pro-American belt, anticipating the US Green Belt doctrine of the 1970s and 1980s. Infinitely more important was the second: only three years after Menderes's brutal removal from office, in September 1963, Turkey and the European Economic Community signed an Association Agreement, better known as the Ankara Treaty. The treaty confirmed Turkey as an associate member and laid out a time frame for Turkey's gradual accession to the EU common market. After a preparatory phase, a transitional period would allow Turkey to adjust its legal framework, enter a customs union by 1995 and eventually become a full member.

At around the same time, one of the most important societal changes of the era began for Turkey, as for many European countries: Turkey followed poor southern European countries such as Spain, Italy and Greece and signed a series of bilateral recruitment treaties, first with Germany in 1961 and then with most western European countries in need of cheap labour to fuel their post-war booms. In the ensuing emigration, a substantial part of Turkey's labour surplus emigrated towards the west, and Turkish diasporas emerged with up to three million in Germany, half a million in France, the United Kingdom and, albeit later, the United States. Netherlands, Austria, Belgium and Switzerland would soon be home to Turkish communities of several hundred thousand. These diaspora communities created additional channels of engagement with 'Europe' beyond the republican elite discourses of 'contemporary civilization', while they also created a nucleus of religious thinkers and activists, who could not operate freely in Turkey. Eventually, Germany would become an important launching pad for the Turkish Islamist movement, the *Milli Görüş* (national view).

*The guardians against the Democrats* In the 1950s and 1960s, the electorate consistently voted for the conservative Democrats, and their successor, the Justice Party. In these years, public opposition came mostly from the left and from socialist groups. This opposition was exploited and in part channelled by the guardian state, which saw its power at risk if the government of the Democrats were to continue. The military coup of 1960 was hence seen as a 'left-wing coup'. When the socialists were elected to parliament in 1965, however, and after the military coup of 1971, the left became the prime target of the guardians, while the Justice Party under Süleyman Demirel became the protector of its best interests. Throughout the 1950s to the 1970s, however, the guardian state, in a mostly clandestine alliance between the military, the judiciary and the bureaucracy, manipulated politics on several levels and used mass violence to destabilize governments. The military interventions of 1960, 1971 and 1980, as well as the events leading up to them, cannot be fully appreciated without taking the guardian state and its actions into consideration.

One of the key plots, which created the conditions for the military intervention of 1960, for instance, was the 6/7 September Pogroms in 1955 (also known as *Septemvriana* in Greek), which supposedly developed as a spontaneous reaction to an arson attack on the house in Thessaloniki where Mustafa Kemal was born and sparked public anger at the situation of the Turkish minority in Cyprus. On 6 September, members of an organization called 'Cyprus is Turkish', who had procured lists of shops and properties of non-Muslims, began looting and destroying them. The attacks started in distant parts of Istanbul as well as in Izmir and Iskenderun – with its sizeable Arab Orthodox population – at around the same time and following the same pattern. They entailed looting of properties, vandalizing of churches and cemeteries, and assault on priests and lay people. More than five thousand businesses were targeted in Istanbul alone, and almost all of the city's seventy-three Greek Orthodox churches were attacked and robbed of their icons. A dozen or more Greeks and Armenians were murdered and no fewer than four hundred women were raped. Hundreds were severely wounded. In fact the events had been planned well in advance by the clandestine 'Council for Mobilization Research' (*Seferberlik Tetkik Kurulu*), better known under its later epithet, 'Special War Office' (*Özel Harp Dairesi*). This was one of the secret organizations which NATO countries created to wage psychological warfare against communism and to prepare the ground defence in the case of a communist attack, but it also stood firmly in the tradition of the secret organizations of the late Ottoman years.

Officer Sabri Yirmibeşoğlu, an undercover agent of the Office and later director of the National Security Council, confirmed that 'the 6–7 September was a job of the Special War Office. It was a marvellous organization. And it attained its goals' (Güllapoğlu 1991). Not only had the attack on Mustafa Kemal's house in Thessaloniki been carried out by an operative of the Turkish intelligence services, even the hundreds of thousands of copies of the *Istanbul Ekspres* newspaper, which galvanized parts of the mob into action, had been prepared well in advance. The pogroms served at least two goals. Even though the government had verifiably only limited responsibility for the events, they served as one of the main charges in the indictment against Menderes and the Justice and Development Party after the coup of 1961. For many non-Muslims of Istanbul, the pogroms were a turning point, after which they realized that hopes of equal citizenship in the Turkish Republic were futile. For the Greeks of *Polis* (the city), 1955 marked the intensification of emigration to Greece, and for Istanbul the end of its Ottoman cosmopolitanism.

The coup of 27 May 1960 was the guardian state's next intervention: on the morning of 27 May, Radio Ankara interrupted its scheduled broadcast for a special announcement. The officer Alparslan Türkeş declared that the Turkish armed forces had taken over the administration of the country, that the National Assembly had been closed down and that the constitution had been suspended. A group of young officers, calling themselves the National Unity Committee (*Milli Birlik Komitesi*), had acted without the connivance of the Chief of the General Staff, though probably in league with the Special War Office. This was the only military intervention in Turkey's crowded history of military coups that happened outside the command chain, and was hence soon reined in by the General Staff, who commissioned a group of jurists to draft a new constitution. Ironically, the 1961 constitution would turn out to be the most liberal Turkey has had to date. It extended individual liberties significantly, and introduced freedom of association and speech as well as autonomy in universities and public broadcasting.

If the constitution was liberal in terms of individual rights, it also gave a more prominent role to the military: creating vested interests for young officers in the country's economic development (and in order to discourage them from future plots), the Armed Forces Pension Fund (OYAK) was established. OYAK would become a major economic actor. It also introduced the National Security Council (*Millî Güvenlik Kurulu*), and codified the constitutional role of the military as a guardian of the political regime. The newly established Constitutional Court introduced a system of checks and balances that would, however, often be employed against elected governments. Ironically, while the 1924 constitution was being abrogated, President Celal Bayar, the entire Democrat government including Prime Minister Menderes and members of parliament were taken into custody on grounds of 'violating the constitutional order'. The proceedings at a makeshift 'Supreme Justice Chamber' (*Yüksek Adalet Divanı*) began on Istanbul's prison island Yassıada in October and rather resembled the show trials of Soviet Russia or China. Defendants were foredoomed and films and radio shows ridiculed them in the eyes of the general public. Menderes was charged for his role in the Istanbul pogroms, yet the proceedings were not about establishing the facts of the case. A year later, four hundred of almost six hundred defendants were sentenced to lifelong prison sentences, fifteen to the death penalty.

The National Unity Committee approved only three death penalties, and both the president and the leader of the Republican People's Party intervened to stop the executions. They failed, and on 16 September 1961, Turkey's first democratically elected prime minister, Adnan Menderes, his finance minister and his foreign minister were executed. The convicted Democrats were transferred to the Kayseri prison, where many remained incarcerated until the 1970s. The 1960 coup was the first visible manifestation of the guardian state, with the military intervening openly in politics and setting up courts to try its opponents, while the judiciary happily participated and the state bureaucracy did its best to support the new regime. All these powers would ensure the impunity of the putschists.

*Political chaos and military takeover* Despite the military's predilection for the Republican People's Party and successive manipulations to create an atmosphere of 'revolutionary change', the idea of a return to Kemalist autocracy proved futile: the 1965 elections brought the successor of the now outlawed Democrats to power. It was the time of the Justice Party and Süleyman Demirel. The 1965 elections also introduced two new political movements, the Labour Party (*Türkiye İşçi Partisi*) and the Republican Peasants and Nation Party (*Cumhuriyetçi Köylü Millet Partisi*). The former was the country's first legal socialist party, based on a coalition of democratic socialists as well as Marxists, Leninists and intellectuals who believed in a 'National Democratic Revolution' (*Milli Demokratik Devrim*). The latter was infiltrated by the former Nazi sympathizer and putschist colonel Alparslan Türkeş and became the platform of the emerging extreme nationalist right and their paramilitary forces. Both parties would play a prominent role in the radicalization of the political sphere in the years to come.

University students had become politicized throughout the late 1950s. Following the 1960 coup, what had started as a nationalist movement galvanized by the events in Cyprus and exploited by the 'Special War Office' evolved towards the left and the idea of an anti-imperialist revolution. The heart of student politics was beating in Ankara's Political Science Faculty, the former Imperial Administrative School (*Mekteb-i Mülkiye*). There, the student body was polarized between the Socialist Ideas Clubs (*Sosyalist Fikir Kulübü*) and the Free Thought Club (*Hür Düşünce Derneği*). It was around this time as well that the first Kurdish political associations, the 'Revolutionary Culture Hearths of the East' (*Doğu Devrimci Kültür Ocakları*), emerged. Invigorated by the spirit of 1968 in Europe and the protest movements against the Vietnam War in the United States, many followers of the left felt that a global revolution was imminent: it seemed only to be a question of when, and not if, Turkey and the world would become socialist. As elsewhere in Europe, street protests, university boycotts, anti-American demonstrations and the slogan 'Yankee Go Home' – a response to US president Johnson's rebuke to Turkey over Cyprus – had become defining elements of the time.

One of these boycotts created the most iconic and also most tragic leader of the Turkish left: the law student Deniz Gezmiş, who initiated the 1968 boycott at Istanbul University and led negotiations with the Demirel government to achieve some of their demands. What was a peaceful student movement, however, was fast radicalized and became violent, when extreme rightist groups and the Islamist-leaning 'Associations for the struggle against communism' (*Komünizmle Mücadele Derneği*) began to attack them with increasing brutality. This time, the guardian state was using the right wing to attack the left, which had stepped out of the republican fold and embarked on their own path of radicalization. When the visit of US ambassador Eric Comer to the Middle East Technical University was met with a massive demonstration against the USA, Deniz Gezmiş was there on behalf of Turkey's first organization dedicated to armed struggle, the 'People's Liberation Army of Turkey' (*Türkiye Halk Kurtuluş Ordusu*).

With state-sponsored extreme nationalist and Islamist groups on the one side and Marxist students on the other, violence mounted. Students and workers alike were incensed by the prospect of revolution, even if they had little idea about what would happen once power had been taken. Every confrontation led to a more violent response and heightened casualties. At anti-American demonstrations in Istanbul's Taksim Square, right-wing groups declared 'jihad' against the left and bludgeoned demonstrators as the police looked on. Amid the chants of 'Blood for blood, revenge!' (*Kana kan, intikam!*), two protesters were killed and more than a hundred injured. Sunday, 16 February 1969 would enter Turkey's political glossary as its own 'Bloody Sunday'. Despite elections in October, which reinstated the Justice Party government, the arena of politics had moved from the Grand National Assembly to the streets: in June 1970, more than 70,000 members of the Revolutionary Workers' Unions (*Devrimci İşçi Dernekleri Federasyonu*) protested against the government's restrictive trade union law in Istanbul's Kadiköy district. Four protesters and one policeman were killed, and Demirel felt compelled to proclaim martial law in some provinces. As the country was shaken by bomb explosions for which no one claimed responsibility, bank robberies by radicalized socialists and battles between rival student groups, the

Chief of the General Staff and the commanding officers met regularly to agree on the modalities of the looming intervention, but also to keep in check the left-leaning young officers, who were hoping for a revolution along the lines of the Young Officers in Egypt.

*The 12 March intervention in 1971* When the People's Liberation Front, operating from the campus of the Middle East Technical University, kidnapped four US soldiers in March 1971, the time seemed to have come for the generals to strike. Army units launched an all-out attack on the student dormitories, killing three and interning more than two hundred students in the university stadium. Deniz Gezmiş released the US soldiers to prevent further bloodshed, but it was too late: the intervention was already unfolding. On 12 March 1971, during the lunchtime news, Turkish radio stations broadcast an armed forces memorandum that accused the parliament and the government of having led the homeland into 'anarchy, fratricide and social and economic discord'.

Demirel was deposed from office, and a new government was formed to tackle the growing violence in the streets. Socialist intellectuals and Marxist groups initially welcomed the intervention, which they thought had been carried out by the left-leaning colonels sympathetic to the idea of the 'National Democratic Revolution'. They would be proved wrong. The generals' first act was to purge the junta of left-wing officers, the second was the detention of Deniz Gezmiş, and the third the convocation of a cabinet of technocrats from both parties. When protests, bombings and bank robberies continued throughout April, the new government under the appointed prime minister, Nihat Erim, declared martial law in eleven provinces. The interdiction of socialist and nationalist associations and the closure of left-wing newspapers followed curfews and arbitrary arrests, often made during the early hours and conducted with considerable brutality. Prime Minister Erim summarized the new rulers' attitude when he proclaimed that the 1961 constitution was 'far too luxurious for us'. His government quickly changed more than forty articles with an eye to curtailing human rights, individual liberties and university autonomy.

As Ankara reasserted its grip on politics, Marxist youth organizations progressed towards the targeted use of violence. Many had participated in Palestinian training camps in Lebanon and the West Bank, where, like the German Revolutionary Army Faction, RAF, they had become as anti-American as anti-Israeli. It was therefore not much of a surprise when a group related to the People's Liberation Army chose to abduct the Israeli ambassador in Ankara, Efraim Elrom, on 17 May 1971 to force the release of the student leader Deniz Gezmiş. This time, the government was not in the mood for negotiations. After a manhunt and the detention of at least five hundred left-wing intellectuals, Elrom's dead body was found in Istanbul. Mahir Çayan, Hüseyin Cevahir and Ulaş Bardakçı had committed the first political murder of Turkey's Marxist youth movement. Nevertheless, the battle cry 'Mahir Hüseyin Ulaş, struggle till liberation' (*Mahir Hüseyin Ulaş, Kurtuluşa kadar savaş*) continued to make the rounds during socialist demonstrations well into the 2000s, and can still be heard even today.

The armed forces took revenge. Martial law courts opened more than a thousand cases mostly against the left – including the socialists of the Labour Party, against the People's Liberation Front and against some right-wing organizations. Ten thousand political activists were imprisoned. The courts convicted most of them of 'destroying the constitutional order by violent means', and sentenced many to death. Ismet İnönü and the Republican People's Party tried to mobilize the parliament to block the death sentences, but was met with stiff resistance from Demirel and the right-wing parties, which voted in favour of the sentences. As the RPP was preparing a motion to consult the Constitutional Court to quash the decisions, Mahir Çayan and his comrades escaped from prison and kidnapped three British and Canadian army technicians to press for the release of Deniz Gezmiş. At the end of March 1972, the leaders of Turkey's Marxist-Leninist youth organizations and their hostages were surrounded in the village of Kızıldere. According to eyewitness accounts, Turkish soldiers, aided by NATO forces, shelled the hideout with machine guns for more than twelve hours, killing all but one. The leader of the 'Revolutionary Youth' (*Dev-Genç*), Ertuğrul Kürkçü, miraculously survived the carnage. A week later, the president confirmed the death sentence on Deniz Gezmiş and his comrades. They were executed in May. Only three years earlier, Deniz Gezmiş had negotiated a peaceful resolution to the student strike at Istanbul University. At the tender age of twenty-four, he was killed as a prime enemy of the state. A participant in the socialist movement of the time, who was detained and tortured in prison, summarized the escalation:

It was like a game. The kids pretended they were about to lead the country into a people's revolution, and Demirel and the military pretended that the kids would destroy Turkey's constitutional order. Both sides knew deep down that neither would happen. But it was the kids who were killed. (Fatma Sayman, interview, 14 June 2009)

Both sides believed that they were fighting their own battles, and both sides would eventually understand that they had been deceived.

*Descent into chaos* In the wake of the 1971 intervention, the guardian state took over the political sphere. The parliament had survived the coup, but power was now executed elsewhere. In the decade after 1971, eleven governments were formed and disbanded without effectively addressing the mounting violence, strikes, boycotts and the deteriorating economic situation. The longest lasted three years, the shortest was voted down after a month. Four men and the political movements they represented alternated terms in office. Sometimes they cooperated in grand alliances, but more often they fought each other viciously. They included Süleyman Demirel and his centre-right Justice Party and the Republican People's Party (RPP), which had evolved towards the 'left of centre' under its promising young leader Bülent Ecevit. Alparslan Türkeş led the extreme right Nationalist Action Party (*Milliyetçi Hareket Partisi*, MHP). Necmettin Erbakan entered politics with the Islamist National Order Party (*Milli Nizam Partisi*) in 1970, and after its closure by the Constitutional Court on grounds of anti-secular behaviour, with the National Salvation Party (*Milli Selamet Partisi*, MSP), which created the backbone of the Islamist political movement in the *Milli Görüş* ('national view') tradition.

The first post-coup democratic elections in 1973 delivered an odd coalition of the 'left of centre' Ecevit and the Islamist Erbakan, two men who had little in common save for an anti-imperialist and nationalist stance rooted, however, in diametrically opposed ideological traditions. Nevertheless, it was these two impulses which paved the way for Turkey's military intervention and subsequent occupation of Cyprus. The collapse of the constitutional arrangements in the Republic of Cyprus that had granted equal rights to the Greek majority and the Turkish minority resulted in an increasingly precarious situation for many Turkish Cypriots. Backed by the military junta, which had taken over Greece in 1967, the paramilitary National Organization for the

Cypriot Struggle (EOKA-B) and its leader, George Grivas, began attacking enclaves where Turkish Cypriots were trying to defend themselves. The massacres galvanized public opinion in Turkey once again, and by 20 July 1974 the military and the Ecevit government had come to the conclusion that the time for intervention was right. The Turkish air force and navy invaded the island from the north and advanced against little resistance. Two days later, Turkey signed its first ceasefire agreement. When talks on the resolution of the situation on the island stalled in August, Foreign Minister Turan Güneş of the Republican People's Party gave the command for the start of the second invasion on 8 August 1974. This he did with a coded wire suggesting that his daughter Ayşe 'should begin her holidays' (*Ayşe tatile çıksın*). Thirty years later, Turkish Cypriots would demand that 'Ayşe should at last come back from holidays', i.e. leave Cyprus on its own. The invasion ended a week later with almost a third of the island falling under Turkish control. More than five thousand died during the invasion, most of them Greek Cypriots.

The succession of elections and governments was accompanied by further polarization between the political forces on the right – centrist, Islamist and extreme nationalist – and the reconstituted left, ranging from the 'left of centre' and socialist movements to the Marxist-Leninist revolutionaries. Parts of the country were taken over by one group or the other and larger cities were separated into 'liberated areas', which were effectively governed by the different Marxist or nationalist groups. Even police associations were split along 'revolutionary' and 'nationalist' lines. This situation was further aggravated by a succession of three 'Nationalist Front' (*Milliyetçi Cephe*) governments, interrupted by short spells of social democrat cabinets under Ecevit. The Front governments were presided over by Prime Minister Demirel, with Türkeş and Erbakan as his deputies, and followed a viciously anti-communist policy. In spite of the mounting hatred on all sides, however, political violence remained under control, with robberies and shoot-outs often leading to material damage but to relatively few deaths.

It was during Ecevit's third term as prime minister, following the last Nationalist Front government, that the situation got out of hand. The religious community of the Alevis was targeted: on 19 December 1978, a mob made up of Islamists and Nationalist Action Party members in the city of Maraş went on the rampage against 'unbelievers', while the governor's requests for army enforcements were rejected and police and local army units looked the other way. A week later, more than a hundred Alevis were dead, their association buildings destroyed and their properties looted. Most of the survivors had fled the city. The Ecevit government was not in control of events. Allegations of CIA involvement notwithstanding, it is now an established fact that the events were planned by groups within the army and executed by extreme nationalist followers of Alparslan Türkeş.

On the day after the Maraş massacres, the Chief of the General Staff, General Kenan Evren, issued a letter declaring the armed forces' fury over the deterioration in public order, and only after this letter did violence escalate in earnest. Within less than a year, the daily number of victims of shoot-outs between rival factions would reach dozens. Fifteen public personages from the fields of politics, academia, the media and trade unionism were assassinated by covertly acting contract killers of the guardian state. Most of the murders remained unresolved. Among the victims were public office holders such as university rectors, journalists, former prime ministers, trade unionists and even extreme right-wing politicians. Demirel was prime minister again, this time in a minority government supported by the extreme right, but he also failed to regain control. Probably to diffuse public outcry over yet another anti-Alevi massacre in Çorum, the army launched an operation against the eastern Black Sea town of Fatsa in July 1980. Under its Marxist mayor Fikri Sönmez, Fatsa had become a symbol of the struggle of the Revolutionary Path (*Devrimci Yol*), a spin-off of the People's Liberation Army. Instead of the usual municipal administration, 'people's committees' and 'resistance councils' governed the town. And rather than summoning the mayor to court or arranging for the extreme right to attack, Chief of the General Staff General Evren paid a personal visit on 9 July. Two days later, the mayor and three hundred citizens were detained and questioned. Most were later released without charge, at least until the generals returned again in September – not to Fatsa, but to take over the country.

The three foundational periods of modern Turkey, which I have examined in this chapter, have sketched the institutional, ideological and political backdrop to the country that re-emerged after the military coup of 1980. Between imperial collapse and republican reinvention, the Young Turks' modernism and Darwinist take on history shaped the core of Turkish nationalism, which in turn became the hegemonic state ideology up until the 2000s. The heritage of the Committee of Union and Progress was decisive: their political mindset, shaped by existential choices between 'survival or annihilation' and 'independence or slavery', is still present in the repertoire of Turkish politics, if increasingly less frequent. The CUP's fetishization of the state as a precondition for the survival of its people, the denial of the violence done to Armenians and Greeks, the exclusive definition of citizenship, which sees only Turkish Sunni Muslims as rightful owners of the state, all go back to this period.

In the sixty years between the demise of the Ottoman Empire and the re-emergence of Turkey as an actor in the global economy following the 1980 coup, the Anatolian peninsula went through convulsions that in intensity and magnitude are comparable to those of no other country in the region but the Soviet Union. Destined for subjection to mandate rule by the Great Powers, nationalists as well as Kurds were galvanized into resistance by Mustafa Kemal, and most of the territory marked for colonial land grab became the new Republic of Turkey. A republican elite, with distaste for the Muslim peasant masses and the non-Muslim minorities alike, ruled the country with an iron fist throughout the 1930s and 1940s, while imposing reforms by law and decree on a reluctant, but muted population. If many of the modernizing reforms were tokenistic and symbolic, they shaped the trajectory of later phases of political contestation between secular modernizing elites and religious conservatives in the smaller towns, between a Turkish-dominated state and a Kurdish-dominated Kurdistan, between the poor masses and the republican elites, as well as between the hegemonic state bloc – the judiciary, the military, the bureaucracy and the party – and new social classes without representation.

In terms of symbols, the first republic churned out highly emblematic icons, the new capital of Ankara with its radical modernist architecture being the most impressive. Yet in many ways the state of the republic resembled the dichotomy of Ankara itself. In the valley, a new city stretched out with tree-lined boulevards, pleasure gardens and model houses, kept in order by a highly militarized bureaucratic state and populated by men and women emulating European chic as part of their duties as citizens. Above it all towered the Citadel of Ankara with wooden mansions and tiny alleyways opening to irregular squares with age-old mosques and *han*s, where craftsmen practised their trade. Life here continued as it had for centuries, even though the

Armenians and Greeks had been decimated and the Jews had begun to emigrate in the late 1940s. It was as if the old Ankara, or Angara, as the locals called it, was in defiance of the new city developing below. For republican elites, the maze of alleyways was a symbol of the rural backwardness they so virulently detested and of the contempt they had for the common people as a whole.

With the end of the Second World War, the same elites realized the need for change, as they felt cornered by Stalinist Soviet Russia as well as by growing popular discontent with the regime. They gave up their dictatorial powers, and opened the way for openly contested elections. However, a parallel guardian state with members of the bureaucracy, the military, the judiciary and some politicians continued to pull the strings behind the scenes, whether through campaigns of orchestrated mass violence, or in the form of military coups and indirect pressure on elected governments. This unstable system of behind-the-scenes conspiracy – clearly reminiscent of the manipulations of the Committee of Union and Progress – and electoral politics, combined with a heavy-handed state and hatred of communism and socialism, created cycles of state and mass violence. The Marxist opposition movements started off in the benign world of student politics, but before long they were radicalized into armed struggle. Islamist and extreme nationalist organizations were cajoled into acting as protectors of the state, which would drop them when state preservation so demanded. Amid the growing violence and instability, industrial development was slowed down, but the country was significantly changed by massive rural-to-urban migration as well as emigration to western Europe. In the run-up to the great changes of 1980, Turkey was a torn country, whose many conflicts were aggravated by the guardian state's cynical engineering.

# 2 | The Özal years: rupture, promise and missed chances (1980–91)

**The year** 1989 represented the great rupture in the history of eastern Europe, and arguably one of the great defining moments of world history. It led to the demise of an ideology, a form of government, an economic system. It also terminated a world order based on bipolarity. Turkey was part of this historical moment, if only by chance. On 9 November 1989, Günther Schabowski announced the easing of travel restrictions for visits from the German Democratic Republic to West Germany, thereby effectively starting the process that would lead to the collapse of the GDR and mark the end of communism in Europe. On the very same day, General Kenan Evren, leader of the September Coup, handed over power to the democratically elected president, Turgut Özal, the first civilian ever in this position since the foundation of the republic. For the people of Turkey, 1989 marked the symbolic end of almost a decade of brutal military oppression. Yet many of the changes that would be associated with the 1989 transformations in eastern Europe, as well as the great ruptures that would destroy much of the social and political fabric, had already been set in motion by the military coup on 12 September 1980. Turkey's 1989 happened in 1980, if in a much more violent and ruthless fashion.

Turkey in the summer of 1980 was a country at war with itself: political assassinations, communitarian violence, random killings and militant activism had brought daily life to a standstill. On the surface, the military stepped in to save the nation. In fact, General Evren and his co-conspirators assumed power, after they realized that the behind-the-scenes politics of the last three decades had not produced the desired results, i.e. a country and society that operated within the narrow confines set by the military elites and the guardians of the state. The restructuring of the country's political, economic and cultural set-up would be possible only with a direct takeover of government affairs.

The years from the military coup of 1980 to the loss of power of Özal's Motherland Party in 1991 and his subsequent death in 1993 witnessed spells of momentous change that defy straightforward categorization. Its core themes are contradictory: political repression, ideological reformatting towards Islam, economic liberalization, terror against the Kurds and the continued presence of the guardian state. It all began with a brutal military coup intent on reining in a society in turmoil and continued with three years of military government that sought to implement neoliberal adjustment and societal pacification by force. It was modified, however, against the wish of the dictators, by the election victory of Turgut Özal's Motherland Party in 1983, which brought to power a coalition of different societal forces in the tradition of the conservative democracy of the Democrat and Justice Parties. The economic liberalization programme suppressed trade unions and abolished labour rights. Yet the new entrepreneurial spirit, as well as the emergence of new social classes, undermined the dictators' fascist ideology: medium-sized towns in Anatolia were slowly transformed into industrial centres, Turkey's hitherto sheltered economy opened to the world market, creating more poverty but also more wealth. Turgut Özal tried to bring Turkey back into world politics and sought to reconnect with the European Community and its immediate neighbourhood, which included the Balkans and the former Soviet Union. Despite globalization and liberalization, a dark shadow hung over this image of the civilianization of power and return to democracy: in the Kurdish provinces, the military, the police and their collaborators committed the most abject human rights abuses with total impunity, while the bureaucracy and the judiciary sheltered the perpetrators and prosecuted the victims. Until the 1983 elections, the guardian state acted overtly in most of Turkey, in uniform and without. In the Kurdish provinces they did not bother to return behind the scenes and terrorized millions of men, women and children long after the return to democracy in the west.

The key dynamic of this era is the struggle between two actors, the elected government of Turgut Özal and his Motherland Party and the 'guardian state', i.e. the army, the judiciary, bureaucracy and their representatives in politics. This struggle was shaped by three factors: first, the formal reign of the military between 1980 and 1983 and its hold on power until the demise of General Evren as president in 1989 ensured that the elected government was confined to a limited political space and confined itself to economic policies. The generals dictated the foreign policy on Cyprus, as well as key domestic decisions such as the infusion of Islam into the ideology of the state or the modalities of the war against the Kurds. Second, the two actors did not always clash: Özal, with his ideological background in political Islam, happily embraced the generals' Islamic turn. With regard to the Kurdish war and Cyprus, he was in tacit agreement with, or at least resigned to, the hawkish policies of the guardian state. Finally, as Özal consolidated his power throughout the 1980s, and came close to challenging the generals, he also displayed a predilection for authoritarian government and illiberal policies as well as political corruption and cronyism.

It would hence be incomplete to characterize the struggle between guardian state and elected leader as a clear-cut confrontation between the virtuous representatives of the people and brutal, narrow-minded generals – even though the latter characterization of course holds true with regard to the 1980 coup. In this, the Özal era most clearly marked the dynamics of the fight between the guardians and the elected leaders, which we have encountered in the years of the Democrat Party under Adnan Menderes, and which we will see with even more force under the Justice and Development Party in the 2000s. The pattern, however, remains the same and accounts for the often contradictory nature of developments, as any policy shift at times of relative civilian power was countered with behind-the-scene politics either instantly, or when the elected governments failed to garner electoral support, as would be the case in the 1990s. Before examining the resurgence of civilian power, however, let us first turn to one of the great atrocities of contemporary Turkish history, the military coup of 12 September 1980.

## Silence and torture: 12 September 1980

It was between 3 and 5 a.m., well before the curfew would be lifted. Military police were kicking the front door of the flat. The neighbours heard the noise, but kept behind windows and doors. When the woman opened the door, the soldiers stormed in with their guns at face level. Establishing that her husband was not resisting arrest, the officer in charge gave him a few minutes to get ready, while the soldiers searched the flat. Two privates were blocking the door to prevent anybody from leaving the flat. His wife knew there was nothing to do, but her son was crying. Eventually, the officer pointed his gun at him and told him to shut up. When the man was ready to leave, they handcuffed his hands behind his back and took him away. For the next few days, she and her son ran back and forth between police stations, martial law offices and prisons. They tried to block out the tortured screams of men and women echoing through corridors and courtyards. When she finally found her husband, she was as relieved as she was shaken by his battered sight.

The woman behind this recollection is the mother of a good friend. In the early 1980s, variants of this traumatic story were repeated a myriad of times and all over the country. What was happening was unprecedented, even in terms of Turkey's then rather high standards of political violence: in the three years of its reign, the military detained around 650,000 men and women from all walks of life for at least ninety days but often for years without charge. While the regime sought to give itself a veneer of credibility, it employed the courts and found willing executioners in the judiciary: prosecutors opened a staggering 210,000 court cases on often fabricated grounds of membership of communist organizations. Some Islamists and followers of the extreme right, who had thought of themselves as defenders of the state, were also tried. Judges granted around five hundred of the six thousand requests for death sentences. Hangmen executed forty-nine men and women.

Only a few days into the military takeover, the assassinations and shoot-outs ended abruptly. Many ordinary citizens were understandably relieved that the violence was over and that people could go about their daily lives without having to fear stray bullets from assassinations and shoot-outs between rival groups. In the absence of independent media reports, few realized the gravity of the human rights violations, especially if they did not have relatives or friends who faced prosecution. The US administration also welcomed the coup, as Richard Perle, Assistant Secretary of Defence during the Reagan administration, remembered: 'The seizure of power by the Turkish armed forces in September 1980 [was] a response by the Turkish armed forces to the breakdown of order and security and the rise of terrorism and widespread random violence in Turkey [...]' (Perle 1999).

In fact, US involvement was not limited to this warm embrace of the putsch: the coup had been planned with the connivance and probably the active support of the US Central Intelligence Agency. The fact that the assassinations literally ended overnight raised suspicions early on that the guardian state must have instigated these attacks in the first place. The political leaders of the time, including the conservative Demirel and the social democrat Ecevit, later verified this assertion. In fact, it is highly likely that a large part of the violence was caused by clandestine groups and stay-behind armies – combat forces in NATO countries that would defend the territory from within in case of Soviet invasion – which received assistance from the CIA. As a result of the army's onslaught, the streets did indeed become safer – largely thanks to an order that anyone caught on the streets during curfew should be shot – yet the violence did not really abate. It was transferred to the prisons and executed by commanders, soldiers, policemen and prison wardens. They tortured almost all of the detainees, beating more than two hundred to death and leaving tens of thousands with lasting physical and psychological wounds. Diyarbakır Prison, and the jails of Mamak in Ankara and Metris in Istanbul, were only three of the many centres of torture that were set up all over the country.

Tabula rasa: *minarets and monuments* The military command used its first weeks in government to destroy what had been a polarized but increasingly complex civil society and create a corporatist dictatorship under the complete control of the guardian state. All political parties, trade unions and associations were closed down – even the most inconspicuous ones; all active politicians were jailed on prison islands in the Marmara Sea; newspapers were put on a very tight leash and forbidden to publish critical stories about the junta. The next phase in this veritable re-education project was the creation of an appropriate legal framework and an updated state ideology that would reinvigorate people's nationalist credentials and steer them away from the perceived communist threat.

The return to authoritarian government structures was greatly advanced by the replacement of the 1961 constitution, which even in its curtailed form after the 1971 military intervention was deemed too liberal. Put to the vote in November 1982 to sustain a veneer of citizen involvement, the new constitution was based on the principle of 'protecting the state from its citizens' (Oran 2006). It severely confined the rights of association and freedom of expression and introduced an authoritarian ideology that surpassed even the revolutionary fervour of the 1920s. Basic human rights, such as the use of mother tongues, were explicitly forbidden. The constitution was geared towards excluding Kurdish and Islamist parties from government by imposing a 10 per cent threshold and, most importantly, in the infamous temporary Article 15, absolved the leaders of the military coup from any legal responsibility for their misdeeds. Another temporary article stipulated a ban on the political activities of all pre-1980 politicians. Given the prevailing climate of fear at the time, the use of transparent envelopes that showed the colour of the vote, and the presence of gendarmes in front of every ballot box, it is not surprising that only a few – less than 10 per cent – dared to cast a no vote. The 1982 constitution was thereby rubber-stamped with a rigged military referendum.

More than half a million people were in jail and tens of thousands of political activists fled to western Europe, where they would politicize the Turkish and Kurdish diasporas, and create the basis of much of the principled criticism of Turkey which European Social Democrats and Green parties voiced throughout much of the 1980s and 1990s. Around ten thousand refugees were eventually stripped of their citizenship, and regained their passports only in the late 1990s. The generals were close to achieving the '*tabula rasa*' that they required for their new deal: a tightly policed political space, severely limited individual liberties and zero tolerance for political forces that could oppose the neoliberal economic arrangements. Yet there still were left-leaning university professors and assistants, as well as local administrators, who continued to voice their criticism of the junta and were protected owing to their status as civil servants. The military government responded to this last remaining island of resistance with the so-called '1402' regulation, sacking around five thousand civil servants who were suspected of opposition to the September Coup. From now on, a funereal silence would reign in universities and public offices.

Concurrently, the generals took steps to correct Turkey's ideological polarization by mandating a state ideology that was in agreement with the doctrine of the 'Islamic Green Belt'. The policy of US president Jimmy Carter – in office during the coup – and his National Security Council under Zbigniew Brzezinski aimed at weakening Soviet influence in the Muslim world by supporting an Islamic awakening against the Soviet Union. The 'Green Belt' policy crystallized in the form of support to the Taliban and their fight against the Soviet Union, and in the encouragement of Islamist movements in Central Asia. In Turkey, it coincided with the generals' intent to refashion and Islamicize Kemalism, whose attraction as governing ideology of the republic had eroded significantly since the 1950s. The local variation of the pro-Islamist policy would soon come to dominate the curricula, the public speeches of General Evren and the official ideology of the Turkish republic. Significantly, it would shape the next generation of students in the public school system and prepare the shift towards a more prominent role for Islam in the public space. It was called the 'Turkish-Islamic Synthesis', and was an eclectic mix of authoritarian, if incoherent, ideologies ranging from Turkish ethno-racial nationalism, Islamist supremacism and Ottomanism to Kemalist authoritarianism. It had been circulating in conservative circles for a while. Its influence went well beyond the remit of the now mandatory religious education in schools and the many hundreds of religious preacher schools (*Imam Hatip Liseleri*) that were set up to provide a strongly religious curriculum.

During the three years of the junta, thousands of mosques were built to put the idea of an economically neoliberal and socially conservative Muslim Turkey into practice, while the budget of the Directorate of Religious Affairs (Diyanet) was increased by more than 50 per cent. As a result, the Diyanet became one of the biggest state service agencies and an important public actor. As in the case of the Armed Forces Pension Fund (OYAK) in the 1960s, the Diyanet and its many subsidiaries created a strong incentive for the growing number of religious personnel to support the new status quo. The generals made sure that religion received more prominence in the universities and established twenty-three faculties of Islamic theology. They thereby laid the basis for the ideological, institutional and political shift towards religion and ethno-nationalism. In addition to this openly religious reorientation of state ideology, however, the generals also revived the personality cult around Mustafa Kemal, which had been waning in the pre-coup years. The veneration of Atatürk in the form of thousands of new monuments and photos of the founder of the republic reached idolatrous proportions, and created one of the many obvious contradictions that mark today's Turkey: How can one be both a pious Muslim – as mandated by the generals – and show reverence to the likeness of Mustafa Kemal? How can one build thousands of mosques, as well as thousands of idols, which are clearly outlawed by Islamic tradition? Yet the putschists followed a military logic, not the logic of common sense. The General Staff, for instance, declared the Kurds to be 'Mountain Turks', and in 1983, had the use of 'languages spoken in countries that Turkey has no diplomatic relations with' proscribed. Such was the strategy to deny the Kurdish language without referring to it. And it was this kind of thinking which injected a great deal of pathology into the political life of Turkey.

Pathologies were the norm during the September regime: the generals brutalized society where they could. In order to achieve their vision of a 'healthy society', the generals targeted individuals and social groups that they deemed morally deviant. Literally storming nightclubs and music halls across the country, military commanders ordered transsexual performers and singers to be removed and imprisoned. Subjected to torture, compulsory haircuts and sexual abuse by privates and their commanders, they were deported to provincial cities. A transsexual activist recalls:

> The soldiers would arrest us during our performances and force us on the train to Eskişehir. Of course we wanted to get out. We would wait for a good moment to jump off the train once we had left Istanbul. We would jump when the train slowed down. Imagine, our heads were shaven. We were battered and bruised. We were still in our performance outfits and we had no money on us. We got back to Istanbul by hitchhiking. And then, they would catch us again. (Buse Kılıçkaya, interview, 2 April 2009)

General Evren personally ensured that famous cross-dressing singers like Zeki Müren and the transsexual performer Bülent Ersoy were banned from stage and state radio and TV. Film director Sırrı Süreyya Önder captured the brutality of the gender and cultural policies of the September regime in his influential 2007 film *Beynelmilel* (The International). In a key scene, a clandestine but exuberant party in the eastern town of Adıyaman takes place in the back of a truck. The organizers meet in the evening in the truck to circumvent the curfew regulations. The men eat and drink and sing with a cross-dressing dancer (*köçek*), accompanied by a band of local Roma musicians. Suddenly, an army unit storms the party and arrests all men present. Responsible for bringing Adıyaman up to the standard of the new times, the local commander coerces the members of the band to form a military orchestra. For the evenings, the commander sets up a military casino, where a female performer from a third-class nightclub performs nationalist songs to entertain the officers.

Önder's persiflage was not exaggerated. Throughout the years of military rule, state TV regularly featured a clip with the singer Müşerref

Akay. Dressed in a red dress and cap reminiscent of a 1930s stewardess's uniform – complete with the crescent and star and as modern and inauspicious as the combat pilot Sabiha Gökçen – a blonde curly-haired Akay performed the song 'Turkey My Paradise', while tanks and soldiers in combat uniform marched on in the background, alternating with touristic images of Turkey's monuments. The lyrics of the song were a crash course in the ideology of the 12 September regime. Akay sung the first part in an agitated deep voice and with a belligerent expression, and then shifted to angelic mode and smile:

> Betrayal has infiltrated my heroic race
> In all hearts there is suffering and hatred
> My enemies are not brave, they are cowards
> There is no friendly nation to the Turk. [...]
> Let us celebrate the principles of our father [Mustafa Kemal]
> Let us run toward the goals he has shown us
> Turkey, Turkey my paradise
> My nation without compare.

'Turkey My Paradise' was commissioned by the generals and used systematically throughout the junta years as background music during torture sessions in the prisons of the regime. A survivor of such torture, the music producer Cem Yılmaz, bought the rights to the song in 2007 to prevent any further performance of it in public.

*The roots of the Kurdish war* The September regime became particularly vicious in the Kurdish provinces, where it was symbolized by the hell of Diyarbakır Prison. Mass arrests of left-wing and Kurdish nationalists reached thousands in the first months of the takeover, yet initially attitudes among the security services remained much the same. As in other prisons in the country, the administration and staff consisted of civil servants and included left-leaning or simply decent individuals, who generally treated the prisoners with respect, or at least not with contempt. This all changed, however, when Officer Esat Oktay Yıldıran was dispatched from Ankara to adapt the prison regime to the new times. Activist Nebahat Akkoç was a regular visitor to the prison where her husband was incarcerated. She remembers the sudden shift, which occurred all over the country:

> One day, everything changed. When I arrived at the prison, I was told

that a new prison administration had taken over. There were dogs
everywhere. We were ordered to queue up one by one and made to
wait for hours. Villagers who did not understand Turkish and stepped
out of the queue were beaten up. The prison chief, Yıldıran, would
roam around the queues, always accompanied by his dog and dressed
in a black overcoat. Announcements blaring through the loudspeakers
were repeated every minute: 'The time for visits will be limited to two
minutes. It is forbidden to speak any other language than Turkish.'
(Nebahat Akkoç, interview, 13 July 2009)

If survivors and eyewitnesses remember Yıldıran as resembling a
Nazi officer, it is for a reason. During his term in the early 1980s, the
prison turned into a slaughterhouse, where guards and officers committed monstrous crimes against the inmates. Prisoners were obliged
to follow military rules and scream the military prayer before every
meal: 'Praise be to God, thanks to our nation, grace to our army'.
They were forced to declare themselves as Turkish and made to yell
the Turkish national anthem, often while being tortured and violated.
Families waiting outside were forced to speak Turkish and not let near
the prison doors if they failed to do so. Yıldıran's sadism knew no
bounds: At least forty prisoners died, often at his hands and always
under heavy torture. This regime differed from that in prisons outside
the Kurdish provinces, as it directly targeted and sought to crush the
inmates' Kurdish identity. However, it did this by introducing a level
of brutality that cannot be explained by motives of either punishment
or revenge. It was a deliberate attempt to coerce Kurds into hatred
against the state and into violence. The torture at Diyarbakır and in
many other prisons in the Kurdish provinces laid the groundwork for
the radicalization of the Kurdish nationalist movement and created an
ever-growing pool of activists, who would see no other choice than to
join the armed struggle against the Turkish state. Yıldıran was later
promoted by the armed forces and died only when a PKK sympathizer
shot him and his wife in the late 1980s in Istanbul.

The early but seminal verdict on those years was best expressed
in the film *Yol* (The Way or The Road) by Kurdish filmmaker Yılmaz
Güney, who directed the film in 1982 from his prison cell with the help
of an assistant. *Yol* narrates the story of several non-political inmates,
all of them Kurdish, who set out for their home towns and villages
for a few days of parole. Initially, they rejoice at the prospect of a

break from prison. Yet as they make their way towards the Kurdish provinces, they run into curfews, are troubled by the heavy military presence and shocked to see military attacks on villages. One by one, they realize that there is hardly any difference left between the prison and the outside. One of the protagonists remarks that '[t]he whole country has turned into an open-air prison run by the military'.

For the Kurdish provinces, Güney's artistic vision was prophetic. Brutalized by torture and military rule, political activists as well as ordinary peasants were cajoled into joining the Kurdistan Workers' Party (*Partiya Karkeren Kurdistan*, PKK). With the charismatic leader Abdullah Öcalan (Apo) socialized in the Turkish Marxist-Leninist youth movements of the 1970s, a clear programme for Kurdish independence, and a military organization that responded to opposition with violence, the PKK became the place to go for thousands of young men and women, who had been terrorized by the military regime. In 1984, the PKK launched a war for the Kurdish territories and a military campaign that did not stop short of terrorist strategies. In response, the state used even more terror and destruction: in addition to regular army and police forces, semi-clandestine counter-terrorism units came into play, which assassinated Kurdish intellectuals and political activists. The 'Gendarmerie Intelligence and Counterterrorism Centre' (JITEM) was the extension of the army, while the 'Special Team' (*Özel Tim*) was its equivalent in the police force. Both were set up to fight the PKK and its sympathizers using legal as well as extralegal measures. Soon, a violent Islamist group was also enlisted in the effort to fight the Kurdish insurgence: the Kurdish 'Hizbullah' (Party of God). Unrelated to its Lebanese namesake, and increasingly powerful thanks solely to the generous financial and logistical support of the guardian state, Hizbullah fighters assassinated PKK activists as well as Kurdish intellectuals, and attacked women in breach of the party's Islamic dress code.

## Motherland promise: wealth and stability

The generals had devised an almost perfect plan for the return to civilian government after three years of direct rule: a three-party poll with two parties established by the junta, the one chaired by a former general and called the 'Nationalist Democracy Party', the other by a bureaucrat and called the 'Populist Party'. In the military mindset of General – now President – Evren and his co-conspirators, these two parties were supposed to represent the left and the right, while the Nationalist Democrats were expected to win as the party of the military. Evren himself had endorsed the army's candidate, Turgut Sunalp, on state TV the night before the polls. The third party permitted by the National Security Council to run, if only to keep up a semblance of democratic competition, was the Motherland Party (*Anavatan Partisi*, also ANAP), deemed too insignificant to disrupt the generals' calculations. To their dismay, however, the December 1983 elections resulted in the victory of the one man they had not considered fit for the job: the technocrat and interim economy minister of the coup years, Turgut Özal. He was the only choice not promoted by the military, and he was voted for by 45 per cent of the electorate. As the puzzled generals looked on, Motherland emerged as victor in all national and municipal elections, a position it would hold for the next six years. Even if the European Community, taken aback by the coup and not convinced of the democratic credentials of the elections, remained sceptical, a new chapter in Turkey's incomplete transformation to democracy unfolded.

Much like the Justice Party after the 1960 coup, Motherland became the melting pot for the followers of Turkey's right-wing political traditions (conservative, nationalist and Islamist), held together by Özal's charisma and his very personal and eclectic ideology: a mix of religious piety and economic liberalism, a sense of entrepreneurial spirit and individual achievement and a more inclusive understanding of Turkishness which created some breathing space for Kurds and other non-Turkish communities. His view of the state resounded with earlier Democrat principles:

> A strong state does not mean a patriarchal state. The aim is not richness of the state but richness of the nation. If people are rich, it means that the state is rich. In economy or political spheres the state should not compete with the people, but support them. The people are not the servants of the state, but the state must be servant of the people. (Sever and Dizdar 1993)

Born to a Kurdish mother and Turkish father, Özal was educated at the Istanbul Technical University and in the United States. He had a distinguished career in the State Planning Administration and the World Bank. Especially in the 1970s, he was a successful businessman working with US companies, but also within the leading Turkish business conglomerates such as Sabancı Holding. He was also well connected to Islamic brotherhoods like the *Nakşibendi* and had run, if unsuccessfully, for the Islamist National Salvation Party in 1977. This background in business and in the state bureaucracy, as well as his connections to religious brotherhoods and his US orientation, placed him in the unique position of being able to lead Turkey out of the military dictatorship and through the global transformations of 1989. As the architect of the '24 January Decisions' – prophetically described by former prime minister Ecevit as unenforceable under the conditions of democracy – Özal did benefit from the suspension of trade union activities and the destruction of the left after the 1980 coup, and the restrictive measures of the 1982 constitution. He had no opposition to fight, at least in economic affairs, where General Evren gave him a free hand.

*Liberalizing the economy, 'cutting the corners'* Yet even with much of the political space policed by the generals and wide popular support, Özal's task of carrying Turkey into the age of global capitalism was little short of Herculean. The import substitution industrialization (ISI) of the 1960s and 1970s had created an inefficient private industrial sector thanks to its protection from international competition. It produced relatively expensive and low-quality goods for internal consumption. This sector remained dependent on foreign suppliers for machinery, and more importantly dependent on the state in a regime of patronage and clientelist relations. This dependent bourgeoisie did realize that it could not develop further under the tight regime of import substitution and in the context of continuous social unrest. The Istanbul-based entrepreneurial sector hence cautiously welcomed the coup and Özal's premiership. Yet many key industries – sugar, paper, coal, spirits – and hence much of the production were still in state ownership or under strict state control. Almost the entire economy was directed from Ankara, and only a few commodities were traded under market conditions. The veteran of economic journalism in Turkey, Osman Ulagay, remembers that his colleagues were surprised at the very idea of a dedicated column on economic affairs when he first started writing it in the newspaper *Cumhuriyet* in the early 1980s.

It was the time when Ankara reigned supreme and the only regular economic news in the papers referred to the fluctuations in the daily gold rate. The economy was an extension of politics and the state. But the state failed to deliver: civil servants had to wear their overcoats in the office, because the state lacked the funds to pay for heating fuel. Very few economists believed that Özal would be able to transform the economic system, and even fewer really understood the gravity of the changes he was introducing. In economic terms, the 'Decisions of 24 January' meant the dawn of a new age. (Osman Ulagay, interview, 9 July 2009)

With annual growth rates of more than 5 per cent, Özal managed to drive inflation down from three-digit rates to one. More importantly, he opened the way for new social classes to emerge: scrapping many of the protectionist measures and terminating state monopolies, he facilitated the emergence of a new class of industrial capitalists in Anatolian cities. 'Big capital' had been invested in a few centres of industrial production in and around Istanbul, Izmir and Adana, and hence was often designated 'Istanbul capital'. Most Anatolian cities were centres of trade and commerce, at best hosting a state-owned industrial enterprise that served as the major job creator. This set-up changed substantially in the 1980s. Thanks to a growing textile sector, as well as construction and engineering companies exploiting particularly Middle Eastern markets and after 1989 Russia and eastern Europe, many medium-sized cities in western and central Anatolia made a leap forward in industrial production. Cities like Gaziantep, Denizli and Kayseri became the centres of this third industrial revolution, after the republican effort at industrialization in the 1930s and the liberalization under Menderes in the 1950s, creating the so-called 'Anatolian tigers'. In the 1990s, they would come to be known as 'Islamic Calvinists'. It was in the same period that big family conglomerates like Sabancı, Koç and Eczacıbaşı entered competition in international markets and transformed themselves into global actors.

Both sectors, 'Istanbul capitalists' and conservative Anatolian newcomers, contributed to the sevenfold rise in Turkish exports from just below US$3 billion at the beginning of the 1980s to US$20 billion at their end. The share of industrial production in exported goods doubled from 40 to more than 80 per cent. Until the collapse of communist regimes in eastern Europe, Turkish businesses were particularly active in the Middle East. If in the late 1970s only 15 per cent of Turkish export goods were assigned to the region, and the European Community was the biggest export market for Turkish goods, by 1985 more than 40 per cent of Turkish exports went to Iran and neighbouring Arab states in the east. After 1989, Russia and the Turkic republics of Central Asia would supersede the Middle East as the eldorado for Turkish businessmen, even though the staunch authoritarianism in Central Asia limited the potential for quick expansion. Much of Central Asia remained more of a symbolic issue in Turkey's foreign policy, while growth rates with Russia were real. Özal's export strategy and the immediate returns were nothing short of miraculous. Yet imports also jumped from US$3 three to US$22 billion, presaging the foreign trade deficit, which would put significant strains on the economy in the later years of the decade.

Another significant transformation that would not only change Turkey's economy but its 'feel' occurred in the tourism sector: a marginal activity in the late 1970s and curbed by the conditions of political strife, tourism contributed only around US$200 million to Turkey's gross domestic product. By 1989, the tourism revenues had reached US$3 billion, the number of tourist establishments had doubled to more than a thousand and the volume of annual visitors had seen a threefold rise from one and a half to five million. Despite the prevalence of large companies, small and medium enterprises from pensions, cafés and bars to transportation companies benefited from the tourism boom on the Aegean and Mediterranean shores – not so much in Istanbul, which was considered too dangerous – and created job opportunities for young men and women. Many of the construction workers and the employees in the hospitality sector in the resorts were of Kurdish origin, and the possibility of interacting with European visitors created a space of opportunity in terms of political and personal exchanges that was not available elsewhere. In any case, the growing tourism sector contributed significantly to society's cultural globalization.

There is no doubt that the Özal years unleashed a new mindset of capitalist development that set free the creative forces of the market. Yet the *nouveaux riches* often thought of capital accumulation in terms of immediate gains and high profits. The emblematic phrase of those years was 'cut the corners' (*köşeyi dönmek*), to make easy money, as much as possible and as fast as possible. Fictitious exports by dummy companies, fake investments to siphon off state incentives and countless cases of embezzlement in the administration enriched some, while they impoverished many. The economic restructuring especially affected wage-earners and led to a significant growth in the numbers of the poor. This poverty took on a decidedly urban character, as immigration to the large metropolises accelerated and brought a growing number of Kurds to the cities in the west. Nevertheless, a pauperization of the masses did not occur, despite the failure of the Özal administration to keep the inflation rate in check. The exception to this could be found in the Kurdish provinces, where the war between the PKK and the Turkish army destroyed rural livelihoods and local economies.

Inflationist pressures stemmed from the foreign trade deficit and the side effect of ambitious infrastructure projects, which the Motherland government carried out through the 1980s, often with a nod to the iconic development projects of the Democrat and Justice parties. The most symbolic of them was Istanbul's second Bosporus Bridge, completed in 1988. In keeping with the pro-Ottoman leanings of the prevalent 'Turkish-Islamic' ideology of the time, it was named after Fatih Sultan Mehmet (Mehmed the Conqueror). The government also took the first steps towards the construction of a comprehensive network of motorways, building on the ambitious first wave of national roads of the 1950s. Finally, the whole telephone system was renewed while literally all villages were connected to the phone and electricity grids. Emulating the developmental model of his predecessors (road and communication networks) and especially of Adnan Menderes (the boulevards of Istanbul), Özal and the Motherland mayor of Istanbul until 1989, Bedrettin Dalan, reshaped Istanbul with the construction of the city's second circular highway and the infamous 'Tarlabaşı' Boulevard, which he had had bulldozed through the urban fabric of the formerly Greek and Armenian areas of Beyoğlu. For years, this main thoroughfare struck visitors as an open wound, with entire building blocks flattened and massive empty spaces recalling the destruction of war zones. Many of the mostly poor inhabitants were forced out of the city centre, where they had had easy access to public services and to informal networks of trade and services. They had to resettle at the periphery, where they were joined by increasing numbers of Kurdish refugees, who were fleeing the military's brutal rule in the south-east. Istanbul's periphery started to expand at a visible pace, initially with semi-formal and increasingly high-rise housing and eventually with skyscrapers and office blocks.

*Özal's new man and the 'Dallas model'* The free market policies of the Motherland revolutionized the terms of engagement for the production and consumption of all goods and services, including popular culture, lifestyle and worldviews. For investigative journalist Ece Temelkuran, who witnessed the late 1980s as a teenager, the Motherland under Özal created a new '*Homo oeconomicus*', a project that had become possible only after the generals had destroyed the left and discredited all alternatives to neoliberal capitalism:

> Özal's project was to create a new man for a new social and economic model. It was the 'Dallas model' [after the popular US TV series], consumption oriented and centred on both the United States and Islam. It was the motto of the time: Let's work hard, let's earn lots of money, let's watch TV, let's drink a lot of tea. Let's cut the corners. (Ece Temelkuran, interview, 15 June 2009)

Indeed, many of the processes of market liberalization and commodification, which are commonly associated with the transformation economies in eastern Europe, happened in Turkey in these years. The first large-scale shopping mall based on US models was built in Istanbul on the recommendation of Özal, who inaugurated it in 1988. Located on the main entry road connecting the city centre with the airport – called Atatürk since the military coup – the Ataköy Galleria was as much a promise of the wealth that was soon to reach all Turks, if only as marvelling visitors, as it was a mall. While imported luxury goods entered the markets – putting pressure on the hard currency reserves – and brash statements of wealth in the form of expensive sport cars and lavish villas marked the new middle classes, popular culture as well as public debate was invigorated by the emergence of commercial TV channels.

An indicator of the prevailing mindset of the time, the emergence of the commercial TV market occurred beyond the confines of the law: with the continuing presence of Kenan Evren as president with substantial veto powers until 1989, a constitutional amendment for the liberalization of radio and television services was beyond the pale. The first commercial TV station, 'Star', was started by later media mogul Cem Uzan and, significantly, Özal's son Ahmet in 1989, and began to transmit from Germany in 1990. Even though the state broadcaster TRT had already prepared the change in popular culture consumption in the mid-1980s with US series such as *Dallas* and *Dynasty*, it did stick to the generals' red lines and banned belly-dance shows, programmes including Arabesk, the music of the urban underdog, and transsexual singers like Bülent Ersoy and Zeki Müren. Everything that was banned made its way into the living rooms of the nation thanks to Star. The new generation of the 1990s, especially if they lived outside the war-torn south-east, was socialized into a light fare of US series like *Miami Vice*, *The Bold and the Beautiful*, music shows and erotic TV programmes that were broadcast in the late hours. The generals' taste disappeared from the screens. But it was only in 1993, and after another commercial TV station called 'Show' went on air, that the parliament finally lifted the state monopoly on radio and TV broadcasting. Three more channels went on air as the new law was announced.

*Pushing the boundaries: the beginnings of civil society* Throughout the 1980s, the National Security Council and General Evren ensured that politics were confined to the straitjacket of military oversight, despite Özal's policies of liberalization. As the torturers went about their daily work in prisons and police stations, the school curricula were militarized, retired and acting officers were invited to teach 'National Security' at high schools, tens of thousands of political prisoners remained in jail and ever more socialists and Kurdish activists were sentenced to inflated jail terms. The judiciary was a particular enforcer of the generals' will. Yet civil society and new political movements emerged nevertheless. While the pre-1980 revolutionary left was being crushed with never-ending court cases and military propaganda, some socialists explored the possibilities of political action beyond armed struggle and Marxist ideology.

The first visible social movement after the military coup was organized by feminists, who were enraged by the comments of a judge, who had suggested that husbands had a right to use corporal punishment against their wives. On 17 May 1987, around two thousand women and their supporters took to the streets in Istanbul's Kadıköy district, chanting slogans against the violence inflicted on women by their fathers, husbands and brothers, as well as by the guardians of a patriarchal society. They were belittled by the police and the military authorities, who failed to understand the radical nature of this opposition: not only did the feminists break the funereal silence surrounding the post-coup arrangements by reclaiming the streets in the name of potentially subversive ideas, they also attacked the core values of the 12 September dictatorship – militarism, unquestioned obedience to authority, fetishization of the state, and the language of patriarchy – which had taken over institutions and shaped the public debate, despite Turgut Özal's more permissive politics. Others established civil society organizations such as the Human Rights Association (*Türkiye İnsan Hakları Derneği*) in 1986, which would play an important role in exposing the crimes of the military regime and successive civil administrations throughout the Kurdish war. It supported individuals suffering from the effects of torture and helped their reintegration into society. Often, its members would face pressure and mistreatment from security services and state agencies.

Özal's liberal outlook, if tempered by the religious and nationalist forces within his party, was not limited to the free market and global orientation, even though these were probably his driving motivations. Where he could, he did push the borders imposed by the military overlords: in 1987, the parliament ratified the individual right of appeal to the European Court of Human Rights (ECHR), opening the way for citizens of Turkey to take cases of human rights abuse into the international sphere. For the first time, they had the right to seek redress from a state whose police and military were using torture and ill treatment as regular techniques of interrogation and discipline, and whose courts habitually protected the perpetrators of torture from the victims. In the same year, a close referendum vote allowed for the abrogation of the articles in the constitution banning the pre-coup leaders from political activity, and cleared their way for a return to politics. In 1991, two years after Özal's election to the presidency and the long-awaited demise of General Evren – the most visible reminder of the 1980 military coup – the Motherland government under Mesut Yılmaz finally revoked the ban on the Kurdish language.

At the same time, however, the war in the Kurdish provinces was raging, and neither Özal nor the Motherland governments under Yıldırım Akbulut and Mesut Yılmaz had the power or will to stem the tide of violence. It was under Özal that the government made the fateful decision to establish the 'Village Guards' (*Köy Korucuları*), paramilitary forces that would fight the PKK under the command of the Gendarmerie and eventually reach almost 100,000 members. The village guards, like the Hamidiye troops (*Hamidiye Alayları*) of Sultan Abdühamid, were tribal contingents and, like their predecessors, would soon become part of the rule of terror in the region. And so would the 'State of Emergency Regional Governorate' (*Olağanüstü Hal Bölge Valiliği*), introduction of which effectively cut off the Kurdish provinces from the rest of the country and established a regime that was based on different laws and state behaviour: as the decade came to a close, even the limited freedoms of the 1982 constitution would be suspended in the Kurdish region.

## Re-engagement with the world: the US, Europe and 1989

Turkish foreign policy in the 1980s was complex and contradictory, shaped by the often conflicting agendas of two actors: the military command, inept in foreign relations, and the more globally thinking and acting Özal. In the three years of military rule, Turkey became an isolated country, save for the military support of the USA. The two differential trajectories of the neighbours Greece and Turkey are a case in point: Greece had signed an Association Agreement with the European Community in 1961, only two years before Turkey. The accession process was frozen during the regime of the colonels, but after Greece's successful return to democracy in 1974, it was admitted to the European Community in 1981. In the same year, to most European observers Turkey looked like a pariah state with a military government at war with its own people, and rightly so. As the military retreated and Özal gained power, however, the country's standing abroad was at least partially restored. Turkish foreign policy shook off its timid manner and the country emerged as a more confident actor. For a brief time, Turkey seemed to successfully create a new role for itself in the emerging post-Cold War world. Many of the debates on a shift of axis, on Turkey's role between the East and the West, of neo-Ottomanism and pan-Turkism, but also on the diplomatic conflicts over the Armenian genocide and Cyprus, can be traced back to these years. The debates of the late 1980s would serve as a blueprint for the foreign policy of the Justice and Development Party in the 2000s.

*International isolation and civilian return* The generals had only the US army and NATO as their friend, but even the Pentagon was not supportive on all fronts. The US administration had helped prepare the coup and supported its leader. Turkey was deemed too important to lose as a US ally in a region where US hegemony had been waning since the 1979 Islamic Revolution in Iran. When it came to Cyprus, however, under Turkish occupation since 1974, the generals were completely isolated. An administrative entity had emerged in the northern part under the control of the Turkish army. When the

European Community suspended financial aid and relations with Turkey in January 1982, owing to the junta's continued hold on power and their defiance in Cyprus, the generals were compelled to look for new allies. The Foreign Ministry tried to win over Arab leaders and showed a heightened engagement in the Organization of the Islamic Conference. Yet the generals' foreign policy failed to garner support for their occupation of Cyprus. In November 1983, only a month before the elections that would transfer the government to civilian hands, the generals persuaded the Cypriot Turkish leader Rauf Denktash to unilaterally declare the Turkish Republic of Northern Cyprus (TRNC). This declaration further stigmatized Turkey in the international community and especially in Europe, where Greece – a full member of the European Community since January 1981 – became a prominent actor mobilizing against Turkey's European aspirations. With the declaration of the TRNC, the generals had created a major stumbling block for Turkey that would sour relations with Greece and the European Union for decades to come.

Another such stumbling block stemmed from the efforts of Armenian diaspora organizations to pass a US Congress decision acknowledging the Armenian genocide. The Armenian Secret Army for the Liberation of Armenia (ASALA), as much Marxist-Leninist as Armenian nationalist, had targeted and killed thirty-six Turkish diplomats since 1979 to compel the government to acknowledge publicly Turkey's responsibility for the Armenian genocide. The attack and hostage-taking in Ankara's Esenboğa airport in August 1982 was a particularly shocking event as it occurred during martial law and in the capital's well-guarded airport. It resulted in the death of eight passengers and one of the two assailants. From now on, Turkish Foreign Ministry officials would equate campaigns for the recognition of the Armenian genocide with the assassination campaigns against its diplomats. It was President Evren who initiated the beginning of a pattern of threats, cross-talks and behind-the-scenes lobbying that from now on would recur almost annually around 24 April: Armenian lobby groups would try to convince Congress to promulgate a resolution on the Armenian genocide and Turkey would retaliate by withdrawing its ambassador in Washington. In 1987, President Evren called off a trip to the USA in the wake of one such resolution, which was eventually quashed by the White House. By the end of their rule in December 1983, the generals had isolated the country from both their western and eastern neighbours. Only the military alliance with the USA and NATO had survived the generals' meddling.

Once in power, however, Özal took a personal interest in the conduct of foreign policy and sought to restore Turkey's damaged international standing step by step. He restarted the opening towards the Arab world, which the military government had failed to sustain, particularly in terms of bilateral trade and the export of services in the form of Turkish construction companies. Relations with Europe in general and the European Community (EC) in particular eased only slowly. Above all, unlike the USA, European governments, and particularly social democrats and the German Green Party, were vocal in their criticism of the military coup and the massive human rights abuses, which continued throughout Özal's rule in the 1980s. Many left-wing organizations and intellectuals had re-established themselves in exile in Germany and neighbouring countries and supported the opposition against the regime. The censored newspapers of the time, and the generals' media machinery, ensured that large parts of the public misunderstood justified European criticism of the junta as hostility towards Turkey and its people. For most, however, the European Community was simply not at the top of the agenda: large parts of the country were still under martial law and the Kurdish provinces were subjected to violent state terror and PKK reprisals. Europe was still far away, and it had not yet become part of the daily political debate, as it would a decade later.

As prime minister, Özal had both a vision for Turkey in Europe and a sense of its economic and political realities. He was aware of the need for an anchor for the country's rapid but volatile economic development. A customs union as well as EC membership prospects would provide a stable framework for the country's transition to democracy and its economic take-off. His vision for a Turkey that was proudly Muslim *and* European, i.e. at peace with its own identity in a largely Christian club, was progressive and probably ahead of the times. It also anticipated the EU policy of his political heirs in the Justice and Development Party which would win hearts and minds in the Turkey of the 2000s. Yet his government's application for EC membership in April 1987 was premature. Neither for Turkey, with its awful human rights record, nor for Europe was the time ripe: the Commission took more than two years to respond. By the time it did, in December 1989, it was busy with the much more immediate challenge of integrating eastern Europe. The Commission refused to begin accession negotiations on the grounds of the country's human rights situation and the deadlock in Cyprus, but it did reinstate Turkey's prospects of eventual accession. EC membership was postponed for now, only to become a major foreign policy goal a decade later.

*The harbingers of 1989* The transformations in eastern Europe and the dissolution of the Soviet empire provided economic and political opportunities for Turkey, which Özal instantly recognized. As early as 1982, he had been on record doubting the sustainability of the Soviet experiment, believing

> [T]hat state planning would not keep the country afloat. He was convinced that the Soviet Union would be incapable of adapting itself to the changing world economy and that it was hence bound to perish. For him, Turkey needed to transform immediately so that it could be an assertive actor when the Iron Curtain fell and take part in shaping the world. (Osman Ulagay, interview, 9 July 2009)

Yet Turkey's encounter with eroding Communism began even before the first governments fell. The harbingers of 1989 arrived on the western borders of Turkey in the last days of May. Subjected to the forcible 'Slavicization' of their personal names and the prohibition of their linguistic, religious and cultural identity since the launch of a 'rebirth' campaign in 1984, Bulgarian Turks had started to organize mass protests in the north-east and south-east of the country, where close to 800,000 Turks lived. Todor Zhivkov, general secretary of the Bulgarian Communist Party, the architect of the 'rebirth' campaign, reacted to the growing number of demonstrations and acts of civil disobedience with brutal repression. After at least seven deaths, and in consideration of the escalation, Zhivkov decided to open the borders with Turkey. More than 300,000 ethnic Turks from Bulgaria instantly rushed to the Turkish–Bulgarian border, where they were welcomed – at least initially – with open arms by Turkey. The refugees created long convoys on the highway to Istanbul and the camps, which were set up in Thrace.

The first wave of arrivals consisted of political activists and critics of the regime, who were forcibly deported. They were followed by more than a third of the Turkish population of Bulgaria. Their arrival not only resulted in the creation of a large immigrant community with different cultural, social and religious interpretations of Turkishness and Islam, it also invigorated the older communities of Bulgarian Turks in Thrace, Bursa and Istanbul, where most of them settled. Most significantly, this first episode of the ruptures of 1989 came as a stark reminder of Turkey's deep connection with the Turkish and Muslim communities of the Balkans and their extreme vulnerability. This sense of Turkish responsibility for the Muslims of the Balkans would be further augmented by the Bosnian war in 1992, when the government of the day opposed the US arms embargo against the warring sides – which benefited the Serbian army – and supported the Bosniak war effort, albeit working through NATO and only behind the scenes with the Bosnian army.

*Restoring Turkey's neighbourhood* Since 1923, Kemalist governments had followed a cautious foreign policy based on regional and global balances. During the four decades of the Cold War, Turkey had effectively been separated from its neighbourhood: the Balkans, the Caucasus and Syria were part of the Soviet sphere of influence. Greece was an ally but not a friend and Iraq first a series of weak monarchies and then a brutal dictatorship under Saddam Hussein. The transformations of 1989 and the decrease in Soviet power in Central Asia and the Caucasus made accessible Turkey's historical areas of influence. The time was ripe for Özal's 'Turkish century', which was to restore Turkey as a key player in the post-Ottoman geography of the Balkans and the Middle East. Even though members of the opposition levelled allegations of 'Ottomanism', suffused with a decidedly pro-American outlook, against him, Özal's foreign policy, like his general politics, was based on a pragmatic mix of business and ideology: increasing economic, educational and cultural relations, tapping markets for Turkish companies, as well as devising new roles for Turkey as guardian of Turkish communities in the Arab world and Central Asia and the Muslim people of the Balkans.

Sensing the inability of the foreign service to engage in a proactive, rather than a defensive, Cold War policy, Özal personally initiated government agencies that created channels for the country's engagement with the neighbouring countries and beyond: the Development Assistance Agency of Turkey (TIKA) became the major instrument of development aid for the Central Asian republics, the satellite TV channel TRT Eurasia brought Turkish broadcasting to homes from

Azerbaijan to Turkmenistan, and the flag carrier Turkish Airlines was one of the first 'Western' carriers to fly to destinations such as Almaty, Astana and Baku. The foreign service's uneasiness stemmed also from the identity of many of its members: considered a bastion of Kemalist modernity, Turkish ambassadors and consuls were not positively predisposed towards the Islamic networks and the Ottoman outlook, which were central ingredients of Özal's foreign policy.

It was in this vacuum that Turkey-based religious groups like the *Nurcu* (members of the brotherhood of the charismatic scholar Said-i Nursi) and the followers of the charismatic cleric Fethullah Gülen began to establish schools, businesses and newspapers in most neighbouring countries and beyond. Particularly the Gülen schools, with their secular curricula and their ethos of 'service for the common good' (*hizmet*), became the preferred educational choice in many post-socialist countries. Acting much like the Protestant missions that had brought modern education to even the most distant regions of the empire in the nineteenth century, these schools prepared the advent of Turkish-speaking and pro-Turkish business and political elites in the entire region. In the years that followed the Soviet collapse, more than a hundred such schools opened in the Turkic republics of Azerbaijan, Kazakhstan, Kyrgyzstan, Turkmenistan and Uzbekistan, as well as in Russia's federal republics in the Caucasus. The Gülen schools also opened in countries on the Black Sea littoral and in the Balkans, namely in Albania, Bosnia-Herzegovina, Bulgaria and Macedonia. Wherever the schools operated, business relations with Turkey would intensify and an increasing number of graduates would choose to study at Turkish universities. Much of the initial investment in the region came from large Istanbul-based companies, which were soon joined by the smaller upstarts from Anatolia.

While Özal's new institutions and the educational networks created the basis of Turkish soft power, which would become much more pronounced during the AKP governments of the 2000s, the retirement of General Evren as president and his succession by Özal created the conditions for a brief period of strong foreign policy that was inspired by Özal's vision of Turkey as a regional power. Despite the recent refugee drama, Turkey normalized relations with Bulgaria in 1989 and soon reached an agreement to disengage military units from the Thracian border. Rapprochement with Greece, in place since the narrow avoidance of war over a Turkish research boat in the Aegean in March 1987, was complemented by a more competitive policy in the Balkans. Turkey was fast to recognize Macedonia in 1991 and also to develop a promising relationship with Albania.

One of Özal's most important foreign policy projects, which he devised with the intent of building up the country's own power base in the Black Sea littoral, was the 'Black Sea Economic Cooperation' (BSEC), with its seat in Istanbul in 1992. The economy-oriented organization for all Black Sea and Caucasus countries, including significantly Russia, as well as Albania, created a non-political forum for neighbouring countries, many of which were and remain at odds with each other. When Turkey suspended diplomatic relations with Armenia in May 1992 after the capture by Armenian forces of the Azeri town of Shusha, for instance, the BSEC was the only institution based in Turkey, where Turkish and Armenian diplomats continued to meet. Little of this spirit of cooperation and proactive engagement, however, would survive after the sudden death of Turgut Özal in April 1993.

Not surprisingly given its growing global political significance, the Middle East became the most important foreign policy arena, where Özal made a daring if risky departure from the balance politics of the Kemalist republic. Relations with Israel had been improving slowly since the mid-1980s, when Özal first publicly spoke about upgrading relations and suggested Turkey act as peace broker between Israel and the Arab world. It was Özal who saw Israel as a necessary partner if Turkey was to play a role in the Middle East. He was also aware of the potential benefits of cooperation with the pro-Israel lobby on the issue of Armenian lobbying in the US Congress, as well as with Israeli intelligence services in the campaign against the PKK. With the start of the Madrid Peace Conference in 1991, relations with Israel could become public without upsetting the Arab governments too much.

If better relations with Israel were part of Özal's Middle Eastern policy, the looming Gulf War against Iraq and the expectation of a US blueprint for a new regional order in the Middle East was at its very core. In order to be able to influence this new order and become America's key ally in the region, Turkey would need to be on the winning side. In August 1990, Özal hence succeeded in cajoling the parliament into authorizing Turkish troop movements into Iraq to join the American war effort. It also authorized the use of American bases on Turkish soil during the invasion. He did this against the express wishes of the General Staff and in contravention of Turkey's reluctance to intervene in intra-Arab affairs. In a remarkable event in Turkey's political history, the Chief of the General Staff, Necip Torumtay, who openly criticized Özal's decision to join the US war effort, was compelled to hand in his resignation after a public showdown. This was the first and so far the only time that a Chief of the General Staff has had to resign because he challenged the president. In the end, the Turkish army did not enter Iraq. But when Iraqi forces took revenge for Kurdish support for the aborted US campaign, hundreds of thousands of Kurdish civilians began to flee towards the Turkish border. The border was closed in April 1991, but eventually the refugees were allowed in at Özal's behest to avoid a humanitarian disaster on Turkey's doorstep. Özal was hence also a supporter of the no-fly zone over northern Iraq, which was established to protect the Kurds from Saddam's reprisals. It would eventually become the seat of the Kurdistan Regional Government, which Turkish diplomats and governments in the 2000s initially eyed with great suspicion.

Notwithstanding his success in the stand-off with the Chief of the General Staff, however, Özal's participation in the ill-informed and interrupted war effort against Iraq was a failure on grand scale. US forces left after ousting Iraqi troops from Kuwait, but without removing Saddam, hence leaving Turkey with a destabilized neighbour. First of all, the grand plan for a restructuring of the Middle East collapsed with the quick retreat of the US military and the survival of Saddam Hussein as dictator of Iraq. The destruction of Turkish–Iraqi pipelines and of Iraqi oilfields deprived Turkey of significant revenues, and ruined the economy of the already impoverished Kurdish regions on the Iraqi–Turkish border, while the USA did little to honour Turkey's support. In the Iraqi campaign, Özal lost. The example of Turkey's involvement in the First Gulf War, however, would become a stark warning to future parliaments not to follow US policies blindly. Another important outcome of the war and the refugee problems it caused was the realization that Turkey's interests lay in the stability of its neighbours and that, as was the case with the Balkans, Turkey would not be able to ignore its eastern borders and the people living beyond them.

**Turgut Özal** became prime minister by chance: because of a miscalculation on the part of the generals, and because of the determination of the electorate not to accept the diktat of the guardians. Once in power, and in a context where a socialist critique of neoliberalism had become impossible, he managed to capture the imagination of ordinary people and respond to their hopes and fears. Thanks to his charisma, he succeeded in keeping together the post-coup coalition of conservative and economically liberal forces. He integrated them into his eclectic enterprise to restore Turkey's respectability and to improve its economic and political standing in the world. During the six years of his premiership, he achieved many of these goals, even though his crude capitalist restructuring of society created many losers and destroyed the values of solidarity and mutual obligation which had held society together. The relaxation of his government's budget discipline soon resulted in growing debts and inflation.

Özal was not able to contain the Kurdish war and the widespread human rights abuses it triggered, nor did he have the power to hold the perpetrators of the September Coup responsible. When he was elected president, he ruled the country through his proxy prime minister, Yıldırım Akbulut, but had to give up much of his power when Motherland lost the 1991 elections. Until his death in 1993, he tried to push Turkey towards a proactive engagement with the major transformations in its neighbourhood, with the collapse of the Soviet Union, the conflicts in the Balkans and the restructuring of the Middle East. Yet in the 1990s, politics in Turkey once again fell under the spell of the guardian state: the military and their partners were soon back in positions of power. The chance to harness his developmental model – political conservatism, economic liberalism and global engagement – had been missed for now, and so had the opportunity to begin a more meaningful partnership with the European Community. A decade of political stagnation was about to begin, even though massive changes in the socio-economic conditions had been set in motion and new social classes were about to play a more important role in the years to come.

# 3 | The 'lost decade': wars, crises and weak coalitions (1991–2002)

**The years** from the election defeat of Özal's 'Motherland' Party in November 1991 to the election victory of the Justice and Development Party in November 2002 were mostly desperate. The liberalization of Turkey's economy and the cautious opening of the political space, Özal's proactive engagement with the post-communist world emerging after 1989, the retreat of the military and the guardian state: all these processes of modest normalization were interrupted. Instead, weak coalition governments chose to collude with the military, the mafia and hundreds of contract killers, ostensibly to fight the Kurdistan Workers' Party, yet effectively unleashing war and terror on their citizens. Why the situation in the Kurdish provinces escalated into such levels of violence and destruction so rapidly remains partly obscure, yet it is almost certain that the war that the generals' Kurdish war was a used to perpetuate the rule by the guardians of the republic. In the 1990s, the economy was as vulnerable as the political sphere, to whose manipulation it was often subjected: a significant but undisclosed part of the budget went to the military and the war against the Kurds, unfettered by public scrutiny. In this atmosphere of semi-legality, where mafia criminals and governors were deemed worthy members of the alliance against terrorism, politicians were able to siphon funds from banks and rely on populist redistribution and patronage. The markets' confidence in Turkey was at a very low point throughout much of the 1990s, when brief periods of rapid growth alternated with economic crises that destroyed people's livelihoods, while inflation hardly ever dipped below a staggering 70 per cent.

Lives were lost in the tens of thousands: people died in the Kurdish mountains, in the cities, through war, massacre, assassinations, torture and earthquakes. Different but interconnected structures of governance effectively divided the country into two parts: the Kurdish south-east was effectively ruled by the guardian state with its special governors, anti-terrorist specialists and criminals, while in the west the institutions of the state were mostly constitutional, yet prone to manipulation by the guardians' meddling. When the cracks in this amoral state of affairs became unmissable and civil society aware of its impact, the powers that be intervened: the Susurluk scandal brought to light the criminal networks that the guardian state had established to fight the Kurdish uprising. It was duly camouflaged by a 'postmodern', i.e. bloodless, military intervention in 1997. The anger at the state's incapacity and the defiant mood of the months after the devastating earthquake in the Marmara region in August 1999 faded under the pressure of the economic crisis. By the beginning of the new millennium, the mood was tired and wary, much like the terminally ill prime minister, Bülent Ecevit, whose return to politics in that decade had turned into a tragic farce. The last year of his government, however, provided moments of comfort: the economy began to recover under the glamorous economy minister, Kemal Derviş, and the frosty relations with neighbouring countries and Europe warmed under the committed pro-European foreign minister, Ismail Cem. The customs union of 1995 with the European Community had been the result of the long-term calendar of association foreseen in the Ankara Agreement of 1963 and concluded as an administrative act, yet it nevertheless marked an important turn in relations between Turkey and the European Community. By the end of the decade, political reform was to pave the way for a new era in Turkey–EU relations.

It was the election of November 1991 which brought the relative stability of eight years of 'Motherland' rule to an end. What followed looked like an uncanny replay of the unstable coalitions and the political violence of the 1970s. The 'lost decade' would see eight coalition governments and two five-month stretches of single-party rule. All parties would eventually share power with another partner, no matter how contradictory their political persuasion. The True Path Party (*Doğru Yol Partisi*, DYP) was led initially by Süleyman Demirel, and after his election to president in 1993, by Tansu Çiller. It acted as senior partner in almost all coalition governments of the time and forced through a counter-terrorism policy that all but destroyed Turkey's shaky rule of law and paved the way for the parallel governance structures in the Kurdish provinces. The Social Democrat Popular Party of Erdal Inönü, predecessor to the Republican People's Party, and its rival, Bülent Ecevit's Party of the Democratic Left (*Demokratik Sol Parti*, DSP), were often the ineffectual junior partners. In the second half of the decade, the Islamist Welfare Party (*Refah*) of Necmettin Erbakan and the extreme Nationalist Action Party of Alparslan Türkeş joined the governing coalitions, while the 'Motherland', led by Mesut Yılmaz, made a brief comeback. In the mid-1990s, Tansu Çiller, in order to escape legal proceedings, even entered an oddball coalition with Welfare. All parties represented in parliament were part of government at some point in the decade, and all of them had their share in political and economic scandals.

In reality, however, the governments often had only limited leverage: the parliament in Ankara became the stage for sterile political infighting and the nepotistic distribution of public moneys. Most politicians enriched themselves illegally in one way or another, and sooner or later they were drawn into the 'fight against terror' that cast a spell over the entire decade. The military and the police called the shots in the Kurdish provinces: they ran the war against the Kurdish separatist PKK, yet increasingly this war turned against the Kurdish people as a whole and against everyone defined as the enemy. Clandestine organizations such as the 'Gendarmerie Intelligence and Counter-Terrorism Centre' (JITEM) and the 'Special Forces' (*Özel Tim*, also *Özel Harekat Dairesi*), as well as contract killers, state-enlisted Hizbullah fighters and village guards, targeted the very intellectuals and moderates who could have mediated between the PKK's maximalist demands for independence and the Turkish state's insistence on territorial integrity. Extrajudicial killings, the wholesale destruction of villages, the burning of forests, and human rights abuses reached a level not seen in Turkey since the atrocities of the early twentieth century.

Nor did the violence stay in the east. In Turkey's western provinces, traumatized soldiers returning from the front began to brutalize their surroundings. They were suffering from the scenes they had witnessed in the Kurdish mountains and from the acts of violence they had been ordered to commit. News of former servicemen who went on killing rampages crowded the 'third pages' of Turkish newspapers, which are usually dedicated to non-political crime stories. Security agents and anti-terrorism operatives, who were redeployed from the war zone, were trigger happy and ready to use torture techniques even against innocent teenagers. The media became both forum and amplifier of the brutalization: a generation grew up with violent radio and TV news that began with announcements stating that 'thirty terrorists were captured dead in the countryside around village x', or 'twenty-one soldiers were martyred by terrorists at control point y'. The names of the villages and the numbers of the casualties changed, but the images of dead bodies and the euphemistic language remained: it was an offence to call the PKK by name, guerrilla fighters were 'captured dead' rather than killed, while the members of the Turkish army were presented as martyrs in the name of God. Some media outlets, including the state broadcaster TRT, went farther and labelled the PKK leader 'Baby killer', and the PKK a bunch of 'brigands and bandits'. The predominant use of the passive voice in these news items gave a diffuse impression of agency, even though the victims were well aware of the identity of the perpetrators.

Soon after Özal's election to president in 1989, a series of assassinations began. As debates on the Islamicization of society were running high, three public intellectuals with critical views on religion were killed: in January, the law professor Muammer Aksoy was shot dead in front of his house; in September, the atheist and anti-clerical writer Turan Dursun was gunned down; and in October, the theologian and columnist Bahriye Üçok was killed by a parcel bomb. None of these murders was resolved, but with the benefit of hindsight, and in the light of recent revelations during the Ergenekon trial (see Chapter 5), it is now next to certain that they were committed by contract killers working for the counter-terrorism units of the military and the police. More than a dozen prominent Turkish and Kurdish intellectuals, political activists and journalists were killed during the course of the decade. Several thousand lesser-known Kurds, whether political activists, Kurdish nationalists or simply people of local standing, were assassinated in the south-east by the covert and increasingly not so covert executioners of the gendarmerie special units. Even though these murders are still referred to as 'unsolved murders' (faili meçhul), ordinary people in the Kurdish provinces knew that the perpetrators were working for the state and the military. According to some sources, including his wife Semra, even the sudden death of President Turgut Özal was highly suspicious. In September 2010, the chief prosecutor of Ankara began investigations into these allegations.

On the local level, significant shifts occurred when the Islamist Welfare (Refah) Party replaced the Social Democrat Popular Party in many municipalities. With the March 1994 elections, the metropolitan councils of Istanbul and Ankara and hundreds of districts and towns came under the control of Welfare. The vote was partly a response to the clientelism of the Social Democrats, and partly a function of the fact that two social democrat parties competed against each other. The Islamist mayors initially resorted to a politics of provocation: their proposals for separate spaces for men and women in public transport, and head-covering for female employees of the municipality, irritated many. A special case of Islamist mobilization was the poor suburb of Sultanbeyli in Istanbul, where Welfare activists had sought to build an Islamic fortress as early as the 1980s. As the Welfare administrators settled into power, however, they focused on the provision of good urban governance and social services and largely abstained from imposing Islamist ideology. And it was in the rather more pragmatic environment of municipal politics where a new generation of politicians was formed that would eventually rule the country.

## State of emergency in the east: the Kurdish war in the 1990s

Late at night on 5 July 1991, policemen apprehended Vedat Aydın in his home in Diyarbakır. He was a respected human rights activist and the Diyarbakır chair of the pro-Kurdish 'Labour Party of the People' (*Halkın Emek Partisi*, HEP). Two days later, his tortured body was found dumped on a roadside in Maden, a district of neighbouring Elazığ province. He was not the first Kurdish political activist to fall victim to the rising tide of 'unsolved murders' which the various counter-terrorism units had committed since the late 1980s. Yet he was the most prominent victim so far, and significantly he was a man who had sought to fight for Kurdish rights through the legal channels of party politics and human rights activism. His funeral on 10 July was a turning point in the history of the Kurdish struggle, as an executive of Diyarbakır City Council recalled four years after the event:

> I was there during the funeral. It is impossible to forget. There were at least a hundred thousand people. We walked from the mosque towards the cemetery, outside the city walls. We approached the Mardinkapı gate, and saw hundreds of special team policemen on top of the city walls and the police station. We couldn't see their faces, because of their white face masks. And anyway we didn't have much time to look at them, because they started shooting at us. It turned into a bloodbath. You can ask everybody here in the district. They have all witnessed it [...] (Şeyhmus Bey 1996)

In the ongoing Ergenekon investigation, acting agents and a former minister of state have given testimony that the bloodbath was carried out on the orders of the city's regiment commander and members of a cell working for the state, a version of events that has been emphatically confirmed by eyewitnesses. Even though officially only three deaths were acknowledged, local observers testified to having seen several dozens killed. After the bloodbath, Vedat Aydın's body was eventually buried in the Mardinkapı cemetery. In 1996, I visited the graveyard, which sits on the slopes falling down from the city walls to the valley of the Tigris river. When I asked my contact whether he could show me Aydın's grave, he hesitated and agreed only on the precondition that we simply walk by it. He was concerned that we might be detained or even get shot at, as the grave was under observation from the nearby police station.

*The policy of scorched earth* On 19 August 1992, 300 fighters of the Kurdistan Workers' Party (PKK) attacked the city of Şırnak in the extreme south-east of the country, shelling the army barracks, the police headquarters and the gendarmerie command. In response, the army razed the entire city, with a population of 25,000 mostly Kurdish residents. From now on, and until the late 1990s, attacks would provoke counter-attacks. Murders would trigger retributions, and ceasefires would be announced and broken. It became impossible to discern who was responsible for which atrocity: guerrillas attacked villages, whose elders had decided to side with the government, and they killed teachers, whom they saw as representatives of the Turkish state. Village guards had a particularly ambivalent reputation: paramilitary forces set up initially by Turgut Özal to complement the regular army, they soon became semi-tribal bands settling scores with their enemies and expelling villagers who refused their protection. The guards became a complicating factor in the conflict, and their decommissioning would still be a problem more than twenty years after their establishment. As well as committing political murders, the anti-terrorism units and their hit men expanded into drugs trafficking, sometimes even in cooperation with traffickers working for the PKK, as a number of narcotics experts suggest. Hundreds of Kurdish intellectuals, activists and PKK sympathizers were tortured and killed, allegedly by members of the Gendarmerie Intelligence and Counter-Terrorism Centre (JITEM). Their bodies were dumped into disused wells of the state-owned Petroleum

Pipeline Corporation, BOTAŞ, in Batman, and stayed there until the remains were exhumed in 2010 as part of judicial probes into the JITEM murders. The army fought the PKK, but also burned villages and tortured their residents before forcing them to flee. The cities were ruled by fear, and by murderers, who used white Renault 12s: 'There were these men, and their duty was to kill. The Special team. Their faces were masked. They were out there. And there was no one you could complain to' (Nebahat Akkoç, interview, 13 July 2009).

The violent Islamist Kurdish Hizbullah, supported by counterterrorism agencies, killed dozens of PKK sympathizers as well as members of the public, whom they considered 'amoral'. They were particularly feared for their utter lack of remorse: in Diyarbakır and Batman, where the group was initially established, Hizbullah fighters not only liquidated their enemies with great brutality, they also shot at and destroyed their graves.

The murder of prominent personalities continued with the assassination of the octogenarian Kurdish writer Musa Anter in September 1992, and the Kurdish trade union activist Zübeyir Akkoç in January 1993. In September, the member of parliament Mehmet Sincar of the pro-Kurdish Labour Party of the People was shot in Batman, while on a mission to investigate the 'unsolved murders'. Another victim was the investigative journalist Uğur Mumcu, who was believed to have found empirical evidence of the clandestine networks that were responsible for the wave of suspicious killings. Finally, the commander of the gendarmerie forces, General Eşref Bitlis, known for his critical stance towards the indiscriminate killings in the Kurdish areas, died in a hitherto unsolved plane accident. In the autumn of 2010, senior retired army officers suggested that Bitlis had been liquidated by JITEM.

In the eyes of many politically aware Kurds, the possibility of a legal engagement within the Turkish political system had collapsed. As the mayor of the Diyarbakır district of Suriçi remarked:

> After Vedat Aydın's murder, ever more men and women decided to join the guerrillas. Those who wanted a political solution were forced into the mountains. The murder of Mehmet Sincar gave another sign. You can be elected, you can be an MP, but we can kill you. And yet another sign came with Ape [Uncle] Musa. You can be eight or eighty, but we will kill you. (Abdullah Demirbaş, interview, 11 July 2009)

For the next six years, the armed forces used a policy of scorched earth to depopulate Kurdish territories that were deemed retreat areas of the PKK. Another objective, in tune with the anti-Kurdish policies of the 1930s, was to disperse Kurdish populations among Turkish speakers in order to speed up their eventual cultural assimilation. The worst atrocities, however, happened during the coalition government of the True Path and the Social Democrat Parties from 1993 to 1995, with Tansu Çiller as prime minister and Erdal İnönü, son of Ismet İnönü, as her deputy. Çiller appointed Mehmet Ağar as chief of the national police force, who established the Special Action Branch (*Özel Harekat Dairesi*) and reached an agreement with the military to coordinate the operation of the various anti-terrorism units.

More than three thousand villages in the south-east were destroyed and their inhabitants evicted either by security forces or, to a lesser extent, by the Kurdish guerrillas. Close to three million Kurds fled their homes, as the rural economies based on agricultural production and cattle-breeding were destroyed. By the end of the decade, at least 35,000 men and women were dead. Most of them were Kurdish fighters, many thousands were servicemen of the Turkish armed forces – often of Kurdish origin themselves – and several thousand were non-combatants, whom the state had failed to protect.

*The urbanization of the Kurdish war* The Kurdish war spiralled out of control so fast that few observers at the time were able to grasp what was happening. There was little hatred between Turks and Kurds, levels of intermarriage, especially in cities, were relatively high, and even the PKK's ideology was based not on race and ethnicity, but on Marxism and anti-feudal mobilization. Yet newspapers and media outlets increasingly fell under the manipulation of the guardian state and contributed to the atmosphere of chaos, in which the PKK was depicted as solely responsible for the troubles. They obfuscated massive processes of uprooting and population movement, which would alter Turkey's demographic set-up. Ever more Kurds were being driven from the villages into the towns of Kurdistan, to western Turkey and to Europe. A new urban landscape resulted, with emerging Kurdish metropolises in the east, and substantial, yet impoverished, Kurdish communities in the cities of western Turkey.

Most of the deportees fled to the urban centres of the region. In Diyarbakır, the population more than doubled from 400,000 in the 1980s to over a million in the mid-1990s. Comparable cases of war-fuelled hyper-growth occurred throughout the region. If the cities of the south-east were already poor in terms of funds, manpower, know-how and infrastructure, the extreme population pressure led to a further deterioration in living standards. A heightened competition over scarce resources changed the rules of engagement in what used to be manageable urban societies operating on principles of mutual trust and traditional obligations. The governments of the time ignored the situation in the Kurdish cities, as they denied the existence of internal displacement in the first place. The Ankara politicians, who were by now caught up in the counter-terrorism struggle, failed to support the municipalities in dealing with the challenge of internal refugees. As a result, municipal councils resorted to informal solutions that included the acceptance of unregulated construction of high-rise flats in the middle of medieval towns. Diyarbakır in the mid-1990s was anything but a pleasant place: the terror of counter-terrorism units was tangible, as police tanks patrolled the streets, village guards in paramilitary uniforms roamed around and police and military personnel directed heavy artillery at passers-by. Business ceased at sunset and an eerie silence fell over dark and overpopulated cities, where the fumes of burning tyres irritated eyes and noses. In the narrow alleyways, street crime, forced prostitution and begging children set the scene for the city's sorry everyday life.

Kurds who had the means or family connections fled to the industrial centres of western Turkey, where they sought to build new lives in makeshift suburbs. Earlier rural-to-urban migrants had settled in the west after selling plots of land or some livestock, and maintained economic and personal relations with their village of origin. Once in the cities, they built small houses on public land and eventually became homeowners, jumping up a rung on the social ladder and joining the growing middle classes. The displaced Kurds of the 1980s, however, had barely escaped physical destruction: they had only what they managed to save from their homes and no village community to rely on in times of economic hardship. In Istanbul, the housing market had changed substantively and moved from self-help housing and eventual integration into formal urban structures towards a primitive capitalist production of urban space: mafia groups were building semi-formally and selling overpriced accommodation to the incoming immigrants. The arriving Kurds had little capital and few skills that would have allowed them to thrive in the urban economies of western

Turkey. Some spoke only rudimentary Turkish. Their numbers gave urban poverty in western Turkey a Kurdish face. That said, many eventually succeeded in setting up businesses and ensuring education for their children, laying the foundations for the rise of a generation of well-educated and self-confident young Kurdish women and men, who would soon enter mainstream Turkish society.

Tens of thousands with family or political connections made their way to western European countries such as Germany, France and Sweden, where they received asylum as political refugees. Kurds in the diaspora soon realized that to mobilize support for Kurdish rights it was necessary to lobby European and US governments. It was also in the relative freedom of the new Kurdish diasporas – first in western Europe and towards the end of the 1990s in western Turkey – that a more self-confident Kurdish identity and a network of institutions – called 'Euro-Kurdistan' or 'virtual Kurdistan' (Ayata 2008) – emerged. Kurdish TV and radio stations, culture centres, a 'Kurdish Human Rights Project' and women's organizations, and even the Kurdish Red Crescent, were established. Many, but not all, were sympathetic to or connected with the PKK. As the Kurdish war destroyed the bases of predominantly feudal Kurdish identity, nationalist mobilization and the experience of uprooting and exile created a modern sense of transnational Kurdishness.

A succession of legal Kurdish political parties began in 1990, when a group of Kurdish MPs left the Social Democrats and established the People's Labour Party (*Halkın Emek Partisi*, HEP). They provided an important vehicle for political mobilization and modernization. Even though one pro-Kurdish party after the other was eventually closed down by the Constitutional Court, and even though the first pro-Kurdish woman MP, Leyla Zana, was dragged from the Speaker's desk of the parliament and stripped of her immunity when she dared to welcome the house with a greeting in Kurdish, the parties provided some basis of legality for political activism. Especially when mayors of the 'People's Democracy Party' took most Kurdish cities in the 1999 local elections, a new political space emerged beyond armed struggle and marginalization. But until the relative détente of 1999, there was still a long way to go.

*Foreign policy without vision* Foreign policy was a limited field of activity at a time when the Turkish army was effectively fighting its own citizens in the Kurdish east, the guardian state was running the political show and elected politicians had turned, if not into puppets of the guardians, at least into extras with limited powers. In the absence of the kind of vision which Özal had devised for Turkey's role in the emerging new world order, and with the succession of insignificant foreign ministers, cluelessness and anxiety reigned supreme. In a repetition of the early 1980s, Turkey's guardians saw only enemies, both in the East and the West, and consequently foreign policy choices were based on perceptions of threat and zero-sum stand-offs. In December 1995, Turkey came to the brink of war with Greece over the rocks of Imia/Kardak, off the Turkish Mediterranean coast. Relations with Syria and Iran soured over support for the PKK and, in the case of Syria, disagreement over the use of Euphrates water. Not surprisingly, relations with the European Community were not at their best either.

Yet it was not all doom and gloom on the foreign policy front. Relations with 'low-conflict potential' neighbours like Bulgaria, Georgia and Azerbaijan were generally good and supported by growing economic interaction and military and security cooperation. Russia also emerged as a major trading partner. And there were two significant exceptions to the timidity and cluelessness of the many coalition governments: one was Turkey's bold rapprochement with Israel, and the other was the coming into force of the customs union with the European Community. The former was the result of a number of factors: George Bush Senior's US project for the Middle East, launched with 'Operation Desert Storm' and aborted with the incomplete campaign against Saddam Hussein, had left Turkey with an even more belligerent Iraqi neighbour and few friends in the Arab world. Rising tensions with Iran and Syria also nudged Turkey towards the only other key US ally in the region. Finally, with the Madrid Conference and the 'Oslo Accords' of the Rabin–Arafat peace deal in 1993, the stigma of cooperation with Israel, at least in the eyes of the Arab world, had been removed. In November 1994, at the height of the Kurdish war, Tansu Çiller was the first Turkish prime minister to visit Israel. At the time hailed as Turkey's public commitment to the Israeli–Palestinian peace process, the visit laid the foundations of a 'strategic partnership' that would last well into the next millennium.

Even though the Turkish–Israeli rapprochement was accompanied by a massive rise in bilateral trade – fourfold between 1990 and 1995

– and some cultural and educational initiatives, it was soon hijacked by security and intelligence circles and shaped by a common perception of threat from Arab governments and unruly minorities. In her visit, Çiller not only secured major arms deals that would equip the Turkish military with weaponry to beat the Kurdish insurgents, she also inaugurated a phase of cooperation between the intelligence services of the two countries that would eventually lead to the detention of the PKK leader Abdullah Öcalan. Cooperation went beyond immediate security threats, as parts of the pro-Israel lobby in the United States were enlisted to fight the passage of resolutions on the recognition of the Armenian genocide in the US Congress. Co-opted by senior military commanders and lobbyists, the 'partnership' took on a rather cynical feel, as first the Kurds and then the Palestinians were subjected to comparable forms of violence and repression in the two countries. The most vocal critics of this cynical coalition were found among the Islamist Welfare Party: as any other Islamist movement would have done, it exposed Turkey's relationship with Israel to criticize the army and pro-Israel parties such as Çiller's True Path and mobilized its followers through events commemorating the suffering Muslims of Jerusalem. Yet once Welfare's Erbakan entered a coalition with Çiller in 1996, he not only tuned down this anti-Zionist rhetoric but – compelled by the guardians and very much in violation of his political beliefs – signed off on further military deals with Israel.

The second, and more surprising, exception was the start of the customs union with the European Community on 31 December 1995, at exactly the same time Turkey and Greece were about to mobilize their navies and air forces in expectation of a war in the Aegean over a pair of rocks. That the narrowly averted conflict did not stall the customs union is a testament to the long-term nature of decisions within the European Community. The Ankara Agreement for the Association of Turkey had set out a calendar for Turkey's gradual accession to the Common Market that began in 1963. In 1973, customs duties on industrial goods of Turkish origin had been removed, and by 1995 the transition phase has been completed. At the end of this transition phase, and in fulfilment of the time frame agreed three decades earlier, Turkey eliminated customs duties for industrial goods from the European Community, entered a full customs union – the only non-member state to do so – and thereby made an important step towards full economic integration and eventual membership. For the country's economy, this was a significant step in the neoliberal restructuring and the globalization of Turkish industry. Beyond that, the customs union was a ray of light in what were still pretty desperate times.

### Fighting terror: the guardian state in western Turkey

The Çiller government decided to combat the Kurdish nationalists with all means at its disposal in 1993. After this date, the country was effectively divided into two distinct territories with different legal and administrative arrangements: in the Turkish-dominated west and in the central Anatolian provinces, in the Black Sea and in the Mediterranean littorals, a civilian administration was in place, and though torture and ill treatment in police custody remained widespread, most people were able to go about their daily work. The Kurdish-dominated provinces of the south-east were in a state of continual emergency. The provinces were ruled by the 'Governor for the State of Emergency Region', who – at least in theory – coordinated the different counter-terrorism units of the police and the gendarmerie. Buses, the main means of public transport at the time, were searched by gendarmes upon entering the region, and then stopped again at least every forty to fifty kilometres. Passengers had to produce their identity cards at every checkpoint. The few domestic flights with Turkish Airlines went through Ankara airport, where passengers were subjected to special searches and identity controls. Even though the two regimes were initially kept apart, the violence soon spilled over into other regions of the country. As the Kurdish war claimed ever more lives, massacres also targeted communities of Alevis (a heterodox religious group) in eastern Turkey as well as in Istanbul. The human rights situation deteriorated everywhere in the country, even in the ostensibly peaceful and touristic Aegean provinces.

*The Alevi massacres: Sıvas and Gazi* On 2 July 1993, Alevi spiritual leaders, intellectuals, artists and lay people from all over Turkey arrived in the eastern Anatolian town of Sıvas. They came to celebrate a festival of ideas and songs in commemoration of the legendary fifteenth-century poet Pir Sultan Abdal, who is believed to be a son of Sıvas. The festival had been held for many years, but this time it was sponsored by the Social Democrat minister of culture, Fikri Sağlar. The governor, Ahmet Karabilgin, had also welcomed the socialist writer, atheist and translator of Salman Rushdie, Aziz Nesin, which Islamists of the Welfare Party took as an offence. Two weeks before the festival, handouts appeared in great numbers, denouncing Nesin as a defiler of the faith and as a dog that should not dare to visit the city. They urged Muslims to join a 'jihad' against the unbelievers, against Aziz Nesin and against the governor, who had invited Nesin in defiance of the popular will. By the time of his arrival, a mob had already formed around the mosques, organized by members of the Welfare Party and of the municipal council.

Protesters interrupted the opening event in the cultural centre, yet the police stepped in and used force to repel the attackers. When the guests left for the Madımak hotel in the centre of town, however, a mob of many thousands began to march towards the hotel, chanting slogans against Aziz Nesin. They also threw stones at the governor's seat and demanded his resignation. Upon arrival, they first set fire to the cars in front of the entrance and hurled stones against the windows. For hours, close to a hundred people were trapped in the hotel, while the organizers and the governor conducted frantic phone calls with Ankara to get in troop or police enforcements. After more than five hours, the attackers eventually understood that they faced no opposition from the security forces, and started to hurl burning devices through the windows. As the flames spread through the building, thirty-five men and women were incinerated or asphyxiated. Among the dead were leading folk singers and poets. Aziz Nesin, together with another fifty people, managed to escape, yet was attacked by a member of the fire brigade and pushed towards the crowd. This time, the police stepped in to save him from the mob.

Even though the governor communicated personally with the Chief of the General Staff, General Doğan Güreş, a 6,000–strong army brigade in the city did not intervene to disperse the crowd. The prime minister, Tansu Çiller, the president, Süleyman Demirel, and the Chief of the General Staff were all reportedly informed about the escalating situation, yet support was not forthcoming. Eyewitnesses later alleged that the police and fire brigades refrained from taking action. While the prime minister and the president tried to downplay the massacre, a court case was opened in the State Security Court of Ankara the same year. The defendants were local office holders of the Welfare Party and were represented by the later justice minister of the Welfare–True Path Party coalition, Şevket Kazan. The defendants all received extremely low prison sentences given the crime in question. After the sentence was quashed by the Supreme Court and the case retried, thirty-three defendants were sentenced to death, automatically commuted to life sentences when capital punishment was abolished in 2002.

In Sıvas, the perpetrators had acted overtly: the attacks had taken place in broad daylight, and the Welfare Party defended the attackers even after their guilt had been established. Many Alevis rightly blamed the Islamists for the death of their fellow believers. Only much later would they ask the question: why had the entire state apparatus allowed the massacre to happen? The answer was spine-chilling: this appeared to be yet another conspiracy of the guardian state and its strategy to govern by turning neighbours into enemies. This time, Alevis were to be galvanized into joining the guardian state in its fight against the Islamists, who by now had been identified as the new prime enemy of the state.

Since the local elections in March 1994, some of Turkey's largest cities – Istanbul, Ankara but also Diyarbakır – were governed by the Islamist Welfare Party. Even though Welfare was only the third-largest party in most cities, it was the fragmentation between competing social democrat and conservative parties which helped the Welfare candidates to be elected as mayors despite votes of around only 20 per cent. This fragmentation of the established parties also helped Welfare to become the biggest party in the 1995 national elections with only 21 per cent of the votes. The sudden power amassed by the Islamists led to concern not only among the military but among the almost 80 per cent of the electorate who had not voted for Welfare. The Alevis were certainly among them.

Hence, when another assault on Alevis took place in Istanbul's Gazi quarter in 1996, few were surprised. This time, the connections between the state and the perpetrators were much more clear cut, but the mainstream media would choose to ignore these relations and depict the Gazi incident as a case of unavoidable counter-insurgency measures against Kurds and terrorists. Since the late 1980s, Gazi had developed as one of Istanbul's main Alevi neighbourhoods. Around 35,000 Alevis, many of them recent immigrants from the Kurdish provinces, lived in the densely built-up quarter with high-rise flats and little public space. They were poor, and especially the younger folk felt excluded and disadvantaged by the Sunni Welfare municipality. Suspected of involvement in socialist organizations, and owing to the Kurdish origin of many of them, they were regularly harassed by police officers, who searched and often humiliated especially the younger men. Above all, it was the heavy police presence in a poor neighbourhood, where other state services were sparse, which many residents of Gazi resented.

The build-up to the riots started when a socialist activist from the neighbourhood was killed in police custody. On 12 March, assailants targeted cafés and shops in the neighbourhood in a drive-by shooting in broad daylight that left two dead and more than twenty-five injured. Not surprisingly, residents were taken aback to see that the police, omnipresent at other times, proved unable to intervene. Angry crowds started gathering around midnight, while community leaders tried to get in touch with government officials to solicit a gesture that would defuse the tension. Yet, as in Sivas, attempts to prevent looming acts of violence fell on death ears. Overnight, burning barricades were erected and set on fire. By the morning, thousands of demonstrators had gathered, mostly from the neighbourhood, but also from farther afield. They were facing police deployments armed with water cannon, guns and tanks. Activists led the frustrated crowd, chanting slogans against the police, which they blamed for the murders: 'Police out of Gazi. Gazi will be a graveyard for Fascism.' Some boys also threw petrol bombs. Yet rather than retreating, the police responded with live ammunition and started shooting into the crowd. Seventeen were killed. The journalist Aliza Marcus was an eyewitness:

> The sound of gunfire echoed around us and suddenly police swept down the streets from both sides, firing their guns as they ran. We took cover in the shadow of a half-finished house and held our press passes in two hands, shouting that we were journalists. The police ran by us, shooting at people we could not see. (Marcus 1996: 25)

The authorities, who were later accused in the press of having refused to take the calls of the alarmed community leaders, were prominent men: Hayri Kozakçıoğlu, governor of Istanbul, was the former governor of the State of Emergency Region. Mehmet Ağar was head of the national police force and architect of the counter-terrorism strategy of the Çiller government, and Necdet Menzir chief of the Istanbul police. They were charged with conspiracy in the late 2000s, but charges were eventually dropped. One of the policemen who were tried and found guilty of the killing would later claim that the orders to shoot had come from them, while other witnesses also suggested it was the triumvirate which directed operations, though such allegations have not yet been proved.

*The Manisa trial and the state of human rights*  The extent to which the Kurdish war and the state's counter-terrorism strategy had brutalized the security agencies became apparent on 26 December 1995, when sixteen teenagers were apprehended in the Aegean town of Manisa. The police charged them for putting graffiti on a train carriage with the words 'No to education fees' and with 'writing political slogans on walls, distributing illegal leaflets, throwing Molotov cocktails and being members of an illegal organization'. For the next few days, policemen in the counter-terrorism department of Manisa tortured the sixteen boys and girls, one of them as young as fourteen. Hüseyin Korkut, one of the Manisa teenagers, was a second-year student of electronics at the time. He stayed in prison for three and a half months. When he was asked in court to describe the torture he was subjected to, he requested to speak to the judge in privacy, because he was too ashamed to talk about it publicly. He recovered from depression only after ten years of psychological treatment. As part of his healing process, he wrote a novel based on his and his friends' agony, which was published in 2007. His description of the first encounter with his interrogators is chilling:

> Ertuğrul was silent. When the cop failed to get an answer, he grabbed Ertuğrul's hair and hit his head against a metal plaque on the wall. After waiting for a few seconds, the cop lifted the black strip on Ertuğrul's eyes slightly. He saw a bulky man with strong, curly hair. He bent Ertuğrul in front of the plaque to prevent him from seeing his surroundings. He started swearing. 'Read it. Read it, you fucking son of a bitch.' It read 'Counter-Terrorism Branch'. He was barely able to whisper the words. 'I have read it,' he said. (Korkut 2007)

As the teenagers remained in custody, the parents gained access to their children after appealing to the prosecutors and receiving support from the member of parliament for Manisa, Sabri Ergül of the Republican People's Party. They could see at a glance that their children had been subjected to torture. Ergül visited the interrogation office of the prosecutor and spoke to the chef interrogator, who disclosed that he had served in the south-east before. He said the teenagers were largely cooperative and would hence be treated well. When Ergül heard a scream followed by the sound of Ottoman military marches, he left the room and tried to locate where the scream had come from. Chancing upon an open door, he saw several boys and girls, stark naked and blindfolded, in the interrogation room of the prosecutor's office. Some of them were lying on the ground, others had been made to sit on a bench and were being interrogated by plainclothes policemen.

A series of court cases followed: the public prosecutor opened proceedings against ten policemen involved in the interrogation in June 1996. Yet as the accused openly defied the writs of summons, the judge acquitted the defendants in October 1998 owing to lack of evidence. Only after the Supreme Court quashed the acquittal twice did the Manisa court sentence the policemen to a total of eighty-five years. Yet this was only one side of the legal struggle: the State Security Court of Izmir tried the teenagers for membership of a terrorist organization, and passed sentence in 1997. Ten of the teenagers were convicted, receiving prison sentences of up to twelve years. Again, it was the Supreme Court which ordered a retrial, and thereby paved the way for the acquittal of all accused in October 2000. The opinion of the court was based on the concession that the evidence heard in court had been extracted under torture. Three months before the policemen's crimes would have lapsed, in April 2003, the Supreme Court overruled their final appeal, and they were then finally imprisoned, eight years after they had committed the crime.

The Manisa trial came as a shock. Many members of the Turkish public were ready to believe that the war in the south-east was a fight against brutal terrorists, who wanted to kill 'our boys' and divide the country. Yet when the state terror reached the prosperous city of Manisa, a half-hour drive away from Turkey's third-largest city, Izmir, and the tourist beaches of the Aegean, even the more jingoistic newspapers and commentators were genuinely taken aback. Never before had the issue of torture had such an 'innocent' face, never before were torturers caught so red handed and yet remained so impertinent, never before was the relation between torturers and judges so obvious. The images of parliamentarian Sabri Ergül, who in front of the Manisa police department unrolled a placard reading 'There is torture in this workplace', captured the news headlines. Dozens of journalists, artists and public intellectuals attended the Manisa trials and ensured with their presence that the torturers did not get off and that the 'kids' were eventually saved from prison.

Hüseyin Korkut, the Manisa student whose life was shattered by the henchmen of the police and the court, gave his novel a title which suggested what many had feared: 'The fire has also fallen on Manisa'.

*First setback for the guardians: the Susurluk incident* In June 1996, the most ominous of the decade's coalition governments took office: the Islamist Welfare Party joined forces with the True Path Party. With Turkey's foremost leader of anti-secular political Islam, Necmettin Erbakan, as prime minister, and Turkey's first female prime minister, Tansu Çiller, as his deputy, this government was bound to run into difficulties. And run into them it did: on 5 November, a road accident in the north-western town of Susurluk killed three people and injured one. The dead were: Abdullah Çatlı, an extreme nationalist former hit man, grey wolf (as members of the rightwing paramilitaries were called), mafia leader, drug trafficker and contract killer in the 1970s and 1990s; his girlfriend, the model Gonca Us; and Hüseyin Kocadağ, a leading police officer and director of the Istanbul police education centre. Çatlı, who was officially sought for murder committed while he was apparently working for the police, had on him a proper passport with a false identity. He was the mastermind of the commandos that carried out assassinations of more than a hundred Kurdish business-men suspected of relations with the PKK in 1994. Kocadağ, a volatile character with a contradictory track record – he was a left-wing police activist before the coup and played a key role in curtailing the escala-tion of the Gazi events, but was also a close confidant of the fascist mafia – had been police director in Siverek in the 1980s. Finally, the sole survivor was Sedat Bucak, a Kurdish warlord from the district of Siverek in the south-eastern province of Urfa. He was also the leader of the Bucak tribe and commander of a unit of 'village guards', who played a central role in the state's counter-terrorism strategy, but had effectively come to rule Siverek. He was also a member of parliament for the True Path Party.

Suddenly, the secrets of more than a decade of clandestine opera-tions and covert actions lay exposed to the public eye. How to explain such collusion between a contract killer – wanted by the authorities – a policeman with a shady track record and a politician with a private army, who were united by one thing: their role in working for the state and against the PKK by using extrajudicial methods of murder and intimidation? The government could not. Tansu Çiller tried to defend Abdullah Çatlı at the launch of the parliamentary inquiry into the Susurluk accident with the now infamous words: 'Those who fire bullets or suffer wounds for this state will be remembered with utmost respect by us. They are honourable men for us' (*Milliyet*, 27 November 1996).

With this robust defence of a killer and drug dealer, Çiller had sealed the eventual end of her political career. Her party was further compromised when her interior minister and former counter-terrorism expert Mehmet Ağar was implicated in the inquiry and eventually forced to resign.

A number of investigations, parliamentary inquiries and court cases brought to light some of the clandestine networks and a few covert operatives and contract killers. Mesut Yılmaz, prime minister before and after Çiller, even proclaimed that he would personally guarantee a thorough investigation into the scandal. Yet he retracted his statement after a Turkish assailant attacked him during a visit to Budapest that had not been announced publicly. And so did everyone else: apart from a few prison sentences for those lower down in the command chain, the prominent names were all cleared. By September 1997, most defendants had been released from jail. For critical observers of the time it seemed clear that the allegations were too explosive and that the investigations had been aborted, before too much information was exposed. The government of Erbakan and Çiller actively discouraged further debate on the case, even though photos emerged in the newspapers in January 1997 that showed Abdullah Çatlı in the company of members of the counter-terror Special team forces.

By February 1997, many in Turkey were appalled by the in-your-face attitude of the Welfare–True Path government, as Çiller was defending as heroes of the nation what seemed to be brutal criminals, and as Erbakan was pushing a bellicose but incoherent Islamist agenda at home and abroad. His 'Islamic Opening' to Muslim countries in the neighbourhood, and especially to Iran, was primarily economic in nature and owed a lot to Özal's mixture of neo-Ottomanist rhetoric and economic pragmatism. Yet his ill-advised visit to Libya and the humiliation he suffered at the hands of Mu'ammer Gaddafi enraged even some of his most ardent supporters. In Tripoli, Erbakan was expecting support and brotherly praise from Gaddafi for his Islamist credentials and a collective declaration about a common economic area based on an Islamic currency. What he got was a litany of severe criticism for Turkey's pro-Israel policy and for oppressing the Kurds, who, Gaddafi said, deserved a state of their own. With Erbakan significantly reduced in stature, and his coalition partner Tansu Çiller busy fighting parliamentary investigations against allegations of heavy embezzlement, Turkey once again looked more like a cynical Third World dictatorship than a country with a European future.

It was hence not entirely unexpected when the European Community, at the Luxembourg European Council in 1997, decided to start accession negotiations with the central European countries and Cyprus, but did not even recognize Turkey as a candidate country. The shock was nevertheless considerable: according to the Ankara agreement, and after the realization of the customs union, the next sensible step could only be full integration into the single market and membership of the European Community. Pro-Europeans in Turkey felt particularly offended that not only former socialist countries, which were hence also poorer than Turkey, were invited to full membership negotiations but also the Republic of Cyprus, whose status was still in limbo. This first snub against Turkey's European prospects coincided with the Turkish media's discovery of the European issue. The realization of the customs union in 1995 had been noted only by experts and businessmen, but newspaper editors did not consider it front-page material. The rejection in 1997, however, became a major media event, which was rendered emotive and blown out of all proportion in full-page headlines, hour-long discussion programmes on TV and a flurry of publications. Suddenly, if in ambivalent fashion, the European Union had become a core theme of domestic debate and a highly emotive conflict, which sparked off the Turkish debate on the European Union.

*A brief interlude of vox populi* When the lawyer Ergin Cinmen started a citizenship initiative to protest about the moral decline in state and government, and to bring the politicians involved in the clandestine counter-terrorism scandals to justice, he was probably not expecting the level of public support which his protest would attract. Cinmen and the 'Citizen's initiative for enduring light' issued an open letter on 1 February 1997, which was widely distributed in the media:

> We, the citizens of the Republic of Turkey, have been taken as the silent majority. And some conclude that our silence means that we approve of all that is happening. On the one side, there are those

who have nothing to say but speak, while on the other side there is a society that has a lot to say, yet is kept quiet. [...] As a society, this time we refuse the role of the silent majority. Instead of those who erode all values, whether patriotism, justice, democracy or rule of law, and speak on our behalf, we want to speak for once. We want an end to the dirt that has invaded out lives. [...] Instead of images and news of suffering and rottenness, we want to hear good, enlightened, quality news. In spite of the complexity of all these issues, our requests are simple.

Bring those to justice who establish and employ criminal organizations. [...] Do not conceal the dirty issues and relations on the pretence of state secrets. Do not establish state agencies that work against the well-being of its citizens.

We do not want our country to be known internationally for its unresolved murders, extrajudicial killings and for hosting 80 per cent of the world's drug trafficking. And we want all this to be achieved soon, within the context of democratic life and democratic methods. [...] As the merchants, pensioners, employers, workers, civil servants, students, artists, writers and professionals, these are the issues we want to explain with our signature. (Translated from Pulur 1997)

The organizers asked their supporters to switch off the lights in their homes for one minute at 9 p.m. By mid-February, close to thirty million citizens were thought to be taking part in the protest. In some neighbourhoods, women went out on the streets and banged their saucepans, others used whistles and torches to support the action. 'One minute of darkness for enduring light' was Turkey's first mass action of civil disobedience and a peaceful but powerful public protest. The ruling coalition tried to ridicule the campaign, and the justice minister from the Welfare Party even depicted the protesters as immoral, causing yet more people to join the action. Yet before the protests could spark a more thorough investigation of clandestine networks and criminals in state positions, and challenge the state of affairs, the political space was hijacked yet again by the guardians of the republic.

## Postmodern coups and cracks in the system (1997–2001)

In the first months of 1997, the political atmosphere became agitated, and once again a crisis situation emerged and unfolded very rapidly. On the one hand, there were the citizen protests. On the other, news programmes and special reports in mainstream media outlets began to stoke fears of an imminent Islamist takeover. News and images of an obscure religious brotherhood, the Aczmendi, dominated the headlines. Nobody had heard of them before – including the leaders of established brotherhoods – but they caused confusion and anxiety owing to their demeanour, which was reminiscent of members of the Afghan Taliban. A 'Jerusalem Night', hosted by the Welfare Party mayor of an Ankara suburb on 30 January, became prime-time news: a typical case of Islamist mobilization and political rhetoric, the event included fiery speeches against a 'Zionist conspiracy' ruling the world, against Israel, and for the 'just order' of Islam, as well as for the 'liberation' of Jerusalem. There was nothing new in these arguments. But it was one of the invitees who made the event particularly unfathomable for a majority of the public: the ambassador of the Islamic Republic of Iran, Mohammad Reza Bakiri. At worst, a local Welfare politician had overplayed his hand and fallen victim to the politics of the Iranian embassy. Yet when tanks rolled through the suburb of Sincan only a few days later, the message was clear: the military was very displeased.

*The 'postmodern' coup of 28 February 1997* On 28 February, the members of the General Staff conferred with government leaders in a regular meeting of the National Security Council. Necmettin Erbakan and Tansu Çiller, unsuspecting of their imminent public humiliation, were told that 'religious reaction' (*irtica*) had become the greatest threat to Turkey's integrity and that the republic was in serious danger of being taken over by radical Islam. The generals presented newspaper snippets and media photos – including those of the awkward Aczmendi sect – to strengthen their case. At the end of the meeting, they proclaimed a list of measures which the cabinet would have to implement. Above all, the generals requested tighter control of Islamic brotherhoods, curtailment of religious preacher schools (*Imam Hatip Liseleri*) and Qur'an courses, the marginalization of 'green' capital – the conservative businessmen of Anatolia – and the closure of radio and TV stations deemed anti-secular. The military command ensured full implementation of their requests by establishing an oversight body headed by the Second Chief of the General Staff, Çevik Bir, and entitled 'Western Working Group' (*Batı Çalışma Grubu*). Not surprisingly, Prime Minister Erbakan was reluctant to sign the document, which was calling for control of and a crackdown on bodies that were naturally allied with the 'national view' tradition of political Islam and his own Welfare Party. After a few days of intense pressure from the General Staff and the mainstream media, however, the leader of Turkey's foremost Islamist movement, Necmettin Erbakan, caved in and signed the plan to fight Islamism.

Not unlike the junta of 1971, the generals had preferred to shape government policy indirectly rather than take over power personally. For the next couple of years, the 'Western Working Group' coordinated a reordering of Turkey's political, cultural and economic landscape with the aim of weakening the influence of religion and Islamism. The propagation of the military and militarist values was also part of their task. Immediate measures focused on the educational sector: as compulsory primary education was extended from five to eight years – a plan that was to be implemented sooner or later regardless of the intervention – the first three grades of the preacher schools were scrapped, thereby substantially reducing the scope, power and appeal of these schools. Most of them had only been established after the military coup of 1980 on the behest of the generals and in order to educate new generations of pious men and women who would withstand the dangers of communism. Now they were declared seditious and closed down at the behest of the very same military.

But it was at the universities that the military command and their willing executioners installed a regime of fear and militarist madness: the chair of the Higher Education Council (Yüksek Öğretim Kurulu, YÖK), Kemal Gürüz, proscribed the wearing of the headscarf at all universities. The police were advised to prevent veiled students, who had been able to attend their classes in the preceding semester, from entering the campus. At the University of Istanbul, Deputy Rector Nur Serter set up so-called 'persuasion rooms' (*ikna odaları*), where hand-picked female staff tried to dissuade the students from wearing any form of hijab. Women who refused to take off their head covering were not allowed to matriculate or attend examinations. My mother, who was working as a lecturer at Istanbul University's Foreign Language School, remembered the atmosphere of the time:

We were all compelled to attend a briefing on religious reaction. I went there because I wanted to see what was going on, but also because we were forced. It was unbelievable. A high-rank officer was lecturing us on political Islam, how it can be detected and what we, as faculty, would need to do to counter it. There were all these well-respected lecturers and professors, and they listened, and no one said a thing. It was surreal. In the end everybody clapped. As if it was the most normal thing in the world that an officer comes to your university and briefs you on what you should think and do. (Tezer Öktem, interview, 10 February 2003)

And indeed, it was the time of briefings: the generals organized massive gatherings of executives from different professions, starting with the universities, the media and the judiciary. They lectured them on the dangers of political Islam and spoke against the Welfare Party, and requested that the participants join their crusade against religious reaction. Again, they got rounds of applause, while big media barons, university rectors and judges of the Constitutional Court got the message. The Constitutional Court duly banned the Welfare Party in January 1998, and thereby closed down the largest party in parliament. Many Islamist TV and radio stations lost their licence on the grounds of their anti-secular outlook.

The most serious consequence of the 'postmodern coup' was the system of surveillance, which the Western Working Group set up to ascertain the political beliefs of individuals. It reached Stalinist proportions: mobilizing the networks of the gendarmerie and collecting information from municipalities, governors and university administrations, the military put several million individuals under observation and had as many files created, which established the political, religious, social and even sexual preferences of the person under observation. Investigations at universities, schools and public offices isolated civil servants with Islamist tendencies, and created an atmosphere of insecurity wherein colleagues started to spy on and sometimes denounce each other. This was all rather reminiscent of the last years of socialist repression in eastern Europe.

Much of the mainstream media played its part in the military's social re-engineering project: there was almost no criticism of the junta and general support for the fight against the Islamist enemy. Only a few columnists and journalists dared to ask questions and remind their readers that what was happening was not a last-ditch attempt to save the secular republic but above all an illegal military coup. Cengiz

Çandar, Mehmet Ali Birand, Nazlı Ilıcak and Ahmet and Mehmet Altan, some of the most eminent names of the Turkish press, were among them. The general secretary of the National Security Council personally called them and their newspapers and threatened them with consequences should they continue their critical stance. Soon, they would see their names in the headlines: in April 1998, the PKK's second-in-command, Şemdin Sakık, was apprehended. His statement was leaked by military operatives to suggest that these and other journalists, as well as a number of Islamist newspapers, were on the payroll of the PKK. All of them lost their jobs overnight. When Sakık declared at his first court hearing that the statement was a forgery, few listened, and the damage had been done anyway. For the next few years, the mainstream outlets of the big media conglomerates appeared to do little more than follow orders from the Chief of the General Staff. According to secret files later published by the newspaper *Taraf*, the Western Working Group was also planning to discredit the Human Rights Association, the pro-Kurdish Democracy Party of the People (*Halkın Demokrasi Partisi*, HADEP) and the Welfare Party in the same manner.

One of the key issues, which the indoctrination officers dwelt on during the briefings, was what they called the 'green capital', made up of the mostly small and medium-sized enterprises in conservative Anatolian towns, whose owners felt a natural bond with the Welfare Party. In the early 1990s, they had started to organize in parallel organizations to the existing Turkish Businessmen Association (TÜSİAD), the Independent Association of Businessmen (MÜSİAD) and TUSKON, the Turkish Confederation of Businessmen and Industrialists. Now they were under attack for providing the funding for what the National Security Council saw as the Islamist dismantling of the secular republic. One task of the Western Working Group was hence to identify businesses whose owners were suspected of ties with the Welfare Party and ensure that they would be excluded from government and army tenders. In the ensuing turmoil, a number of private banks also changed hands, and the retired generals on their management boards made sure that they were sold off to individuals and capital groups of the appropriate persuasion.

February 28 1997 was one of those moments in Turkish history when the guardian state, this amorphous one-party parallel state rooted in the early republic, made an overt comeback. The Western Working

Group, a body established to spy on and terrorize a significant section of society, would be all but unthinkable in a democratic polity. At this point, however, the guardians of the republic did not see the necessity to hide behind clandestine organizations. Another fateful event would soon help them sustain the militarist wave that they had launched.

*Capturing Öcalan* Erbakan had stuck to his guns, hoping that he would be able to weather the storms of the February coup. By the end of June, however, and in the face of mounting pressure from the General Staff and the mainstream media, he resigned from his post as prime minister. President Demirel, in all likelihood under pressure from the high command, did not invite his former protégée Tansu Çiller, the ruling coalition's junior partner, to form a new government. Instead, he appointed Mesut Yılmaz, who cobbled together a grand coalition with the Democratic Left Party of former prime minister Ecevit and the Democratic Society Party, the pro-Kurdish party of the time. When this coalition collapsed owing to a no-confidence vote, a brief one-party government under Ecevit followed, which lasted for barely five months from January to May 1999. Yet something extraordinary happened a month into the rule of the ailing Ecevit: on 15 February, the leader of the Kurdistan Workers' Party, Abdullah Öcalan, was apprehended by members of the Turkish National Intelligence Agency (MIT) in Kenya. His capture was preceded by a long manhunt involving many of Turkey's traditional foes.

Until October 1998, Syria had provided a safe haven for Öcalan and the PKK as part of a strategy to keep Turkey under pressure. When the Turkish government threatened President Hafez al-Assad with a military operation and amassed combat troops on the Syrian borer, al-Assad almost instantly gave in and evicted the Kurdish leader. Subsequently, the two countries signed an agreement of cooperation. After an odyssey through Russia, Italy and Greece, he was cornered in the Greek embassy in Nairobi and kidnapped by MIT operatives, who were probably acting together with Israel's intelligence organization Mossad and the CIA. As this was a covert operation, there is no incontrovertible evidence establishing the support of the US and Israeli intelligence services, but it is a fact that the capture took place during the heyday of Turkish–Israeli–US military and intelligence cooperation. Öcalan's capture sent shock waves through the world: owing to their involvement in the flight of Öcalan, and in his illegal stay in Greece, three Greek ministers were forced to resign, while Turkish–Greek relations reached a frosty low point. On the global level, riots and demonstrations erupted throughout Europe and Asia. Angry Kurds chose Greek and Israeli embassies and consulates as well as Turkish institutions as targets. A large number of Greek consulates in Germany were occupied. In Berlin, security personnel shot dead three unarmed Kurdish protesters, who were trying to storm the Israeli consulate.

Back at home, Prime Minister Bülent Ecevit was relishing the moment. With virtually all newspapers and media triumphant over Öcalan's capture, a language of vengefulness invaded the public debate. Media outlets like *Hürriyet* branded the PKK leader as 'baby-killer' and 'head of the terrorists'. Turkish governments since the 1980s had concentrated all their blame on the personality of Öcalan. Now that he was in custody, people were made to believe that Turkey's worst nightmare, the Kurdish war – euphemistically called the Kurdish problem – was over. Families of soldiers killed in the conflict were encouraged to campaign for the death sentence and the mainstream media sported humiliating images of a blindfolded Öcalan. Humiliation and grief were indeed the feelings that galvanized many nationalist Kurds, especially in the south-east, to join protest actions against their leader's imprisonment. Such behaviour was seen by the Turkish public as yet another indicator of the treacherous behaviour of the Kurds generally.

Amid the surge of these deeply divided emotions, Öcalan's first statements came as a surprise: instead of the armed struggle for an independent Kurdistan, he was now promoting Kurdish–Turkish brotherhood, and called for the PKK to lay down their arms. Observers at first wondered whether Öcalan made these statements under duress. Yet the trial suggested otherwise: it took place at a special State Security Court set on at the prison island of İmralı – the prison from which the protagonists of Yılmaz Güney's film *The Way* had set out in the early 1980s. The indictment referred to the armed insurgency, which Öcalan had started in 1984, and included charges of treason and separatism. Throughout the proceedings, which took place amid high drama and were followed by the excitable widows of servicemen, the Kurdish leader called for an end to the armed Kurdish struggle and for a democratic engagement with the Turkish state. A week into the trial, he even pleaded for mercy and asked to be spared the death penalty to be able to fight for peace and prevent more bloodshed.

Öcalan's reconciliatory advances did not prevent the judges from delivering the death sentence for treason in their verdict at the end of June 1999. The trial had taken place in a heated atmosphere, and it was quite obvious that the State Security Court was not an 'independent and impartial tribunal', a conclusion which the European Court of Human Rights (ECHR) reached in 2003. Yet his execution never took place: after a second trial, and an appeal both to the local court and the ECHR, his death sentence was commuted to life imprisonment in October 2002, after Turkey abolished capital punishment. This was part of a larger package of legal and human rights reforms induced by the European Union. The PKK cadres unilaterally called for a ceasefire, and for some time the National Liberation Front of Kurdistan, the PKK's armed wing, abstained from major attacks against Turkish military targets.

Two parties benefited from Öcalan's capture – the Democratic Left Party, which claimed it as a success for Prime Minister Ecevit, and the Nationalist Action Party of Alparslan Türkeş, who had always called for a tough anti-Kurdish policy. In the April 1999 elections, they came first and second, gaining 22 and 18 per cent of the votes respectively. Together with the Motherland Party, they formed another odd coalition, which tried to harness the prevailing nationalist sentiment. Many older supporters of Ecevit, who remembered his 'left of centre' politics in the 1970s, were dismayed at the jingoistic tone which he had acquired since the capture, seeking to outstrip Türkeş in his nationalist credentials. Beyond the emotive Öcalan trial, the government, with Ecevit again as prime minister, faced an economic worst-case scenario: inflationist pressures had been rising throughout the decade and had stabilized around an annual rate of 70 per cent. People had become used to thinking in terms of millions and billions of Turkish lira, with one US dollar equivalent to over 600,000 lira. The economy was fast becoming 'dollarized', and a majority began to convert their savings into foreign currency. As if this was not enough, the government would soon see itself engulfed by another calamity, this time neither of the generals' making nor because of its inconclusive fiscal policy.

*Killing tremors: the Marmara earthquake of August 1999* In the early hours of 17 August, an earthquake struck the town of Gölcük in the province of Izmit, around a hundred kilometres east of Istanbul. The Marmara earthquake, as it would be called, had a magnitude of 7.5 and was one of the most devastating ever recorded in the region. Heavy aftershocks would be felt for days to come. Nobody was prepared for an emergency of such proportions, as the earthquake affected the heavily industrialized and densely populated eastern Marmara region. Official figures on the destruction came late, as did the aid and relief efforts, but months later the government conceded that close to 18,000 had died and more than 300,000 buildings were partially or fully destroyed. Some argued that the number of deaths may have exceeded 40,000.

The government proved incapable of organizing a concerted relief effort in the most crucial first three days. In fact, it even failed to dispatch to the area the hundreds of international rescue teams which arrived at Istanbul's main airport and were often made to wait for hours before being sent on to the region worst affected. The airport's crisis centre felt more like a dusty government office, where the requests of incoming teams were dealt with in a bureaucratic manner. This all changed, however, when a small ad hoc civil society initiative formed around the academic Tanay Sıtkı Uyar took possession of one of the many desks and telephones in the crisis centre. I was part of this group. We immediately started to organize the dispatching process. A fluctuating number of young men and women, we began posting announcements on private radio and TV stations to enlist translators and volunteers for the incoming rescue teams. Soon, hundreds of volunteers were camping in front of the centre, waiting to be sent to the disaster region. They were members of all of Istanbul's communities, Turks, Jews, Armenians, Arabs, Kurds, Bosniaks, and of all classes and walks of life, and they insisted on helping. While we were able to send hundreds of volunteers to the region, which greatly facilitated the work of the rescue teams, some civil servants in the centre were upset by the unconventional situation and the lack of respect for hierarchy among members of the initiative. An ambassador representing the Foreign Ministry even tried to evict us on the grounds that we occupied a larger desk than he himself had.

If the ambassador's stubborn insistence on etiquette in the face of human suffering captured the complete failure of state agencies during the earthquake, it was the spontaneous reaction of the civil society which represented the mood of the public: from day one, thousands of individuals, ad hoc groups and organizations would drive to the region to help the locals and relief teams in their rescue efforts. Food, water and blankets arrived from everywhere in Turkey.

Many private enterprises allowed their employees to take leave and join the rescue teams. Bus companies carried relief supplies without charge. Municipalities from all over the country sent heavy vehicles and work equipment, and students organized the delivery of goods needed in the region. For a couple of weeks following the tremors, and amid the suffering and pain, Turkey woke up to the realization that it had a vibrant civil society that was more capable and efficient in organizing people's life than the state. What they also realized was that the world was not their enemy: the response from all major countries in the world and from Turkey's neighbourhood – Greece, Bulgaria, Egypt, Israel – was overwhelming. The state, with its pompous self-aggrandizing narrative, had faltered miserably. The chimera of Turkey as a beleaguered country hated by the whole world, carefully nurtured by the guardians of the republic and much of the media in the years since the coup of 1997, lay exposed. Surely, nothing could be the same again. Surely, things would have to change. Three years after Susurluk, the people had had another taste of their power.

A first indication of a new beginning was the 'earthquake diplomacy' which developed between Greece and Turkey. The massive aid effort of Turkey's neighbour, which quickly expanded from government agencies to municipalities and NGOs, was received enthusiastically in Turkey. Less than a month later, an earthquake struck a suburb of Athens. It was much smaller in scale, but it triggered an immediate solidarity campaign in Turkey. For publics as well as politicians, the two earthquakes came as a striking reminder that the two countries were bound by geography, even if they had been divided by history. The spontaneous outpouring of mutual sympathy among members of the public on both sides of the borders paved the way for official contacts to develop. Less than three years after the Kardak/Imia crisis, when the two countries had been on the verge of war, and barely six months after the embarrassment of Greece's involvement in the flight of PKK leader Öcalan, Foreign Minister Ismail Cem and his Greek counterpart Giorgios Papandreou laid the foundations for the Greek–Turkish rapprochement.

### Crises, hopes and saviours (2000–02)

After the earthquake, things could only get better, or so large parts of the public felt. The capture of Abdullah Öcalan had removed the key obstacle in relations with Syria and had left the PKK headless.

The earthquake diplomacy had unfrozen relations with Greece. And another, even more important external development changed the framework of Turkish politics and strengthened the hope that the country was moving towards new horizons: the Luxembourg Summit of 1997, at which European leaders had refused to confirm Turkey's candidate status, had been a shock for many in Turkey. It had also been the first major appearance of the European issue in the Turkish media. Foreign Minister Ismail Cem, arguably the most progressive mind in the triple coalition of the Democratic Left, the Motherland and the extreme right-wing MHP, was aware that the Turkish–European relationship could not be left to its own devices, and that Turkish frustration at being excluded was not helpful in any way.

It was largely thanks to Cem's negotiating skills that the Helsinki European Council in December 1999 declared Turkey a candidate for EU accession on an equal footing with other potential candidates. The Council also requested the abolition of capital punishment and a readiness on Turkey's part to resolve the Cyprus issue. The decision was welcomed enthusiastically throughout much of the mainstream and even parts of the Islamist media. Prime Minister Ecevit, who had increasingly fallen under the spell of the nationalist frenzy following Abdullah Öcalan's capture, spoke of the hope that membership was now closer than ever. Thus began the roller-coaster of the public phase of Turkey–EU relations, a love-hate story which incensed and galvanized men and women everywhere in Turkey, and soon also in Europe. Before world events of a different magnitude – the 9/11 attacks in New York, the Iraqi War and the rise of Islamophobia accompanying the two – would significantly complicate this happy vision of Turkey's European future, however, a home-made crisis destroyed much of the confidence that had built up in the wake of Helsinki.

*A national crisis: the turmoil of 2000 and 2001* For much of the 1990s, Turkey's economy had been growing erratically, with bursts of rapid development interrupted by minor and major crises. Public spending was driven up by military expenditure and the war in the Kurdish provinces, as well as by generous handouts, especially in the agricul-tural sector, and corruption in the remaining state enterprises. The coalition governments financed their growing budget deficits with heavy borrowing, while banks adapted to this environment and made a growing proportion of their profits by lending to the government.

The state-owned banks in particular were operating behind a smoke-screen of political patronage and were prone to political meddling and opaque credit practices. They have also been accused frequently of the channelling of illegal funds related to the war on the Kurds, and these allegations were being investigated at the time of writing. Towards the late 1990s, a consensus emerged gradually that the institutional set-up of the economy as well as the government borrowing strategies would need to be reformed. Negotiations between the triple coalition under Prime Minister Ecevit and the IMF produced an austerity programme with the key elements of budgetary discipline, a currency peg, privatization of state enterprises, a reduction in agricultural subsidies and finally, and most significantly, the regulation of the banking system. These were badly needed reforms, which were bound to have an adverse effect on the core constituents of the parties in government. Even though there was general support for the programme, the commitment to its implementation was at best lukewarm.

November 2000 saw the first wave of the crisis. Liquidity problems in some major banks sparked a general loss of confidence in the banking system, leading to the flight of foreign currency and the devaluation of the Turkish lira by almost a third of its value. When the central bank reacted by injecting millions of dollars into the system – in violation of its own currency policy – confidence in the currency peg and the programme collapsed. The ensuing panic on the markets could be stalled only by another emergency package from the IMF. In return, Ecevit's government reaffirmed its commitment to lower inflation, speeding up privatization and preparing a comprehensive banking reform. By early 2001, the situation appeared to stabilize as much of the foreign capital that had exited during the crisis was now flowing back. Some observers suggested that the 2000 crisis had not been deep enough to generate the badly needed radical changes, as only wage-earners and lower- and middle-income groups had been affected, while the upper middle classes had weathered the storms well. This would soon change.

In February 2001, a row between the president, Ahmet Necdet Sezer, and Prime Minister Ecevit triggered a second period of turmoil that greatly surpassed the crisis of 2000. Images of an enraged Sezer throwing a copy of the constitution at Ecevit soon dominated the news. Sezer was no friend of the IMF and furious about the government's plans to privatize state enterprises such as Turkish Telecom.

For Sezer and the military, the privatization of state assets and the rehabilitation of the state banks amounted to a dangerous interference in Turkey's national security. At least part of his anger was also due to his suspicion of Ecevit's political instincts, which he deemed not sufficiently sympathetic to the army's anti-Islamist strategy. When news spread about this clamour at the top of Turkish politics, the entire economic system collapsed, with grave consequences for all sectors of society.

Large quantities of capital left the country in an instant. Overnight interest rates soared to close to 5,000 per cent and the lira plunged yet again, this time by 50 per cent. People who still held their savings in Turkish lira lost half the value of their money, while real wages were reduced by more than 20 per cent overnight. People woke up the next morning only to realize that they had effectively become poorer by a third. In the coming months, more than a million wage-earners lost their jobs, and tens of thousands of small and medium-sized enterprises were forced to declare bankruptcy. Many banks went out of business as well, leaving thousands of hitherto well-paid bankers unemployed. As factories closed and the domestic market collapsed, the economy contracted at almost the same speed as it had grown over the last few years. Ecevit's coalition government was incapable of stemming the downward spiral. Yet this time the crisis was severe and encompassing enough to create large public consent for a sweeping reform programme.

Public support was crucial, yet the gravity of the crisis would probably not have been mastered without one person, who played a key role in negotiating a major IMF package and in ensuring that it was thoroughly implemented: Kemal Derviş. Derviş was a vice-president of the World Bank with indisputable credentials, a top-level economist with thirty years of work experience, and excellent links to the transnational financial community. He was hence a perfect candidate to smooth the adjustment of Turkey's economy after the crisis. In March Prime Minister Ecevit appointed Derviş as an above-politics technocrat against vicious opposition, especially from the Republican People's Party, and left- and right-wing isolationists, including President Sezer, who saw in his appointment a conspiracy to sell out Turkey to the United States.

In less than half a year, however, Derviş managed to implement the wide-ranging structural reforms which the government had been postponing. In moves reminiscent of Özal's determination to impose the 24 January Decisions of 1980, he succeeded in convincing his government (and crucially also the AKP administration, which would follow in 2002) to implement the IMF programme in its entirety. Part of the programme aimed at deregulation through further privatization of state enterprises and infrastructure, liberalization and abolition of state monopolies. It also aimed at the reduction of agricultural subsidies and barriers to foreign direct investment. At the same time it introduced elements of re-regulation, which the government and the opaque public banking systems had so far defied: a transparent and disciplined fiscal policy and a stronger autonomy for the central bank were crucial components of his programme. It was complemented by tight regulation of the banking and finance systems through a 'Bank Regulatory and Supervisory Agency' and other regulatory agencies in the energy and telecommunications sectors. After these reforms, Turkey's economy increasingly took on the appearance of a transparent and liberal market. Two years after the crisis, inflation had fallen to single digits from over 80 per cent, growth rates were back to their pre-crisis levels and the exchange rate of the lira had stabilized. Despite recurring political crises, the economy was on its way to turning into a real success story in terms of export-led growth and diversification, though not in terms of job creation.

*A world crisis: 9/11 and the clash of civilizations* If the impact of the 2001 economic crisis was felt instantly by the overwhelming majority of society, whether rich or poor, wage-earner or self-employed, Kurd or Turk, the effects of the attacks on the World Trade Center in New York on 11 September 2001 took some time to reach Turkey. The immediate response was shock, fear and disbelief as the images were transmitted on TV screens throughout the country. Probably the first question most people had on their mind was whether there were Muslims behind the attack, and once they understood that it had been carried out in the name of Islam, they probably felt that this would eventually also impact on Turkey. The second question, which few dared to ask, was whether Turks were involved. The sense of relief was palpable when it was established that the attacks were an all-Arab affair. In the following weeks, responses diversified, adding to the public debate a host of conspiracy theories, anti-imperialist criticism of the United States and also some Islamist attempts at justification. Generally, however, these explanations generated little sympathy for the perpetrators, despite the Turkish public's solid anti-American attitude.

At this moment, few would have foreseen the pervasive changes in the global political environment which were about to be unleashed by the US administration of George W. Bush. Yet instinctually many felt that 9/11 would alter their lives sooner or later. And alter they did throughout much of the coming decade, and on a number of levels: the US invasion and occupation of Iraq would bring the 'war on terror' into Turkey's eastern backyard, many global political conflicts would become shrouded in the language of civilization and religion, a major Islamist attack would jolt Istanbul, and the creeping Islamophobia in European publics would eventually jeopardize Turkey's EU bid. People in Turkey, as elsewhere in the Muslim world, were made to feel more 'Muslim' and more different by their European and American interlocutors. Many of them began to think of Islam as a security issue – ironically, much along the lines of Turkey's guardians, whose anti-Islamism could have inspired many of the policies of European governments fearful of their Muslim communities.

At the same time, the global obsession with religion and Islam, and the fear of everything radical, would also create opportunities, which 'moderate' Islamist movements in Turkey, from the Justice and Development Party to the Fethullah Gülen movement, harnessed for their global emergence as respectable Muslim actors. Turkey soon became referred to as a 'model of moderate Islam', and was enlisted by the United States to export its brand of High Islam to contain radical elements from the Balkans to the Middle East. For many Muslim currents in Turkey, the post-9/11 period marked a phase of expansion. In the years to come, when much of Europe and the USA slid into a deeply illiberal mindset of securitization and anti-terrorist campaigning with little regard for human rights, Turkey would buck the trend and engage in radical legal reform and democratic consolidation.

By July 2002, however, Prime Minister Ecevit had become frail and tired. He nevertheless refused to step down despite mounting criticism from his own party. When eight of his ministers resigned, early elections became unavoidable and were scheduled for September. In a final and bold act, parliament approved a government reform package designed to ease the way for EU membership: the death sentence was abolished except in times of war and the bans on education and broadcasting in Kurdish were lifted. The burden of almost two decades of war and state terror in Kurdistan was finally coming to an end. Significantly, the Nationalist Action Party supported this package, which saved Abdullah Öcalan from the gallows.

**The decade** between the end of the post-coup Motherland government of Turgut Özal and the triple coalition under Prime Minister Ecevit was dominated by a forceful return of the guardians of the republic and their meddling in politics and society. As a result, the country was effectively split into two: the Kurdish provinces were ruled by a brutal emergency state, which trampled on basic human rights and radicalized ordinary members of the public through torture and humiliation. The rest of the country resembled a democratic polity – albeit one with major human rights issues and widespread use of torture – but the violence of the emergency state frequently spilled over. Eventually, no one was able to escape the general brutalization of the country through war and arbitrary state action. And the wounds of the terrors of the 1980 coup only a decade earlier had not even begun to heal. The politics of the guardian state became particularly visible when the military intervened in 1997 to rein in the Islamists, whose resurgence in the post-coup environment of 1980 they had supported so strongly. Guardian politics reigned supreme after the intervention, when the high judiciary and the bureaucracy, as well as parts of the political spectrum including the Republican People's Party, became willing executioners of the blueprint to rewire Turkish society along militarist and secularist lines.

Yet all the meddling and manipulation were for nought: by the end of the decade, the country was ready for normalization. Cautious steps towards reform under an otherwise quarrelling triple coalition were interrupted, however, by a series of internal and external crises of increasing magnitude: from the exposure of the workings of the deep state to military interventions, from the near-war experience with Greece to a devastating earthquake, and from crushing financial collapses to the shock of 9/11, Turkey was deeply shaken. In the fateful three years between 1999 and 2002, the country experienced the Marmara earthquake, which not only killed close to 40,000 people but destroyed much of its industrial heartlands, a complete collapse of its economy and its banking system and the public humiliation of its entire political class, which lay exposed as corrupt and unable to defy the diktat of the generals. It would not be an exaggeration to suggest that people's confidence in what they had come to know as their homeland was deeply shattered. And still, the deeper the crises were, the stronger the constituencies for change and reform seemed to become. After a decade of manipulations dictated by the masterminds of the guardian state, Turkey was about to return to the world of politics.

# 4 | Justice and development: 'Islamic Calvinists' versus the guardian state (2002-07)

The succession of guardian state intervention and civilian challenge during the terms of Turgut Özal in 1980 had given way to the weak governments of the 1990s. After the multiple ruptures of 1999–2002, however, civilian control was on the rise again. This chapter discusses the emergence of a new, and probably the toughest, challenge to the power of the guardians: the Justice and Development Party (*Adalet ve Kalkınma Partisi*, AKP), whose leaders presented themselves to the world and to their electorate as adherents of a 'conservative democracy'. After the relative isolation of the 1990s, the first decade of the 2000s was characterized by Turkey's return to participation in world historical events. If the impact of 9/11 seemed to have bypassed Turkey initially, in the 2000s the big debates about the compatibility of 'Islam and democracy' all focused on Turkey and ascribed to its 'Muslim' leaders a different weight and authority. A great deal of sympathy was offered to the leaders of Turkey's 'Muslim Democrats' of the AKP. At the same time, the globalization of Islamophobia also shaped perspectives on Turkey as a Muslim rather than a European country and sparked the debate about whether 'Islam and Europe' could ever be reconciled. Yet as world history was unfolding, Turkey's guardians realized that the combination of a sympathetic global environment, rapid economic development, strong electoral support and EU membership prospects would ultimately lead to a challenge to the Kemalist state, which the guardians might not survive. The cycle of manipulations and social unrest was hence unleashed once again, though this time too many observers were aware of what was going on. Had the guardians of the republic overplayed their hand this time?

Elections have marked significant turning points in Turkey's history, as much as military interventions. The general elections of 3 November

2002 created such a key moment: in one sweep, 90 per cent of MPs lost their job and all parties of the preceding parliament – Çiller's True Path, the Nationalist Action Party, Motherland, Ecevit's Democratic Left Party, as well as the pro-Kurdish Democratic People's Party – failed to reach the 10 per cent threshold. The almost complete change of political elites led to the constitution of a two-party parliament: the Republican People's Party (*Cumhuriyet Halk Partisi*, RPP) of chairman Deniz Baykal acquired a third of the seats with almost 20 per cent of the vote. The victor was the newcomer Justice and Development, which had parted ways with the Islamist Felicity Party after its ban in 2001. It took the remaining seats with 35 per cent of the vote. Their two leaders would shape the outlook of the decade to come: Abdullah Gül, who became the interim prime minister until Recep Tayyip Erdoğan, the former Welfare Party mayor of Istanbul and chairman of the AKP, became prime minister after a by-election in March 2003. Abdullah Gül also served as foreign minister and was elected president in 2007.

For many, observers and men and women on the street alike, the new constellation marked the end of a decade of strife. There was a credible promise of stability in the new two-party parliament, boosted by the AKP's commitment to continue the policies of the preceding government in two crucial policy areas: the IMF programme of economic recovery delivered by former economy minister Kemal Derviş and the pro-European Union reforms, which were part of Turkey's long-term European policy, but begun in earnest under former foreign minister Ismail Cem. For a period of almost three years, and despite concerns of anti-clerical critics that the secular republic might be in danger, a majority of people in Turkey and many sympathetic observers abroad were in high spirits: the country seemed to have overcome political fragmentation, and had a government intent on development and Europeanization. True, the AKP had its roots in political Islam and the 'national view' (*Milli Görüş*) tradition of the Welfare and Virtue parties, yet their leaders had disassociated themselves from the more radical tenets of their ideological forefather Necmettin Erbakan and defined their party in the tradition of 'conservative democracy'. Observers were using different terms to frame this new phenomenon of religious piety, democracy and market commitment and came up with labels ranging from 'Muslim democrats' to 'moderate Islamists' (the preferred US term) and 'post-Islamists' (owing to the break with the Islamist Felicity Party). They were all trying to give a name to a phenomenon that was just unfolding. The most expressive term which came up in the debate was that of 'Islamic Calvinists', i.e. hard-working, moneymaking but pious entrepreneurs, who refrained from sumptuous lives, exerted discipline over their bodies and time, and reinvested their earnings into their businesses as well as into education and Islamic charity.

EU membership looked closer than ever, as the military, with its pro-reform Chief of the General Staff, Hilmi Özkök, now also supported the accession process. The EU had become an issue of major public interest since the 1999 Helsinki European Council meeting. The Copenhagen European Council in December 2002 was one of the happy moments in the Turkish–European relationship, which turned the relations into a public love affair. In Copenhagen, European heads of state confirmed that accession negotiations with Turkey would go ahead, if the European Council in December 2004 were to decide that Turkey fulfilled the Copenhagen political criteria of a functioning democracy. Amid the ensuing media frenzy, the premature expectation of almost imminent membership took hold, which explains part of the massive frustration when the process eventually stalled.

Even though the newspaper *Milliyet* called the council decision regarding the start of accession negotiations 'conditional', this did little to spoil the excitement about imminent changes. In fact, many of the conditions set out in the decision had increasingly become part of the internal debate and found more support than ever. The Copenhagen criteria demanded stability of institutions to ensure democracy, the rule of law, human rights and respect for and protection of minorities. In the particular case of Turkey, this meant progress on minority rights, especially for Kurds, the Alevis and non-Muslim minorities, and the total abolition of capital punishment (i.e. also during times of war). Turkey was also requested to support the Annan peace plan in Cyprus. In addition to the stick of conditionality, the delegation also had some carrots to offer: the customs union would be deepened and Turkey was to receive increased pre-accession assistance.

With clear membership prospects, the conditionality of the European Union worked wonders, and the government embarked on a series of legal initiatives and reforms that created a momentum of their own. This was particularly felt in the Kurdish provinces, where restrictions on the use of language were eased. On Cyprus, the AKP government made a bold move: it not only decided to support the

Annan peace plan, but also the Turkish Cypriot 'yes' camp, which eventually dethroned Ankara's long-term proxy, the Turkish Cypriot leader Rauf Denktash. This was, however, not sufficient to persuade the Greek Cypriots to vote for the Annan plan, which was not accepted in the end. And there was also some opposition to the European Union and the reforms that the government carried out. The pending loss of sovereignty and power which membership would necessarily bring was a concern for some. This opposition, however, was confined mostly to the relative political margins of the old Islamists of the Felicity Party, to the extreme right-wing Nationalist Action Party – which ironically had made possible many of the EU reforms of the earlier government, and whose criticism hence rang shallow – and anti-European socialist and Kemalist groups.

When the European Council meeting in December 2004 approached, almost everybody in the country was hoping for a positive signal. Public support for EU membership at this juncture was well over 70 per cent. In the run-up to the meeting, the Austrian People's Party and the German Christian Democrats tried to introduce the idea of a 'privileged partnership', but had to content themselves with a specific mention of the 'absorption capacity', which would have to be taken into consideration once the negotiations were completed. Another issue of concern was Cyprus, where the rejection of the Annan plan by the Greek Cypriots had created a new deadlock. All these last-moment twists and turns notwithstanding, the final decision of the European Council was clear: Turkey had fulfilled the Copenhagen criteria and was ready for accession negotiations. Negotiations were to begin in 2005 with the shared objective of membership. This was a truly historic – if fleeting – moment showing Europe and Turkey at their best.

Accession negotiations did indeed begin in October 2005, but by then the country had already become a different place. In what appeared to be a rerun of earlier guardian state scenarios, the mood suddenly shifted and an unprecedented nationalist backlash against Europe and the idea of European Union membership unfolded. Anti-European sentiment was also fuelled by anti-Turkish debates in many continental European publics. After a blissful time lag of four years, the effects of 9/11 came to be felt in the form of growing Islamophobia in Europe and in the neoconservative politics of George W. Bush. As the debate deteriorated, public support for the EU dropped below 50 per cent. In 2006, a series of political murders took place, as the mood turned back to the desperate isolationism of the late 1990s: violence, character assassinations, the work of hit men and the drama of innocent victims made the headlines once again. Critical observers at the time sensed the signature of the guardians, but much of the mainstream media took events at face value: once again, the language of existential binaries invaded the public debate, and the image emerged of a last-stand fight that was to be waged by republican secularists, if the republic and the achievements of Mustafa Kemal were to be defended against the encroachment of Islamists and the destruction of the country by the European Union. At one point, pro-European views were close to being equated with treason.

Yet as the country descended into this new round of political violence organized and incited by the generals, it was also changing beyond recognition: industrial production boomed throughout the period. Industrial centres outside Istanbul, the 'Anatolian tigers', evolved into highly efficient, well-run cities with tidy, if unimaginative, residential quarters, restored old towns, new airports, motorways, and an expanding railway infrastructure. Istanbul turned into a centre of services, tourism, finance and skyscrapers, with all the displacement processes such development entails. In much of Turkey, and to a much lesser extent in the Kurdish provinces, industrialization became tangible and changed the face of the built environment. Turkey was going through a fourth wave of modernization, after the Kemalist state industries, Menderes's American-inspired entrepreneurialism and Özal's forays into the world of global capitalism. Yet this fourth wave of modernization also brought into the limelight the conservative middle classes of Anatolia with their educational institutions and civil society associations: Islamic codes of dress became omnipresent, as pious women left their homes and explored urban spaces hitherto inaccessible to them. Expressions of public piety became visible and the 'feel' of Turkey shifted towards a more Islamic one. In the early 2000s, all was changing, but much was still the same.

### Islamic Calvinists in office

The election victory of the Justice and Development Party raised eyebrows in Turkey and abroad. The guardian state, the military, the high judiciary and parts of the bureaucracy were dismayed to see yet another Islamist party in office, after the generals had explicitly intervened in 1997 to terminate the Welfare Party government under

Erbakan. Neoconservative observers in the USA predicted a drift towards Iran and hence to the wrong side of their Manichaean world order of 'good' versus 'evil'. Decision-makers in the European Union were stunned, while critics of Turkey's EU candidature were rejoicing at the prospect of an 'Islamist' Turkey. By contrast, the 'unreconstructed' Islamists of the Felicity Party (successor of the outlawed Virtue Party) criticized Erdoğan and his modernizers for selling out to the West:

> The AKP back then was all about being accepted by the hegemonic system. The party became the key actor in Turkey's second neoliberal wave [with Özal's reforms constituting the first], it happily agreed to represent the 'moderate Islam' that the USA was expecting. It was really the 28 February intervention which created the AKP in the first place. (Mehmet Bekaroğlu, interview 13 July 2009)

Yet the Felicity Party had achieved only 2.5 per cent of the votes in the 2002 elections and their criticism was barely audible. AKP leaders sought to publically distance their party from suggestions by the US administration that Turkey was a model for the coexistence of 'Islam and democracy', and the AKP a prime example of 'Muslim democracy'. There is little doubt, however, that the AKP government happily rode the wave of goodwill by harnessing the opportunities it created: under its government, the Directorate of Religious Affairs (Diyanet) as well as the network of schools and charities close to the cleric Fethullah Gülen replaced Arab organizations in much of the Balkans as guardians of the local Muslims and funders of local communities. Much more salient were allegations that the AKP was nothing but a wolf in sheep's clothing, following radical Islamism under the guise of pro-European politics. Were these accusations justified?

*The sources of AKP power: Islamic Calvinists and the Gülen network* The Justice and Development Party emerged out of the ban on the Virtue Party, which had succeeded the Welfare Party after its proscription in 1998. The old cadres of Virtue were staunchly rooted in the 'national view' (*Milli Görüş*) tradition and in close ideological proximity to the Egyptian Muslim Brotherhood. After the Constitutional Court had punished Necmettin Erbakan with a ban on political activities, Recai Kutan continued *Milli Görüş* with the Felicity (*Saadet*) Party. The party's name evoked the reign of Prophet Muhammad, which is often referred to as the felicitous age (*asr-ı saadet*), and hence made a clear statement regarding its commitment to political Islam. A group of modernizers, who had gathered around the former mayor of Istanbul, Recep Tayyip Erdoğan, acted on another premise: they realized that they would be able to shape the country's future only if they reconsidered their relationship with Islam, paid credit to the partly secular order of the Turkish Republic and gave up on the more revolutionary aspects of Islamism, and especially the idea of a 'just world order', i.e. a global Islamic state. Even though the founders had their ideological roots in political Islam, the know-how on good governance and public services, which many of them had acquired during their term in municipal office since the 1990s, made them pragmatists, closer to the legacy of the Motherland Party under Özal than to Erbakan's ideological Islamism. The globalized outlook, the reference to Islam as inspiration rather than political goal, and the proximity to the traditional economic liberalism of Turkey's conservative tradition soon attracted actors from the entire spectrum of the right and from some left-wing liberals.

Another source of AKP power was its embrace – if differential – of two important religious networks: the *Nakşibendi* order (*Naqshibandiyya*), an influential religious brotherhood with a strongly conservative ethos and a large membership, and the followers of Fethullah Gülen. While the former had provided the backbone of the 'national view' parties, and was hence also the first port of call for the AKP, the rapprochement with the Gülen movement, with its millions of members and powerful educational and media institutions, was not as straightforward. Fethullah Gülen, a charismatic preacher hailing from the brotherhood of Bediüzzaman Said-i Nursi, had kept his distance from the National Order because of the latter's global Islamist aspirations. He was close to the Turkish–Islamic synthesis of the 1980s and did not oppose the military intervention in February 1997. He also remained silent when the Constitutional Court outlawed the Welfare and later the Virtue parties, as he believed that the 'national view' parties were too provocative in their politics. It was different with the AKP: there was a significant overlap between the free market orientation, the focus on Turkey and the global reach of the Gülen network, and the political attitudes and modus operandi of Justice and Development.

The Gülen network emerged as an innovation of traditional religious brotherhoods throughout the 1970s, and grew especially in the 1980s, when the Turkish–Islamic synthesis was the preferred ideology of the generals. It extended throughout the 1990s and expanded especially in the areas where the weak system of public welfare left a vacuum; that is, in educational institutions and university preparation schools, in the social services, but also in the media and the publishing sector. Thousands of student halls and reading circles, hundreds of privately financed primary and secondary schools and eventually even universities emerged out of these networks, first in Turkey and, after 1989, in the Turkic republics of Central Asia, then in the Balkans and Russia and eventually also in Muslim-majority countries in Asia and Africa. Finally, Gülen schools also opened in West European countries with Turkish immigrant populations, such as the United Kingdom, the Netherlands and even integration-obsessed Germany. Often targeting the children of middle-class or upwardly mobile parents, the schools played a great role in the creation of the religiously and socially conservative but globally acting middle classes – a realm hitherto reserved for the Kemalist elites – and in creating export-oriented business networks in and beyond Turkey.

In business, and in the face of the weakness of the rule of law, businessmen close to Gülen created networks of mutual trust and obligation:

> There was no state that would enforce business legislation and protect small businesses. Membership in the network made possible trust-based interactions. The businessman in Kayseri can send his products to his counterpart in Van without prepayment, because he can trust his counterpart as he knows that he is part of [the network] and liable to control from his peers. (Şahin Alpay, interview, 13 July 2009)

As the businesses close to the Gülen network grew, new associations emerged: the Turkish Confederation of Businessmen and Industrialists (TUSKON), for instance, a competitor to the Istanbul-based Turkish Businessmen Association, TÜSİAD, became one of the key actors in Turkey's export drive in the late 1990s. With the 'postmodern coup' of 28 February 1997, the military – and, in its tow, the mainstream media – had labelled these associations, as well the businesses they represented, 'green capital' or 'Islamic capital', and had them excluded from government tenders. With the AKP in power, they came back with a vengeance and would eventually staff most of the government's agencies and institutions.

Yet the societal changes that created the support base for Justice and Development went deeper: the backbone of the AKP social base was the religiously conservative but market-oriented middle classes of the Anatolian heartlands, which had transformed from a class of merchants and pre-industrial small producers into an increasingly globally oriented business and industrialist elite. This transformation, which Gerald Knaus of the European Stability Initiative described in a widely discussed report on 'Islamic Calvinists' in 2005, was significant: in the 1950s, Kayseri was a dusty central Anatolian town of 65,000 inhabitants, with two large industrial complexes belonging to the state – an aircraft factory and a textile combine – small furniture manufactories and a large bazaar as the nodal point for business transactions in the province. Remnants of the city's relative wealth – stately homes, proud churches and school buildings – had barely survived the destruction of its sizeable Armenian community in 1915.

In 2000, Kayseri had around 600,000 inhabitants, 40,000 of whom were employed in the furniture industry and related businesses alone. A massive industrial zone outside the city – developed since the 1980s – hosts thousands of small and medium-sized companies, producing denim and textiles as well as cables and light and heavy machinery. The development from the manufactory stage, in which a master craftsman would work with an apprentice, to the level of highly sophisticated industrial holdings and exporters of furniture or textiles happened often within two generations: the founder of the business would be the grandfather – an elderly gentleman wearing a white beard as sign of his piety and his status as haji after the pilgrimage to Mecca. His sons would have expanded the business in the Özal years, benefiting from the new opportunities of the Middle Eastern and Central Asian markets. His grandsons and sometimes also his granddaughters, finally, would probably have studied at the Gülen schools and at university, speak foreign languages and travel the world in search of new business opportunities, and vote for the Justice and Development Party. They would combine effortlessly religious piety and self-discipline with profit maximization and rent generation. In the absence of a better term, they would all be seen as 'Islamic Calvinists' by circles sympathetic to the AKP, and as 'green capital' by the guardian state, which feared their wealth and growing political power.

*Tayyip Erdoğan and the 'war on terror'* The first AKP government constituted after the November 2002 elections was led by Abdullah Gül, as Tayyip Erdoğan was barred from running for political office owing to a religiously loaded speech he had delivered five years earlier. In 1997, he had criticized the military by citing verses from a poem by Ziya Gökalp – ironically, one of the key figures of Turkish nationalism – and was convicted by a State Security Court to one year's imprisonment on grounds of 'inciting hatred'. This sentence not only ended his short but successful term as mayor of Istanbul, but also limited his citizenship rights, and most importantly, his right to run for office. It was only after a constitutional change that Erdoğan could stand for a by-election in March 2003 and was duly elected. As an underdog, deprived of his rights by the judiciary, he had a large proportion of the public on his side when he was then appointed prime minister.

So, was Erdoğan an Islamist firebrand? Born in Istanbul's rough neighbourhood of Kasımpaşa to poor immigrants from the Black Sea town of Rize, Erdoğan was forced to earn his own money early on – as a child he sold lemonade and pastry on the streets, while in his free time he played in semi-professional football clubs. He was educated in a religious Imam-Hatip school – explaining his personal sense of grievance when the schools were branded centres of religious reaction in the 1997 intervention – and became active in the National Youth Foundation (*Milli Gençlik Vakfı*), the youth association of Erbakan's National Salvation Party, in the mid-1970s. His political career began in earnest in 1983, with the foundation of the Welfare Party, and had its first peak when he was elected mayor of Istanbul in 1994. Though he was certainly shaped by Islamist ideology and socialized in the *Milli Görüş* tradition, Erdoğan's ascent to power was a success story more akin to the American dream than a case of Islamist radicalization. A cable from the US embassy in Ankara would nevertheless describe him as possessing attributes of 'overbearing pride', 'unbridled ambition stemming from the belief God has anointed him to lead Turkey' and 'an authoritarian loner streak' (US embassy, Ankara, 2004).

As soon as he had taken over power from his confidant, Abdullah Gül, Turkey entered the stormy waters of the war against terrorism. Since the 9/11 attacks, George Bush and his allies had been pushing the agenda for a war against Iraq on grounds of what is now generally accepted as bogus evidence of the threat of Iraqi weapons of mass destruction. In Turkey, opposition to the war was next to universal. A wide coalition of civil society groups and political movements, which had formed during the 'One minute of darkness for enduring light' campaigns against the Susurluk scandal in 1997, took to the streets to mobilize against Turkey's possible participation in the military campaign. Mediations between the Turkish government and the Bush administration turned sour when the US negotiators realized that they could not rely on their well-established ties with the military: the Turkish generals were largely absent from the negotiations and refrained from a public stance regarding the intervention, probably to let the government walk into a trap and then score points with public opinion in case of failure. Instead, the Pentagon had to deal with an elected government that was driving a hard bargain to ensure that Turkey would not suffer economically, while it insisted on a say on the future of Iraq and the emerging Kurdish entity to its north.

Less than two weeks before Erdoğan's re-election and appointment as prime minister in March 2003, parliament was to vote on a government motion that would have allowed the US military to launch its offensive against Iraq from Turkish territory. Public opinion, including the majority of AKP voters, remained squarely opposed to Turkey's involvement. The vote, also referred to as the '1st of March Permit' (*1 Mart Tezkeresi*), took place as more than ten thousand demonstrators marched through the streets of Ankara. Despite last-minute pleas from the government and Tayyip Erdoğan, the motion failed to attract the majority of parliamentarians, as almost one hundred MPs defected from the party line. Significantly, the Turkish no vote was exemplary: Turkey was the only democratic country where anti-war campaigns and majority opinion succeeded in forcing the government to change its course and give up on plans for war on Iraq, prompting the otherwise not overly pro-Turkish Noam Chomsky to remark:

> Turkey was offered similar inducements [as other countries in the Western alliance]: a huge financial package and the right to invade the Kurdish northern Iraq. Remarkably, Turkey did not fully submit, teaching a lesson to the West that aroused great ire and, as Secretary of State Powell sternly announced at once, instant punishment for the misdeed. (Chomsky 2004: 35–6)

The speed with which civil society had been able to organize the protests marked the self-confidence of a new coalition of activists, expressed by Cengiz Algan of the initiative 'Say No to Racism and Nationalism' (*DurDe*): 'The parliament's vote on 1 March to refuse passage to US troops for the war on Iraq was a success of the new left. We were the only movement in the world which had a significant impact on a government's decisions' (Cengiz Algan, interview, 8 July 2009).

In the USA, however, the Bush administration was enraged, as their crucial northern front had now collapsed.

In a follow-up vote and face-saving gesture for the government, the parliament opened the country's airspace to US fighters, and was rewarded with an aid package to offset the effects of the war. Even though relations were soon back on track, the occupation of Iraq would regularly cause disagreements between Washington and Ankara. The bone of contention was the emerging Kurdistan Regional Government in the north and US dependence on the Kurdish parties as the only pro-US actors in the Iraqi theatre of war. For a long period, US forces refused to tackle the PKK, which had its main bases in the mountains of Iraqi Kurdistan and would be dismantled only towards the end of the decade. If the anti-war mood in Turkey was already decidedly anti-Bush, an incident in the Kurdish town of Sulaymaniah in July 2003 (also known as the 'hood event', *Çuval Olayı*) triggered a staunchly anti-American response. Probably meant as an act of revenge for Turkey's lack of commitment to the war, a US military unit stormed a Turkish military intelligence mission in Iraq in July. Turkish soldiers and intelligence officers were forced to wear Guantanamo-style hoods and were frogmarched to prison. The footage of the imprisonment constituted the Bush administration's most devastating public relations disaster in Turkey. The opportunity costs for a pro-US stance rose instantly for Prime Minister Erdoğan and poisoned US–Turkey relations, as the occupation of Iraq turned into an unfettered bloodbath right on the doorstep of Turkey's Kurdish provinces.

Yet the war on terror came closer still. In November 2003, double bomb attacks jarred Istanbul. They targeted the headquarters of the HSBC Bank, the British consulate and the Neve Shalom Synagogue in Galata. Fifty-seven were killed in the blaze, including the British consul general, Robert Short. This was, by any criteria, an unusual attack which did not have the signature of Turkey's own brand of radicalized Islamist movements. Such movements did exist, but were under observation by the security services and had only limited scope, the exception being the Kurdish Hizbullah, whose relatively high organizational capacity stemmed from its cooperation with the security services. An earlier attack by such groups had devastated the Neve Shalom Synagogue before – driven more by Islamist anti-Semitism than

by a general hatred of the West – but large-scale attacks on symbols
such as banks and consulates were unheard of before the November
bombings and did not happen again thereafter.

More than seventy people were eventually charged and brought
to court in 2007. Most of them were Turkish citizens from extreme
Islamist backgrounds, who worked together with a Syrian middle-
man, who in turn had close contacts with the al-Qaeda operative
Abu Musab al-Zarqawi. Al-Qaeda eventually claimed responsibility
for the attack, which was supposed to target British interests. Even
though the attack may have come as a bloody reminder for Justice
and Development's balancing act between democratic political Islam
on the one hand and violent Islamism on the other – at least in the
eyes of their critics – and even though some overexcited commentators
called the bombings 'Istanbul's 9/11', November 2003 had little impact
on the debate in Turkey. In a later indictment, it was suggested that
the bombers may have received support from within the military – as
part of a cynical plot to denounce the AKP government as terrorist
– but this allegation has so far not been substantiated. Considering
Turkey's intimate exposure to violence and given its crowded agenda
of everyday scandals, it is not surprising that the bombings had
little impact beyond the Jewish community, which had been directly
affected, save probably for one detail: In European reports about the
bombings, the tone was somehow different from the coverage of 9/11
and showed concern about whether Turkey might now go down the
route of Islamist terrorism experienced in Iraq or Afghanistan. It did
not. The November bombings remained a sideshow and were soon
forgotten, but the long-term impact of 9/11 would soon be felt.

*Negotiating the European promise* In December 2002, at the Copenhagen European Council, the effects of 9/11 had not yet trickled down
into the popular consciousness: European heads of state reiterated
their commitment to Turkey's membership and laid out the road map
for the next few years:

> The European Council [...] strongly welcomes the important steps
> taken by Turkey towards meeting the Copenhagen criteria, in particu-
> lar through the recent legislative packages and the subsequent im-
> plementation measures which cover a large number of key priorities
> specified in the Accession Partnership. The Union acknowledges the

determination of the new Turkish government to take further steps on the path of reform [...] The Union encourages Turkey to pursue energetically its reform process. If the European Council in December 2004, on the basis of a report and a recommendation from the Commission, decides that Turkey fulfils the Copenhagen political criteria, the European Union will open accession negotiations with Turkey without delay. (Copenhagen European Council 2003)

This supportive decision implied the understanding between two sides that Turkey would support the Annan plan for Cyprus, which the United Nations were negotiating with the leaders of the two communities.

In the eight months between its inauguration and July 2003, the AKP government introduced four major harmonization packages – in addition to two such packages passed by the preceding administration – including wide-ranging legal reforms to fulfil the political criteria of the European Union and extend personal rights and freedoms. These included the discontinuation of the State Security Courts, which had been prosecuting citizens on shaky charges of terrorism since their inception during the post-coup constitution of 1982. Throughout 2004, the reform of the penal code was high on the agenda. In a measure considered as one of the benchmarks of Turkey's transition towards European norms and procedures, the government consulted – and more importantly listened to – civil society representatives.

> The debates on the penal code were quite amazing. The women's organizations insisted on revising the articles dealing with violence against women. They ensured that the issue of 'honour killings' and sexual violence was dealt with in the interests of the women rather than society. And the government took their advice. This was a true case of deliberative democracy. (Ayşe Kadıoğlu, interview, 8 July 2009)

This was the heyday of the AKP's Europeanization drive: in a radical departure from earlier governments' inflexible Cyprus policy and their fixation on the recognition of two federal Cypriot states, Erdoğan and his foreign minister, Gül, supported the United Nations plan for the peaceful resolution of the Cyprus conflict. In June, public radio and TV started their first broadcasts in Kurdish and a few other minority languages against the vicious opposition of Deniz Baykal, the main opposition leader. Legislation was passed that permitted the teaching of Kurdish in private language courses. Baykal, as well as the leader of the Nationalist Action Party, Devlet Bahçeli, accused the government of having ushered in a process that would lead to the eventual disintegration of the country. By contrast, pro-Kurdish politicians as well as liberals were enraged by the strings attached to these reforms: Kurdish and other language broadcasts would be allowed only on state radio and TV and limited to less than an hour daily. The language courses would have to fulfil high technical specifications and would be closed to schoolchildren. While justified in principle, the latter criticisms ignored the symbolical importance of these steps, which effectively gave Kurdish the official recognition it had been denied during the entire history of the Turkish Republic.

Despite these mounting controversies, the approval rating of EU accession and the reform process ran at an all-time high of 70 per cent and the government enjoyed support at home and abroad. Bureaucrats in the European Union had never seen such a frantic Turkey so determined to do all it could to begin accession negotiations as soon as possible. Even the decision of the European Court of Human Rights in November 2005 on the case of Leyla Şahin versus Turkey did not subvert the prevailing euphoria, at least not immediately: Leyla Şahin was a fifth-year medical student at Istanbul University when she was barred from attending classes and sitting exams in 1998 due to the headscarf ban imposed after the the 28 February military intervention. Many in the AKP and beyond had expected that the court would judge in favour of Şahin and her right to education, thereby paving the way for revoking the ban in Turkish universities. Effectively prioritizing the principle of secularism over the right to education and religious freedom – a decision comprehensible only in the aftermath of the 9/11 attacks in New York in 2001 and the rising fear of Islam – the judges upheld the decision after an appeal from the defence lawyers.

As Turkey was celebrating its European vocation throughout 2004, however, stumbling blocks were building up. In many continental European publics, the mood was turning against the idea of Turkish membership. The looming eastward enlargement of the European Union involving ten countries was raising fears about immigration and financial transfers to the much poorer accession states. Yet the debate on Turkey was not limited to enlargement fatigue and was intimately connected to the emerging unease with Islam as a result of the ripples that 9/11 sent through Europe.

The cultural genie was out of the bottle. Turkey had already fulfilled most Copenhagen criteria, but then a pan-European debate began on Turkey's Muslimness. The discussions were biased, prejudiced and ill informed, but they were necessary for people to learn about Turkey. But then the debates were hijacked by ultra-conservatives with a deep lack of vision, with parochial minds, who really betrayed what the European Union is all about. (Nora Onar, interview, 9 July 2009)

In the light of these critical debates, Turkey appeared too large, too populous and, significantly, too Muslim for EU membership. These points were taken up readily by populist and extreme right-wing parties like Le Pen's Front National and Jörg Haider's Freedom Party of Austria, yet they would soon enter the vocabulary of mainstream conservative parties.

In Cyprus, the almost quintessential roadblock against change in Turkey, time was ticking away as well. This time, however, the roles had changed: if before the Turkish Cypriot leader Rauf Denktash, an ardent nationalist and proxy of the Turkish state, had been the person to block any meaningful negotiations for three decades, this time the Greek Cypriot leader Papadopoulos was trying to prevent a lasting solution. In the months following the formation of the AKP government, something else had changed in Cyprus: the Turkish Cypriots, bullied both by the Turkey-oriented nationalist regime in the north and their unwelcoming Greek Cypriot compatriots in the south, emerged as subjects of history. Throughout 2002 and 2003, massive demonstrations for a solution and against the regime of Denktash and Ankara took place in the island's north. Organized by a broad coalition of trade unions and left-wing parties under the leadership of the platform 'This is our land' (*Bu memleket bizim*), more than 80,000 demonstrators marched in north Nicosia on 27 February 2003 against Denktash and for a common future for Cyprus within the European Union. Considering that there were about 160,000 Turkish Cypriots living in the north at that time (the remaining 100,000 or so inhabitants are thought to be settlers from Turkey), it is hard not to join Thanos Demetriu and Sotiris Vlahos, Greek Cypriot socialists and bi-communal activists, in their assessment that a revolutionary situation was unfolding in northern Cyprus with a mass basis that had little to compare with it in world politics. While this revolutionary moment went almost completely unnoticed in Europe and beyond (hence Demetriu and Vlahos's 2009 book title:

*The Betrayed Upheaval*), and was actively ignored and downplayed in the Greek Cypriot south, it did force Denktash to open the barriers between the two sides in April 2003.

The peace plan negotiated by UN secretary-general Kofi Annan with the leaders of the two communities, and the three guarantor powers (the United Kingdom, Turkey and Greece), stipulated a bizonal, bi-communal republic as a member of the European Union. It proposed a swap of territory between the two federal entities, generous compensation for refugees who had lost their properties, and foresaw that both Cypriot communities would hold a referendum on the plan, and after a yes vote on both sides join the European Union together. After intense negotiations, a timetable was agreed for a referendum on 24 April 2004. Each community would vote separately for or against the plan and for unification, and thereby open the way for the accession in May 2004 to the European Union of a united Cyprus.

The neatly planned script for unification and EU accession collapsed, however, when Greek Cypriot leaders, including the communist AKEL party, united with the president of the Republic of Cyprus, Tassos Papadopoulos, and urged their compatriots to vote against the Annan plan. On 24 April, 65 per cent of Turkish Cypriots cast a yes vote and 75 per cent of Greek Cypriots voted no. To the dismay of many EU officials, who had counted on Greek Cypriot leaders to win over their constituencies for the plan, and to the shock of Turkish Cypriots and the Turkish government, the Republic of Cyprus nevertheless joined the European Union in May 2004, together with eight eastern European countries and Malta, but without a peace settlement. In theory, the entire island became part of the EU, while the acquis was only suspended in the north. In actual fact, the 'Turkish Republic of Northern Cyprus', together with Turkey, continued to administer the island's northern part.

And still, when the EU's December deadline approached, the prospect of the start of accession negotiations was emotive enough to outshine all public concerns. On 15 December, the European Parliament voted for Turkey's EU accession with a two-thirds majority. Even though this was a non-binding decision, it was a highly symbolic message a day before the fateful European Council meeting. During the vote, hundreds of European legislators were holding placards displaying Turkish and European flags as well as the word 'Yes' in the different languages of the Union and in Turkish, hence creating one of the most iconic images of the pre-accession process. And on 17 December: 'The European Council [...] decided that, in the light [...] of the Commission report and recommendation, Turkey sufficiently fulfils the Copenhagen political criteria to open accession negotiations [...]' (Brussels European Council 2004).

This was followed by another highly symbolic change in Turkey's everyday life: with inflation down from 80 to 10 per cent – a result of the economic austerity programme of the IMF and Kemal Derviş – the government decided to slash six zeros from the Turkish lira. A people that had grown accustomed to calculating their expenses in billions and changing their lira instantly into dollars in order to protect them from inflation were now getting used to thinking in units of tens, hundreds and thousands. Confidence in the New Turkish Lira (Yeni Türk Lirası, YTL) returned as savers opted for saving accounts in the local currency. The de-dollarization was also a reflection of the growing confidence of foreign investors. Foreign direct investment rose by 60 per cent between 2002 and 2004 and tripled between 2004 and 2005, though remained confined mostly to the privatization of public assets and companies.

Accession negotiations were to start on 3 October 2005 at the Luxembourg Summit of the European Council, hosted by the British EU presidency. Start they did, though only after rounds of frantic negotiations pushed by UK Foreign Secretary Jack Straw, to prevent the Austrian delegation from derailing the whole undertaking by insisting on the option of a 'privileged partnership'. In the end, Turkey committed itself to continuing to seek for a solution for Cyprus and to extending the Ankara protocol to all new member states, effectively meaning that it would eventually recognize the Republic of Cyprus. Even though the Austrian proposal for a 'privileged partnership' did not enter the accession partnership framework, a new concept called 'absorption capacity' did. For the first time in EU accession processes, and as a result of the massive eastern European enlargement wave in May 2004, the ability of the Union to absorb a new member state without stressing its own resources became a formal factor for consideration, *after* the negotiations were concluded and before accession could become effective. This, together with the prospect of French and Austrian plans for a referendum over Turkey's membership, the German Christian Democrat Union's insistence on a privileged partnership and the hostile attitudes of the Republic of Cyprus, meant that the European promise was losing its appeal at a time when its realization appeared most tangible.

After the emotional roller-coaster of almost six years since the initial European moment in Helsinki, the accession process would turn into an increasingly desperate affair. In December 2006, a set of eight chapters was frozen, because Turkey refused to extend the Additional Protocol to the Ankara Agreement to Cyprus. Turkey did in fact not open ports and airports to Cypriot vessels, because the isolation of northern Cyprus, which the EU was supposed to ease, continued, despite the Turkish-Cypriot yes vot. Further chapters were frozen in the following year, the most unfortunate (the chapter on economy) at the intervention of French president Nicolas Sarkozy in order to avoid a point of no return in Turkey's accession process. Without the carrot of membership, the government had little to gain politically from responding to the EU's sticks.

### War and peace in Kurdistan

The EU reforms were enthusiastically welcomed in the Kurdish provinces. Ever since the capture of PKK leader Abdullah Öcalan in 1999, a ceasefire had been in place, and military operations had all but ceased. With the AKP in power, the atmosphere normalized still further: in the 1990s, shops in Diyarbakır or Batman used to close before dusk to allow customers to return to their homes before sunset. The public space was a place of extrajudicial killings, patrolled by the various security and counter-terrorism units. On winter evenings, life would come to a halt in the late afternoon, while buses to the villages and towns stopped running around the same time. Released from the tight grip of the 'State of Emergency Regional Governorate' (*Olağanüstü Hal Bölge Valiliği*) in November 2002, residents of the south-east experienced, for the first time in almost a generation, basic freedoms, such as travelling without regular identity controls and roadblocks. In the large cities of the south-east, urban life was slowly restored to its pre-1980 vivacity, despite the fact that many cities in the region were suffering from the additional strain of hundreds of thousands of internally displaced people. Notwithstanding the poverty and erosion of traditional social institutions in these cities, however, there was a remarkable relaxation of authoritarian policies and a softening of attitudes among members of the security forces.

The lifting of the state of emergency also opened the way for a more self-conscious Kurdish associational life. The municipalities ruled by the pro-Kurdish Democratic Society Party (DTP) through cultural activities, concerts and film festivals contributed to the emergence of a new public sphere, which had a distinctively Kurdish touch. The images of incessant violence and bloodshed, with which the region was hitherto associated, were replaced, at least in some parts of the Turkish mainstream media, with images of a cultural revival beyond conflict. In Diyarbakır, the mayor of the metropolitan administration, Osman Baydemir, renovated the imposing city walls, which had been wilfully neglected by state agencies because of their iconic importance for Kurdish identity. Abdullah Demirbaş, the mayor of the intramural Suriçi district, began a programme for the restoration of the old town, including its derelict Armenian and Syriac churches. Together with the first transmissions in Kurdish on Turkey's state radio and TV, a 'Kurdish spring' seemed to complement Turkey's European future.

*The Şemdinli affair* Violence in the Kurdish provinces did not cease completely: low-level armed conflict in some areas continued after the end of emergency rule, even if fighting was largely confined to rural areas. On 9 November 2005, a week after the start of accession negotiations with the European Union, this changed when the impoverished town of Şemdinli made it into the headlines: a bookshop, owned by a former member of the PKK, was bombed. A passer-by was killed. It was supposed to look like a PKK attack in the centre of the city, but happening in broad daylight, it failed. Passers-by close to the bookshop were emboldened enough to stop the white Renault which was trying to flee the site of the attack. Three men were captured by the crowd and handed over to the police: two of them were military officers, and one was an ex-PKK informant.

Inside the car boot, the people present at the scene found weaponry, police and gendarmerie uniforms, lists of men under observation, an index of DTP members, and a map of the bookshop and its surroundings. Finally, they also came across the car's registration papers, which indicated as owner the Gendarmerie General Command of Hakkari. Once again, the deep state had been caught red handed, but this time it was harder to deny. What is more, it was abundantly clear that this plot had been planned and executed by members of the armed forces. Newspaper readers in the rest of the country, however, believed that this was an intra-Kurdish affair, and the footage of angry men in

Şemdinli and soon in other Kurdish cities, attacking police stations and throwing stones at gendarmerie posts, seemed to confirm the notion of Kurdish mobs attacking Turkish security personnel. In the ensuing protests in Şemdinli, a gendarme shot dead one protester and more were killed in the wave of protests which erupted throughout the Kurdish region.

The young chief prosecutor of Van, Ferhat Sarıkaya, was intent on throwing light on the affair. Soon he had to face not the gendarmerie but someone else in higher command: the acting chief of the ground forces and later Chief of the General Staff, Yaşar Büyükanıt, supported one of the two officers with the words 'I know him, he is a good boy'. Sarıkaya not only charged the three assailants, he also implicated Büyükanıt for trying to pervert the cause of justice and for his involvement in undercover activities during his earlier term of office in Diyarbakır. In March 2006, the 'Court for Heavy Fines' in Van granted the prosecutor's indictment and imposed heavy prison terms for the three defendants. Yet, as in the case of Susurluk, the legal process was interrupted before justice could be done. In response to an appeal by the defendants, the Supreme Court decided that the case had to be heard by a military court, which in turn dropped all charges. The three assailants, who had been caught in the act in broad daylight, were released. After a request from the Chief of the General Staff, the prosecutor was relieved of his duties in the case. In April, he was deposed from office by the High Council of Judges and Prosecutors, the body overseeing the judges and prosecutors, to the applause of the leader of the Republican People's Party, Deniz Baykal, who equated the indictment with a 'coup against the military'.

*The beginning and the suspended end of the 'Kurdish spring'* If Kurds in the south-east were still hopeful that the Şemdinli affair was a one-off, an unpleasant episode of déjà vu that soon would be forgotten, they were put right instantly: the death in combat of fourteen PKK fighters on 29 March 2006 set in motion a circle of violence that recalled the worst days of the counter-terrorism years. The demonstrations, which had died down after the investigations into the Şemdinli affair, spread throughout the region, publicized by the pro-PKK Kurdish satellite TV channel Roj TV. In the next few days, security forces killed at least fourteen protesters, mostly in Diyarbakır. Many of the victims were young men, yet three were children under ten years of age, who had got caught up in the street fights. At least four hundred were wounded in Diyarbakır alone, and more than five hundred were detained for interrogation. The violence spread to Istanbul, where a petrol bomb killed three women passing by a demonstration in a mostly Kurdish-populated suburb.

In scenes reminiscent of Gaza and the occupied territories, stone-throwing children were at the forefront of street battles with the police units, which the DTP mayor of Diyarbakır, Osman Baydemir, tried to de-escalate, together with the deputy governor. While Baydemir came under criticism from both Kurdish radicals, who accused him of collaboration with the police, and the establishment, who scolded him for not doing enough, Prime Minister Erdoğan signalled a shift in his government's Kurdish policy and a return to hard-line security strategies. He declared that the 'security forces will intervene against the pawns of terrorism, even if they are children or women. Everyone should realize that.' In the wave of detentions and prosecutions following the April protests, 200 children between twelve and eighteen years of age were taken into custody and around ninety were charged with participation in illegal protests and 'aiding and abetting' the PKK, a charge carrying a maximum jail sentence of twenty-four years.

And finally, in a replay of the 'securitizing' reflex of all their predecessors in the 1990s, the government introduced an amendment to the anti-terror law that effectively revoked many of the liberalizing reforms of the penal code. In addition to the 'propagation of terrorist groups', the 'propagation of the goals of terrorist groups' was made an offence. This highly ambiguous formulation could be applied to penalize legitimate requests, such as for education in Kurdish, on the grounds that these demands were also advocated by the PKK. The amendment reintroduced prison sentences of one to three years for the publication of views deemed supportive of terrorist groups. In addition, the chief prosecutor of any province was empowered to suspend publications, an action hitherto possible only with a court order. The wide definition of terror paved the way to charge independent journalists and Kurds engaging in legal politics. Most importantly, and in clear violation of Turkey's obligations arising from UN provisions for the protection of children, as well as the Turkish constitution, the amendment provided for the courts to charge children between the ages of fifteen and eighteen as adults, if the charges included terrorism offences, i.e. throwing stones.

In the following two years, almost two thousand children were prosecuted under the Anti-Terrorism Act and around 10 per cent of them were found guilty and imprisoned. In almost all cases, their offence was to throw stones, and to a lesser extent Molotov cocktails, at security officers. It was only after the law was revised in 2010 that most of these children were eventually released. The judiciary, in its self-declared mission to defend the state, charged dozens of local DTP chairmen and members with terrorism offences and opened hundreds of court cases against DTP mayors. The mayors of Diyarbakır and Suriçi were forced to spend several days a week defending themselves against often fantastic allegations of destroying the territorial integrity of the country. What had happened as a promising new beginning with the Kurdish provinces seemed to have come full circle, if with the significant difference that activists and politicians were dragged to court rather than tortured and dumped on the roadside, as had been the case in the 1990s. A 'Kurdish opening', however, was still to happen.

## Memory and reality: the return of the guardians

The 'European' years of the AKP government highlighted the remarkable cultural and intellectual transformation which had been taking place since the mid-1990s. Cultural production moved beyond the narrow confines of Kemalist kitsch and socialist realism, and artists, writers and film-makers began to participate in public political debates with their work. With the promise of a free and democratic society, and the hope of becoming a 'normal' country, whose citizens could look beyond issues of daily survival, individuals began to turn to history, to their histories. As in the arts, history in the Turkish republic was a sterile exercise geared either towards Kemalist and later Turkish-Islamic nation-building or a Marxist critique of its political economy. In these meta-narratives, there was little space for real stories and for the experiences that the peoples of Turkey shared. The Kemalist project of a unitary identity and historiography had long lost its appeal, but it was in the early 2000s that activists, academics, journalists and members of the public challenged the hegemonic narrative on 'Turkey for the Turks' and that generals, extreme nationalists, mainstream media outlets and Kemalists assembled to defend it. When the challenge to the worldview of the guardians became too threatening, however, their voices were stifled and a violent counter-movement emerged.

*Remembering 1915* In the republican era, Armenians and their contributions to the late Ottoman Empire were effectively excised from history, save for their 'treacherous uprisings' against the ailing Ottoman Empire. Ever since the bomb attacks on Turkish diplomats by the Armenian Liberation Front (ASALA) in the 1970s and 1980s, Turks and Kurds had been educated about 'Armenian conspiracies' and mobilized against the 'genocide lie'. In the 1990s, when the first books on the genocide were published in Turkey – Taner Akçam was the first Turkish author to challenge the established narrative – only very few in the educated middle classes or in academia knew about the genocide at all, even though knowledge of atrocities against Armenians was part of folklore and local history everywhere in Turkey. Outside the Armenian community and those families that had witnessed or taken part in the deportation of Armenians, or had escaped extermination by conversion, few Turks questioned the official orthodoxy and made no connection with the recollections of their grandparents. According to the official narrative, Armenian nationalist organizations had rebelled against the empire and collaborated with Russia in order to establish an independent Armenia on Ottoman soil. In 1915, the Ottoman state had decided to deport Armenians from the eastern provinces to cut their communications with the advancing Russian forces. Many had died owing to hunger and disease, but the state had done its best to protect them. There was no genocide, not even deportation orders, only relocation to the Syrian desert. This was the position of the chair of the Turkish History Association, Yusuf Halaçoğlu, who equated the genocide claim with treason to the Turkish nation.

This narrative, however, was flying in the face of international scholarship, where there was little disagreement about the historical fact that the majority of the empire's 1.5 million Armenians had been destroyed through a programme of deportations and murders organized by the Committee of Union and Progress. The following years would show that the memory of 1915, and of many more instances of state violence such as the Dersim massacres of 1937/38, the Wealth Tax and the Istanbul pogroms of 1955 had not been excised from the collective memory as thoroughly as republican nation-builders would have hoped. It rather appeared that these memories had been dormant, awaiting an opportunity to be related and heard. Once the first books were published, and people started talking about their family recollections, the sterile narrative of modern Turkey seemed to be exposed as what most 'national' histories are: a highly biased and selective version of a history of the victors.

The debate on the destruction of the late Ottoman Empire's Armenian communities began in earnest – cautiously at first and under the sword of Damocles of the penal code's Article 301, which sanctioned the 'denigration of Turkishness' – with an interview in the newspaper *Radikal* in October 2000. The historian Halil Berktay argued that the 'Special Organization' (*Teşkilat-i Mahsusa*) of the Committee of Union and Progress was responsible for conducting massacres on a massive scale in 1915. Literature on the genocide was translated from English and French, while other publications reinstated the Armenians as a historical subject. Books about the Armenian communities of different Turkish cities were translated from Armenian or republished in Turkish. An exhibition and a book of postcards depicting Armenian life in Turkey before 1915 (Köker 2005) was an eye-opener for many who had believed the official version that only Armenians in the eastern provinces had been deported. They now saw the visual evidence of Armenian life all over the empire and contemporary Turkey, and wondered where all these Armenians had gone.

While these books on the Ottoman Empire's Armenians and the public events and talk shows discussing them helped re-establish the factual backdrop, it was the novels and memoirs which brought the human dimension of suffering and coping to the forefront. The novelist Elif Shafak broke the silence as early as 2002 in her allegorical *Flea Palace*, where the unbearable stench of a garbage pile in an Istanbul neighbourhood became a metaphor for the denial of a history full of filth. She continued the theme with her 2006 *Bastard of Istanbul*, in which she explored the possibility of discussing the genocide through the words of a US-Armenian visitor to Istanbul called Armanush. In *My Grandmother*, lawyer and activist Fethiye Çetin told the story of her Armenian grandmother Seher (with the Armenian name Heranush), a survivor of 1915, while Baskın Oran edited the memoirs of Manuel Kırkyaşaryan under the title *Deportation Memories of a Child Named MK*. Published in 2005, these books helped the reading public to recognize the Armenians as people 'like us'. Instead of the demonized Armenian terrorists of the ASALA, and despite the number-crunching on fatalities preferred by Kemalist historians, Armenians emerged as the victims of a sinister policy of extermination.

Opposition to this radical re-reading of the history of modern Turkey did not take long to emerge forcefully and in an organized fashion. It came in the form of an aggressively nationalist-conspiratorial set of debates, publications and court cases that brought back the language of existential binaries and branded the revisionists as 'traitors to the nation'. This mindset was written into semi-factual bestsellers and films that celebrated the history of the Turkish people as a fight for survival against malignant European powers and the neocolonial United States. Turgut Özakman's *These Mad Turks*, depicting the 1919–23 Turkish War of Independence as a heroic, almost supernatural struggle of good against evil, sold more than 700,000 official, and probably as many pirated, copies. If this retrospective response to current developments attempted to repair a 'humiliated national pride' with reference to the 'golden age' of the War of Independence, the box-office hit *Valley of the Wolves in Iraq* dealt with a much more immediate theme. The film, loosely based on the real story of the 'hood incident', followed a Turkish avenger on his mission to restore national pride after the humiliation of Turkish soldiers by US occupying forces. The protagonist operated outside the law, backed not by state agencies, but by clandestine networks extending from mafia-like organizations, extreme nationalists to 'patriotic' individuals within the state apparatus. It was almost a blueprint for the deep state operations, and there is little doubt that behind this cultural shift towards militarism and chauvinism was a guardian state campaign to defend the republic against the challenge of historical revision.

Extreme nationalist lawyers, with Kemal Kerinçsiz, the chair of the ephemeral 'Great Union of Jurists' (*Büyük Hukukçular Birliği*), at the forefront, filed complaints against literally all journalists and writers who challenged the official narrative, and convinced prosecutors to charge them with Article 301, i.e. 'denigrating Turkishness'. The court hearings in 2005 and 2006 saw some of Turkey's most prolific intellectuals – Orhan Pamuk, Murat Belge, Elif Shafak and the Armenian-Turkish journalist Hrant Dink – heckled and assaulted by mobs who were reportedly led by Kerinçsiz and his henchmen. Most of the intellectuals were eventually acquitted, save for Hrant Dink, who was convicted of insulting Turkishness, and then murdered. Suddenly, and beyond the comprehension of seasoned observers, the public debate had come to be dominated by a vengeful language and a hateful polarization that seemed to justify violent acts and hate crimes.

This nationalist hysteria was also manifested in the urban space: if hilltops in Kurdish provinces had been adorned with Turkish suprem-acist slogans since the 1980 military coup, the mid-2000s saw the emergence of massive flagpoles with even bigger Turkish flags the size of a football pitch. Where and how the phenomenon first started remains to be researched, but the first flags seem to have been a state affair. Soon, however, AKP municipalities would catch up, in part because they were nudged to do so, in part because they didn't want to see their nationalist credentials questioned. By 2005, Istanbul's delicate skyline was already littered with dozens of extremely big Turkish flags. After the ugly makeshift mosques of the 1980s and their disproportionately high minarets, even uglier and higher flagpoles dwarfed minarets and office buildings. The Turkish flag was now everywhere, even though it meant very different things to different people. To a dispassionate observer, it simply felt like a sign of a deep crisis of national identity.

And indeed, the year 2005 was a high point of the challenge to the Kemalist narrative: on 6 September, a coalition of civil society associa-tions opened an exhibition of photos on the destruction caused by the Istanbul pogroms in 1955. The exhibition was open to the public and took place in a building off Istiklal Avenue, i.e. right in the centre of Beyoğlu, where the pogroms had begun. In a highly symbolic gesture, a group of men stormed the exhibition and destroyed some of the exhibits, chanting the slogans 'Turkey is Turkish and will remain so' and 'Love it or leave it!'. The assailants, members of an extreme right-wing group, were apprehended by the police and then released. The pressure was now building up: as more and more politicians and mainstream newspapers started attacking the critical intellectuals who declared that 1915 was a moment of shame for Turkey, preparations went ahead for a major conference on the 'Ottoman Armenians in the late empire: the issues of scientific responsibility and democracy'. With a last-minute injunction, Kemal Kerinçsiz tried to prevent the conference, and failed owing merely to a technicality: the injunction had banned the conference from the campuses of two of the three co-organizing universities, Sabancı and Bosporus University. The organizers then made the bold decision to go ahead at the campus of the third collaborator, Bilgi University.

On 24 September, the conference began amid mounting rhetoric from extreme nationalist circles, as well as asides from Deniz Baykal and Kemal Kerinçsiz, who questioned the 'scientific character' of the conference and dismissed it as a political event. The AKP justice minister, Cemil Çiçek, even accused the organizers of 'backstabbing the Turkish nation'. Participants trying to reach the conference venue were pelted with eggs and subjected to verbal abuse by nationalist protesters and members of the formerly Maoist 'Workers' Party' of Doğu Perinçek, who had recently shifted to a politics of extreme nationalism and racism against Kurds and Armenians. Not only was he suspected of being on the payroll of the deep state, and hence ended up as a defendant in the Ergenekon case, he would also be convicted of genocide denial in Switzerland in March 2007. Despite the heavy atmosphere and the fulminations, however, the conference went ahead – indeed, with a written welcome address by then foreign minister, Abdullah Gül. Turkey's most prominent historians, academics and journalists, as well as many students and interested members of the public, took part. There was dispassionate scholarly debate, yet there were also moments when the audience was moved to tears. Hrant Dink, in response to the heckling of a female protester who accused Armenians of territorial claims on Turkey, relayed the story of an elderly Armenian lady from Anatolia, who had left her home in Paris to die in her village of birth. He ended with the conclusion:

> Yes, it is true that Armenians long for this soil. But let me repeat what I wrote soon after this experience. At the time the then president of Turkey, Süleyman Demirel, used to say: 'We will not give even three pebbles to Armenians.' I told the story of this woman and said: 'We Armenians do desire this territory because our roots are here. But don't worry. We desire not to take this territory away, but to come and be buried under it.' (Dink 2005)

The front page of *Radikal* newspaper the next day summed up the atmosphere at the conference: 'At the conference, even the word "genocide" was pronounced, and the world is still rotating and Turkey is still in place' (*Radikal*, 25 September 2005).

Yet Turkey was not really in its place any more. If the start of accession negotiations on 3 October provided a last respite, the next year and a half would bring a complete escalation on all fronts. A wave of court cases and rabble-rousing, of death threats and public attacks against critical minds and particularly against Hrant Dink, swept through the mainstream media. Many columnists joined the hunt for the 'enemy within' and attacked Hrant Dink for his public call for a reconciliation of Turks and Armenians. Throughout 2006, as violence spread through the Kurdish provinces, extreme nationalists stirred up anti-Christian sentiment. As observers were wondering how relatively unknown figures like Kemal Kerinçsiz could have amassed so much power over prosecutors and could act with such audacity and impunity, the first murder occurred. In February, the Catholic priest Father Andrea Santoro was shot dead in the Black Sea town of Trabzon by a sixteen-year-old boy. In May, an extreme right-wing lawyer with Islamist leanings shot dead the Council of State judge Mustafa Yücel Özbilgin, who had been denounced by the radical Islamist newspaper *Vakit* as responsible for an anti-headscarf ruling. None of these murders, however, was what it purported to be at first sight. Initially, they were thought to be have been committed by extreme Islamists or nationalists, who had taken the law into their own hands to 'avenge the Turkish nation' against sedition. The killers themselves believed that this was what they did. But they were only the instruments of others. As in earlier instances, the guardians of the republic opted to enlist killers in the name of 'saving the state', and this time they used members of the extreme Islamist-Nationalist Great Unity Party (*Büyük Birilik Partisi*). And again, Turkey entered a frantic period where hatred spiralled out of control, enmities exploded and people were galvanized into action without knowing exactly why.

*The murder of Hrant Dink* On 20 January 2007, Hrant Dink was murdered. The assassin approached him in broad daylight, in front of the Armenian-Turkish newspaper *Agos*, for which Dink had worked as editor-in-chief since its inception in 1996. The teenager Ogün Samast, who had travelled from Trabzon to Istanbul that day, was apprehended as prime suspect. The murder did not come as a surprise to those close to Dink, who knew that he was receiving serious death threats and that he could not count on the protection of the security forces, who openly intimidated him. Yet the shock waves that his death sent through the world were enormous: throughout Turkey and the Armenian diasporas people were stunned by the murder of someone as humane and sensitive as Dink. Spontaneous vigils and demonstrations took place on the site of the assassination. Many of the columnists who had accused Dink of treason moderated their language overnight and virtually everybody seemed to be mourning his death. Yet none of these spontaneous – and in some less genuine cases calculated –

manifestations of sympathy would prepare the public for the day of his funeral three days later.

Organized by a coalition of civil society organizations including the initiative 'Say No to Racism and Nationalism' and the 'Young Civilians', 100,000 mourners joined the funeral procession that set off in front of the offices of the *Agos* newspaper and stopped at the Armenian Evangelical Church in Kumkapi, eight kilometres away. The mourners, Foreign Minister Abdullah Gül among them, were holding placards with the slogans 'We are all Armenians' and 'We are all Hrant Dink' in Armenian, Turkish and Kurdish. The Armenian Turkish novelist and colleague of Hrant Dink Karin Karakaşlı remembers:

> 'We are all Hrant Dink. We are all Hrant Dink ...' I remember my shock that day, when I heard a hundred thousand people shouting: 'We are all Armenians'. The funeral was not only a matter for the Armenian community. The 23rd of January was an event that took place in the centre of Turkey. [...] It was a reality: this was the society of Turkey. (Karin Karakaşlı, interview, 9 July 2009)

The investigations, eagerly awaited by Dink's wife Rakel, his friends and the mourners, turned into a farce even before the court case had started. Leaked video footage showed policemen and gendarmerie personnel proudly posing for the camera alongside the murder suspect Ogün Samast in front of a Turkish flag. Early investigations suggested that Samast was the henchman of mastermind Erhan Tuncel, an informant for the police and gendarmerie intelligence service, who was connected to one of the suspects of the murder of Father Santoro. Yet the court proceedings dragged on without real progress and turned into an offensive charade, with the suspects mocking the victim's family and their legal representatives. Samast and his accomplices were acting with the same audacity and disrespect with which the lawyer Kemal Kerinçsiz attacked his enemies, the murderer of Father Santoro spoke to the public and the assassin of the Council of State judge behaved in court. This was, as many sensed at the time, the audacity of the guardian state.

*The republic marches* President Ahmet Necdet Sezer's term of office was coming to an end. The new Chief of the General Staff, Yaşar Büyükanıt, had already opined that Turkey needed a 'president who is loyal to the principles of the republic – not just in words but in essence'. With roughly two-thirds of the votes in the Assembly, however, the AKP was bold enough to consider the nomination of Prime Minister Erdoğan as successor. Yet as the deliberation over the future president continued, the public mood came to a head, with allegations emerging from every corner and amplified in the secular media that the AKP, this time, was really trying to destroy Turkey's secular order by having a man elected into office whose wife wore a headscarf. Critical voices were muffled: when the news weekly *Nokta* published a feature on a series of coup attempts by senior officers, only narrowly foiled, the owner was forced – by the military – to halt the magazine's publication. The story referred to the diary notes of retired naval officer Özden Örnek, and much in the blueprints for the coup attempts resembled the series of murders and political polarization that were actually happening at that very moment. Like the liberal intellectuals, *Nokta*'s editor-in-chief Alper Görmüş was charged with the offence of 'denigrating Turkishness'.

A wave of massive protest marches began on 14 April in Ankara: after days of frantic calls to take a stand against the government, most emotively made by some leading columnists in the mainstream secular media, hundreds of thousands poured out into the streets to join the first 'republican meeting' in Ankara. People from all walks of life voiced their frustration against the 'anti-secular agenda of the AKP' and a whole set of other grievances, including its 'sell-out' to the United States and the European Union. There is little doubt that many protesters were genuinely concerned about the AKP's conservative social policies, and about the increasingly self-confident religious stance of their leading members. Yet it is also certain that these protests were not representative, but the outcome of a well-organized manipulation that exploited the fears especially of the secular urban middle classes and the Alevi community – understandably wary of any form of Islamist politics – and used them to prevent Justice and Development from taking over the institutions dominated by the guardian state. The organizing committee was indeed chaired by the Ataturkist Thought Association, an anti-European Kemalist network led by the recently retired commander of the gendarmerie, General Şener Eruygur. Some of the co-organizers, including most trade unions and the influential Chamber of Medical Doctors, withdrew from the event on the grounds that it also included the paramilitary group called 'Turkish Revenge Troops' (*Türk İntikam Tugayları*). Deniz Baykal, leader of the main opposition party, as well as many university rectors attended nevertheless and joined in the choruses 'Turkey is secular and will remain secular' and 'We don't want an imam as president'. Some participants also chanted the slogan 'The army needs to take action'.

A few days after the protests, two Turkish converts to Christianity and a German missionary, all three working for a Christian publishing house in the city of Malatya, were slain in a most horrendous way. As if to make the point that the Justice and Development government had unleashed the worst demons of Islamist rule, the murder further deepened the mounting anti-AKP atmosphere. The suspects were soon apprehended – as in the murders of Father Santoro, Hrant Dink and the Council of State judge Özbilgin – but the masterminds remained behind the scenes and the court cases remained inconclusive. In the aftermath of the demonstration, Erdoğan retracted his candidacy. On 24 April, the AKP nominated foreign minister Abdullah Gül instead. Gül was generally considered a more palatable candidate given his soft-spoken demeanour and his commitment to Europeanization and democratization. Yet he also had his political roots in Erbakan's 'national view' tradition of Islamism, and his wife Hayrünisa also wore a headscarf. It was clear by now that this was not the candidate the generals and large parts of the now incited secular public had in mind.

Something else happened on this symbolically charged date of 24 April, which is usually reserved for angry statements against looming US Congress resolutions or parliaments passing bills on genocide recognition: the Chief of the General Staff published a blunt note on the Internet declaring that the vote for a non-secular president (in other words, Abdullah Gül) would prepare the conditions for a military intervention. Known also as the 'e-memorandum' or the 'e-coup', this note was the final call to arms to the anti-government coalition. Three days later, the parliament was to elect the president. The Republican People's Party did not participate in the presidential ballot in order to render invalid the AKP majority's vote for Gül. To the shock of some of the most eminent constitutional jurists in the country, and at the request of the main opposition party, the Constitutional Court decided that Gül's election was indeed null and void because of the lack of a two-thirds quorum, which no legal scholar of any standing had ever heard before. It was clear that the court's decision was political and responded to the military's preferences. Early elections appeared to be the only way out of the deadlock, together with an AKP initiative to allow for direct elections for the presidency. Although the then president, Ahmet Necdet Sezer, returned the reform package to parliament, the Constitutional Court eventually gave the go-ahead, hence paving the way for a referendum on a direct presidential ballot.

Yet even after the government had called elections for July, the 'republican demonstrations' continued throughout April and May with the largest manifestations in Istanbul and Izmir drawing several hundred thousand participants. In addition to the pro-army and extreme nationalist actors behind the first event, Kemalist women's organizations also joined in, together with many middle-class women and followers of the RPP, who felt threatened by the AKP's mix of pro-market policies and social conservatism. While their concerns were genuine, extreme nationalists, who exploited the mass agitation to air their own slogans, hijacked their agenda. Amid a sea of Turkish flags and posters of Mustafa Kemal, a lynch-mob atmosphere built up, in which not only Erdoğan and Gül were shouted at, but also supporters of the European Union and critics of the nationalist historiography. The ordinary men and women, who had come out to voice their anger at being excluded from the AKP's developmental deal and who felt discriminated against because of its social and religious conservatism values, were being used by the puppeteers of the guardian state.

*The ballot box as remedy* The 2007 elections were the most deftly organized in Turkey since the first democratic elections in 1950. Although 84 per cent of Turkey's 42.5 million voters cast ballots, both the voting and the counting of votes moved along swiftly, thanks to a newly digitized system. By 10 p.m., a tableau had emerged that came as a shock to generals and protesters alike. In a clear vote of confidence and support, Justice and Development had increased its share of the national vote from 34.3 per cent in 2002, when it first swept into power, to a staggering 46.7 per cent. The AKP led the balloting in all but a few coastal provinces in the west. Even in locales with a strong republican persuasion, such as İzmir, the Republican People's Party (CHP) escaped defeat only narrowly. In the predominantly Kurdish south-east, though it did not win every province, the AKP more than doubled its vote to over 50 per cent. Thus, the AKP not only established itself as standing 'in the societal centre' of the country, as Prime Minister Erdoğan proclaimed during his victory speech, it also became the only political party that could justifiably claim to represent all regions of Turkey.

The Republican People's Party, despite a merger with the Democratic Left Party, attained only 20.8 per cent of the vote and fell below 10 per cent in all Kurdish provinces. In Diyarbakır, considered by many as the political centre of Kurdistan, CHP candidates attracted an abysmally low 1.9 per cent. Faring well only in some western provinces, the CHP were relegated by the 2007 elections to the status of a regional party rooted in Turkish identity politics. Benefiting from the CHP's decline, the Nationalist Action Party succeeded in doubling its vote to 14 per cent, doing especially well in western and southern Turkey, where they took over many traditionally republican constituencies. Twenty-three Kurdish candidates, who ran as independents rather than under the banner of the Democratic Society Party to circumvent the 10 per cent threshold, were elected from the south-eastern provinces.

All the manipulation and fear-mongering of the last two years had not only come to naught: they had almost delivered the absolute majority for the AKP which the high command and the secular campaigners had so dreaded. The economy's performance during the AKP's five years in office was pivotal in making up voters' minds: growth rates at a constant 7 per cent, the doubling of per capita income, record highs in foreign direct investment and rising stock markets had built up confidence. But voters also followed a libertarian reflex, which had seen the rejection of parties imposed by the generals, whether in the first democratic election of 1950, or during the 1983 elections after the September coup: 'The ballot box in Turkey is a good site. This is where Sunalp [the candidate favoured by the putschists] was defeated and Özal won in 1983. And this is where the AKP got forty-seven per cent after the manipulations over the presidential elections' (Ayşe Kadıoğlu, interview, 8 July 2009).

The 'window of opportunity' in 2002, which saw a brief period of consensus between the Justice and Development government, the main opposition party and the Chief of the General Staff, led to a cultural and political vibrancy that has few comparisons in Turkish history. It released an intellectual and artistic potential that was unparalleled in the country's recent past and marked a new sense of history beyond Kemalist-nationalist statism, Marxist reductionism and Islamism. The promise of Europe and a better life seemed tangible, and the prospect

of facing the demons of the past seemed real. Yet anti-Turkish sentiment in the European Union – in part a long-term result of the creeping
Islamophobia created by the 9/11 attacks and the US assault on Iraq
– soon created the smokescreen under which extreme nationalists,
and increasingly Kemalists, regrouped to attack any pro-European
policy that was likely to challenge the hegemony of the guardian state.
Political murders intimidated the liberal intellectuals and activists, yet
when they failed to silence them, mass demonstrations were organized,
which sought to prevent the democratic process from taking its course.
A great opportunity had faded in the mayhem of manipulated political
violence. The coalition of the armed forces, the bureaucracy and the
high judiciary had once again succeeded in taking centre stage: as
before, they employed their clandestine networks of conspirators and
hit men, induced leading columnists into manipulating society on
their behalf, and exploited the fears of ordinary men and women to
thrust them into action. Yet the plots did not produce the expected
outcome: Justice and Development was elected again, and embarked
on a new term in office, this time with the former AKP prime and
foreign minister Abdullah Gül as president and Tayyip Erdoğan as
prime minister. If there is an ironic twist in this history, it is in
the adverse effect of the generals' manipulations: more people had
actually voted for the AKP to show their determination against the
meddling of non-elected actors than would have otherwise done so.
By trying to discredit the AKP through judicial spin and pressure on
the streets, the guardians in fact devalued reasoned opposition against
the increasingly visible Islamization of society.

# 5 | Another nation: moving towards the present (2007–10)

**This chapter** is merely a first draft of history. It is written as events are unfolding. And in line with the key characteristics of Turkey's political life, the events are developing so fast and are so diverse, the news in the media so contradictory and the stakes so high, that it is close to impossible to distinguish truth from fiction and fact from manipulation. Yet there is one event of massive importance that has overshadowed the AKP's second term in office: the first open confrontation between an elected government and the guardian state, carried out through the courts and amid a frenzy of disinformation in competing media systems. The evidence, which the court cases against the 'Ergenekon network', another name for the guardian state, began to reveal, were hair-raising but not surprising when considered within the context of Turkey's recent history, which we have discussed in the preceding chapters.

Yet as the revelations continued, and as ever more public person-ages and officers – first only retired personnel, but eventually also serving generals – were summoned to court, and as the number of former bigwigs in custody grew, criticism of the proceedings became widespread. And indeed, there is little doubt that the government used the judiciary – with significant parts now beyond the control of the guardians – in order to settle political scores. Second, some of the indictments did not always correspond to the complex reality: the 'deep state' was often portrayed as a tightly controlled, hierarchical terrorist organization. As we have seen in the preceding chapters, however, the guardian state is much more complex and flexible, a network of people and institutions, albeit under the undisputed leadership of parts of the military. The extreme politicization not only of the case but also of the judiciary, which is now divided between pro-AKP and pro-guardian secularist camps, complicates a resolu-tion of the matter in the courts. Yet the exposure of the guardian state and its workings is nevertheless a momentous turning point in Turkey's history.

The economy continued to grow at record rates of 7 per cent and higher, and even the global financial crisis brought only a temporary slowdown. But two significant fields of conflict remained in the limelight. The first was the evolution of the 'Kurdish issue', which embarked on a roller-coaster ride of its own, but failed to reach a happy end. The second was Turkey's forceful emergence as a regional actor under Foreign Minister Ahmet Davutoğlu, who did not shy away from stepping over some US and EU 'red lines', notably in the case of relations with Iran, Syria and Israel. The question of whether Turkey's axis was 'shifting' became particularly salient when a series of crises brought Turkey and Israel to loggerheads. The result was the end of the Israeli–Turkish partnership, which had begun in the Özal years of the First Gulf War, and accelerated during Tansu Çiller's assault on the Kurds. With the end of this strategic relationship ended a chapter in the geostrategic set-up of the Middle East. It was, however, not the end of Turkey's Western orientation, but a course correction in its Middle Eastern policy.

Before the AKP's reckoning with the guardian state, however, there was first a last-ditch effort on the part of the latter to keep the former from government. It all started with the vote for Abdullah Gül. On 28 August 2007, the members of the Turkish Grand National Assembly elected the former prime and foreign minister as president of the Republic. When Gül was sworn in the next day in parliament, the generals and members of the Republican People's Party boycotted the ceremony. Both the military and the republicans were adamant in showing their contempt for a president who had his origins in political Islam, and whose wife wore a headscarf, even though the party that elected him to office had garnered almost 50 per cent of the vote. In order to circumvent a handshake with Ms Gül, a disarmingly charming person, the generals from now on attended state functions without their wives, forcing the president to do the same. At first sight, these buffooneries called to mind Orhan Pamuk's sharp mockery of a small-town coup in his novel *Snow*. In *Snow*, the military commander of a godforsaken city on the Georgian border and his patriotic supporters use a nationalist theatre play to set in motion a local coup aimed at thwarting a feared Islamist takeover. Yet before long, the enforced invisibility of the headscarf became an established part of state protocol. It symbolized the abyss between elected representatives and self-declared guardians of the state, as it introduced another layer of denial: the generals and the Republican People's Party denied the fact that the overwhelming majority of women in Turkey cover their heads, whether with a headscarf or a veil.

Despite the 47 per cent vote, the guardian state thought it could open another front against the AKP. In March 2008, the chief prosecutor pressed charges against the party on grounds of 'anti-secular activities'. The indictment triggered a cycle of allegations and slander against the government, which were so vicious that they resembled a 'judicial coup' seeking to complete what the 'electronic memorandum' against the election of Abdullah Gül had failed to achieve: ousting the elected government, which the guardians now deemed a major threat to the country's future. The prosecutor not only requested a total party ban but also called for all leading AKP cadres – including the prime minister and the president – to be barred from public office for a period of five years. The Constitutional Court deliberated in July, taking into account a strongly liberal-minded plea for the freedom of political association by the independent rapporteur Osman Can. With a margin of only one vote, the court overruled the prosecutor's request for a ban, yet argued that the AKP had indeed become anti-secular in its activities and hence cut the party's public funding. The coup was narrowly averted and finally it seemed that the scene was set for unfettered democratic rule.

## The guardian state exposed

In June 2007, a chest of grenades belonging to the Special Forces Command (*Özel Harekat Dairesi*), one of the covert actors of Turkey's clandestine security networks, surfaced in the Black Sea town of Trabzon. When the Istanbul public prosecutor's office launched a probe into the circumstances surrounding the find and the people involved, the prosecutors in charge were probably aware that their investigation would change the course of Turkey's history: named after Ergenekon – the mythical Turkish homeland in Central Asia, as it has been imagined by Turkish nationalists since the 1920s – the investigation set in motion a court case that would see hundreds of retired and serving military personnel, including high-ranking officers, nationalist academics and Kemalist activists, being charged for membership of a terrorist organization attempting to subvert the democratically elected government.

Soon, a barrage of allegations and counter-allegations, some of them fabricated by the very actors of the deep state, swept through the public sphere. Policemen excavated arm caches used by the counter-terror units, covert hit men and groups within the armed forces. In the south-east, the remains of hundreds of murdered men and women – victims of the different security agencies – surfaced in derelict wells of the state petroleum agency. New waves of investigations led to the detention of all the actors who had been at the forefront of the covert and not so covert plots which we have encountered in the preceding chapters. These were plots to manipulate public opinion and galvanize support for military interventions in order to oust elected government. The following public personalities appeared in court: Kemal Kerinçsiz, the lawyer who had so shamelessly fomented hatred against Hrant Dink, the leader of the racist-nationalist 'Labour Party' (*İşçi Partisi*) Doğu Perinçek, Kemal Alemdaroğlu, who was made rector of Istanbul University after the military intervention of 1997 and had played a major role in imposing the headscarf ban, and his friend Kemal Gürüz, the former chair of the Higher Education Council with whom he had advocated a takeover of the army. Another crucial actor who was charged was the key actor of the Gendarmerie Intelligence and Counter-Terrorism Centre (JITEM), retired general Veli Küçük.

*The Ergenekon trials* Many of the defendants who had incited public hatred in the preceding months and years, and who now stood accused, continued their threatening behaviour during the court sessions, and attacked both prosecutors and judges. Their provocative attitude was a clear indicator of their trust in the guardians and their conviction that the trial would collapse before the charges could be heard. Parts of the mainstream media, particularly the flagship newspaper of the Doğan group, *Hürriyet* (Liberty), did indeed join a campaign to talk down the Ergenekon trial. In a growing flurry, the leader of the Republican People's Party, Deniz Baykal, and civil society organizations close to the General Staff sought to depict the investigations and court case as a government plot to discredit the secular opposition. Yet as the list of foiled coup attempts grew longer and the emerging details ever more shocking, the criticism abated, at least partly. Probes into coup plans with working titles as illustrious as 'Cage' (*Kafes*) and 'Sledgehammer'

(*Balyoz*) exposed cynical blueprints of plots for the assassination of non-Muslim religious leaders and Armenian dignitaries, as well as the bombing of mosques in Istanbul with the express aim of causing havoc and creating an atmosphere of terror that would bring down the AKP government. Another plan suggested provoking a military confrontation with Greece, as had been tried before in the 1990s, when the countries had been close to war at last twice. The ostensibly independent newspaper *Taraf* played a central role in exposing the coup plans.

The revelations were shocking even for critical observers, who had suspected the hand of the military in many of the brutal ruptures of recent Turkish history, and for most Kurds, who had witnessed the deep state in action in the south-east. For the average member of the Turkish public, however, the cynicism of the plots – bombing mosques to galvanize pious people into attacking secularists – was simply outrageous. After all, every male citizen of the Turkish Republic is obliged to serve in the armed forces for at least twelve months of his life. Ever since the foundation of the republic, but much more forcefully since the military coup of 1980, young recruits have been indoctrinated in the image of the 'military nation'. In fact, a whole society, its everyday life and political culture were shaped around the rhetoric of militarism, male chauvinism and nationalism and the slogan 'Every Turks is born a soldier'. Yet as the details of successive coup plans emerged, and as the belligerent tone of communiqués from the Chief of the General Staff began to fail to impress people, the 'myth of the military nation' started to crumble.

For the first time in Turkey's history, critics also raised questions about the efficacy of the military and its ability to protect the recruits under its charge, particularly after the newspaper *Taraf* revealed military intelligence of two PKK raids on military posts, the first in Dağlıca in October 2007, which had left twelve soldiers dead and eight servicemen abducted and released months later – only to be put on trial for having surrendered to the enemy. The second raid came a year later and resulted in seventeen deaths. Both events triggered pogroms in cities in western Turkey, which saw Kurdish businesses and neighbourhoods attacked by young men, often led by members of the Great Unity Party (*Büyük Birlik Partisi*), which combined the most violent aspects of Islamist and nationalist extremes. The *Taraf* material suggested that the loss of life could easily have been avoided, had the high command taken into consideration available security data.

The armed forces, whose initial reaction was to deny the allegations and to start a witch-hunt for the whistle-blowers, came under further scrutiny, when anti-militarist associations like the 'Opponents of War' (*Savaş Karşıtları Derneği*) – which had largely been ignored in what was still a society with an almost religious devotion to its army – released information about the growing number of suicides among recruits, especially of Kurdish origin. The moral and physical retreat of the armed forces became even more pronounced as commanders implicated in the Ergenekon investigations – among them a former commander of JITEM operations in Diyarbakır – committed suicide. Between 2007 and 2010, ten senior commanders and the former director of the counter-terror Special Action Branch (*Özel Harekat Dairesi*) took their lives. A growing number of whistle-blowers in the armed forces led to the publication of ever more incriminating material about plots to foment hatred between Turks and Kurds in different parts of the country. Inter-ethnic violence between Turks and Kurds was becoming the last resort for the guardians of the republic.

*The Young Civilians are displeased* As the military lost ground, its critics gained strength. Inconceivable only a decade ago, thousands of protesters took to the streets to ridicule the guardians and their meddling in public life. The anti-militarist campaign 'Young Civilians' (*Genç Siviller*) chose a pair of sneakers as their sign of placidity, in defiance of the military boots that marked the armed forces' brutality. Their very name was a subversive pun on the 'serious' concept of patriotic 'young officers'. And their slogan '[t]he young civilians are displeased' – a response to Kemalist newspapers hinting at officers being 'displeased' by political developments – exposed the hollowness of the military language. The young civilians' understanding of politics and their take on the country's recent history were real novelties: they summarized their ideological framework with a reference to the German pastor Martin Niemöller, whose critique of the inactivity of German intellectuals in the face of the Nazi takeover resounded with the German post-war generation:

> We live in a country where from the left to the right, from the Alevis to the Sunnis, everybody becomes a [...] 'high democrat' when their

own rights are violated, but looks the other way and thereby becomes complicit when another group is targeted. Our key reference is our own conscience and our repulsion at all kinds of injustice. We are surprised that people are not able to show the same moral response to different events: to the Madımak massacre [of Alevis], to the intimidation of the Muslim segments of society after the 28 February intervention, to the oppression of the left, to the unresolved murders of the dirty [Kurdish war] and to the actions of the Turkish armed forces east and west of the Euphrates.

We know that Turkey would be a different place today, had these questions been asked when 'they' came to take others away [...] In 1960, they came for the Democrat Party, in 1970 they came for the left and the Alevis, in 1980 they came for everybody. They also came during 28 February, and we see that they come today with their sig-natures. For the Kurds they were always coming anyway [...] Everyone should know that we will be there and will speak out when they come for you one day. Will you also speak out for others, so when they come for you, you will have people to back you? Then you are one of us. (Translated from Genç Siviller 2009)

A growing number of liberals, progressive Islamists and democrats took part in the street protests and anti-military events. True to the spirit of the young civilians, if not to the liking of all involved, they joined forces with feminists, Muslim women's groups and gay and transsexual organizations like KAOS GL and Lambda Istanbul, who had been organizing an annual gay pride march in Istanbul since 2003. Especially in the Kurdish provinces, hopes were running high that this time the 'dirty war' on the Kurds would finally be fully investigated.

The Ergenekon trials, however, remained contested: a continuous media campaign of misinformation led many to believe that most charges were fabricated. The coverage, especially of the Doğan media – Turkey's leading media conglomerate – prompted the government to react with hefty fines, officially on grounds of tax evasion, yet clearly with the intention of reining in the Doğan outlets. A series of blunders on behalf of the security services and the prosecution – the arrest of suspects in the early hours, the temporary detention of the respected professor Türkan Saylan, the constantly expanding list of suspects – diminished public trust in the process. Even more importantly, some

Justice and Development cadres were caught admitting that they did see the trial as an opportunity to take revenge for the military's assault on the Welfare Party and the Islamic segment of society in 1997. The case held the key to a reckoning with several decades of guardian state activity, and hence with the 'dark side' of Turkey's government, but political expedience and legal insufficiencies slowed down the proceedings. The question remained – and remains, as the proceedings continue – whether Turkey's volatile and highly politicized legal system would be able to deal judiciously with a case of such magnitude. Yet it also became evident that the guardian state was losing credibility with every new revelation of its behind-the-scenes manipulations.

### Home affairs: Kurdish, Alevi and human rights

Even though the AKP government was openly challenging the guardian state, its policy in the Kurdish provinces and towards the representatives of the Kurdish national movement, the Democratic Society Party, did not – at least at first sight – differ significantly from guardian state policies of control and intimidation. Yet the policy of 'openings', first Kurdish (soon commuted to a democratic opening), then Alevi, brought some unexpected discursive and eventually also policy shifts, which might well be too little too late, but are significant nevertheless, considering the decades of denial vis-à-vis Kurdish identity.

*Local elections and electoral fine-tuning* The campaign for the March 2009 local elections was particularly aggressive and called for the 'strongholds of the opposition' to be taken by Justice and Development. In addition to the traditional heartlands of the Republican People's Party in the Aegean region, Erdoğan particularly 'wanted' the Alevi stronghold of Dersim and the political centre of Turkey's Kurdish movement, often also called the 'capital of Kurdistan', Diyarbakır. Erdoğan's visit to Diyarbakır on 20 October 2008 as part of his early campaigning started on an uneasy note. His assurances about 'democratic steps', some words of sympathy in Kurdish and the promise of a state TV channel in Kurdish were widely welcomed by the crowd that had gathered to listen to his speech. Yet when he attacked the Democratic Society Party (DTP) for its connections with the PKK and denounced it as terrorist – seemingly ignoring the fact that the DTP was in charge of the city's municipal councils and elected by more than 50 per cent of the city's voters – he sparked a series of angry protests.

Shopkeepers let down their shutters and tens of thousands of protesters took to the streets, while the nationalist Kurdish satellite media was raging with anger. Later in the day, dozens of demonstrators were taken into custody with several children among them. They would soon be charged with trumped-up allegations of 'membership of a terrorist organization' and many would be sentenced to prison sentences. AKP cadres attempted to balance a belligerent security discourse reminiscent of the Kurdish war with a clumsy narrative of recognition and positive engagement. People in the Kurdish provinces were not impressed, as they could see with their own eyes that innocent children were treated as if they were full-blown terrorists and their elected mayors – Osman Baydemir and Abdullah Demirbaş among them – were harassed by courts and inspectors of the Interior Ministry seeking to uncover illegal – that is, pro-Kurdish – activities. The launch of the all-Kurdish-language TV station TRT 6 (or TRT Şeş, in Kurdish), an important step in the government's recognition of Kurdish identity, did little to allay the disappointment of many Kurdish voters.

On election day, 29 March – local elections are held nationwide – visitors at the AKP headquarters in Ankara were nevertheless aghast when they realized how badly they had misread the atmosphere in the Kurdish provinces. Not only did the party fail to win the republican and Kurdish strongholds, but it lost many cities to the Republican People's and the Nationalist Action parties and only narrowly defended its mayoral seats in Istanbul and Ankara. In the Kurdish heartlands, the DTP made major gains, and in Diyarbakır, the metropolitan mayor, Osman Baydemir, was re-elected with 65 per cent of the vote. Erdoğan was deeply frustrated by the Kurdish vote, but at least some in the party took the results as a reality check: a fully fledged hegemonic shift towards the AKP's pro-Islamic developmental paradigm, which Erdoğan had probably been longing for, was not forthcoming. In the extraordinary conditions of the presidential elections, the public had closed ranks behind the AKP. Under conditions of relative normality, differential voting patterns emerged, reflecting the local political milieus and changing ideological orientations.

*The 'Kurdish opening'* Despite its defeat in the Kurdish provinces, the government stuck to its reform promises to the Kurds: in May 2009, members of the cabinet initiated a debate on a 'Kurdish opening' (*Kürt açılımı*) without, however, specifying what exactly this opening would entail apart from more liberal regulations regarding TV and radio in Kurdish. Some of the suggestions voiced – restoration of Kurdish village names, removal of inscriptions on hills celebrating the supremacy of Turkishness – 'Happy is he who calls himself a Turk' – launch of Kurdish language institutes at universities and some sort of amnesty for PKK fighters – constituted a radical departure from the state practices of denial. Yet the debate on these rather enlightened measures came in tandem with a policy of marginalization directed at the Democratic Society Party and their elected representatives in parliament and the municipalities. This ambiguity would characterize the government's policy towards the Kurds throughout the period under study. The banning of the DTP by the Constitutional Court in December 2009, again, as in the case of so many other Kurdish political parties, on grounds of 'undermining national unity and cooperating with the PKK', only aggravated this ambiguous state of affairs. As if responding to the Young Civilians' reproach that in Turkey democracy is only democracy for one's own sake, AKP cadres remained silent when the court outlawed the party that represented close to 50 per cent of all votes in the Kurdish provinces.

Immediately after the verdict was announced, police arrested leading Kurdish politicians and mayors on charges of membership of an alleged urban organization sympathetic to the PKK. The orchestrated images of thirty-five handcuffed mayors and DTP cadres in front of the Diyarbakır courthouse were probably meant to send a signal to the AKP's nationalist constituency that the government was on top of things. In the Kurdish provinces, however, the images were understood as a humiliation of pro-Kurdish politicians by the state. The mayor of the Diyarbakır district of Suriçi, Abdullah Demirbaş, was also among the detained. He would be released only several months later, on health grounds.

That normality was not yet forthcoming and the AKP's Kurdish policy remained sketchy became apparent at the very time when the Kurdish opening was first discussed. On 4 May, a village in the south-eastern province of Mardin became the stage for a massacre that was unprecedented in scope and scale, even in the context of the high level of endemic state and domestic violence in the Kurdish provinces. Masked gunmen stormed an engagement ceremony in the Kurdish hamlet of Zanqirt (officially named Bilge) and opened fire on the visitors. Forty-four men, women and children died instantly. Even though President Gül was quick to blame the massacre on outmoded and regrettable traditions and the prime minister described it as 'abominable, inhumane and beyond words', Kurdish observers were stunned: the attack defied all conventions of traditional tribal justice, which might appear irrational and brutal but operated according to clear rules and norms.

Before long, it emerged that not only were both attackers and victims members of the same extended family, but their men were all enlisted as village guards, the paramilitary force initially set up by Turgut Özal to assist the military's campaign against the PKK. At their height in the 1990s, the village guards had numbered more than 90,000 in the Kurdish provinces, and despite decommissioning, around 50,000 were still in active service by 2009. Once human rights groups and Kurdish activists had established that the massacre was the result of village guards fighting over local resources and territory, a long-overdue debate began on the sustainability of these remnants of the Kurdish war. And indeed, the village guards had turned into a veritable crime machine:

> [T]hroughout the [Kurdish] conflict, village guards benefited from a culture of impunity imported from the Turkish military. As a consequence, village guards became known for their role in drug and arms trafficking, summary executions, enforced disappearances, sexual assaults and seizure of lands and homes of displaced villagers. A striking tactic employed by village guards was to disguise themselves as PKK militants which would enable them to shift the blame onto the PKK. (Eşsiz 2009)

Even if the government did not launch a review of the village guard system, an emotive speech by Prime Minister Erdoğan evoking the shared pain of Turkish and Kurdish mothers – whether mourning the death of soldiers or PKK fighters – had created a window of opportunity for the resolution of the conflict. When a group of combatants of the PKK's armed wing returned voluntarily from their base in northern Iraq in October 2009 to test the authorities' commitment to the 'opening', a peaceful resolution to more than two decades of conflict seemed to be within reach. Yet it was not meant to be: when the PKK fighters – in a misapprehension especially of the Turkish public's rather volatile support for the opening and its fundamental rejection by the opposition parties – were welcomed by jubilant crowds and delivered what many observers took to be victory speeches, the government had little to say to defend its own position. When they were accused of treason by the Republican People's Party and the Nationalist Action Party, the two largest opposition parties, they retreated.

The government nevertheless remained committed to the language of the 'Kurdish opening', if only partially to its implementation. The launch of a Kurdish teaching programme in a newly established university in Mardin and the launch of Kurdish and Zazaki courses in another new institution in Tunceli (Dersim) were exciting departures. Courses for Kurdish started in Mardin in the summer of 2010: at a visit in August I was stunned to see fifty young men and women being educated as teachers of Kurdish under the watchful eyes of the obligatory poster of Mustafa Kemal. Yet the establishment of a department of Kurdish language was still prevented by the Higher Education Council, leading the chair of the Turkish department, Selim Temo, to withdraw from the project. What is more, instead of cooperating with the University of Diyarbakır, where faculty was ready to start teaching in Kurdish, the government opted for two peripheral universities: the Artuklu University was in Mardin, which does not have a majority Kurdish population but rather a large community of mostly pro-state Arab citizens; Tunceli (Dersim) is located in an Alevi centre, where the population is slightly less enthusiastic about Sunni Kurdish nationalism.

Given that only a decade earlier Kurdish students who petitioned their universities for language courses in Kurdish were prosecuted and sometimes had their matriculation rescinded, these steps were significant nevertheless. The key frustration, which academics in charge of the Kurdish programme at the Artuklu University in Mardin voiced, was with the half-heartedness of the government's commitment to the project. State representatives first suggested support for a project for a full department of Kurdish language and literature, but retreated when the Higher Education Council – chaired by an AKP appointee – insisted on downgrading the department into a programme for 'living languages' and demoting Kurdish to the level of a local dialect rather than accepting it as a language with a written literature. These frustrations notwithstanding, it was a remarkable experience for me to sit in on a seminar on the Kurdish language, delivered in Kurdish, to Kurdish students in a state university, after almost nine decades of denial of Kurdish identity.

The AKP's 'Kurdish opening' created some important – if incomplete – departures from decades of oppressive policies, and created new fora for the negotiation of Kurdish identity and Kurdish needs, even though it also took great care to avoid being seen as giving in to Kurdish nationalist demands. At the same time, however, the public visibility of Kurdish identity, and its depiction in the mainstream media as connected to the armed operations of the PKK, alienated ordinary Turks. Before long, mutual distrust began to proliferate, and soon plots multiplied to foment hatred. The growing nationalist reaction exposed the Kurds, especially in areas where they constituted sizeable minority groups, calling to mind the guardian state policy against Alevis in the 1970s. Tensions between Turks and Kurds and everyday racism against Kurds in western Turkey became widespread. Simple neighbourhood brawls and football games, especially between Turkish and Kurdish clubs, often turned into ethnic confrontations and were exploited by extreme nationalists to stage pogroms and attacks on Kurdish businesses. A paradigmatic case in point was the murder of four policemen in the district of Dörtyol in Hatay province, allegedly by members of the PKK, in July 2010. In response to the event, a mob organized by the Nationalist Action Party attacked Kurdish businesses and neighbourhoods in the town. The pogroms continued for two days, when it emerged that the mastermind of the pogroms was not only a member of the Nationalist Action Party, but also an informer of the local gendarmerie unit.

The fact that the provocation was so immediately revealed suggested that the capacity of the guardian state to create instances of mass violence to manipulate society had been significantly diminished by the Ergenekon investigations and court cases, but also by a network of whistle-blowers and informants, who exposed the plots as they unfolded. The AKP's initial reluctance to negotiate with the key personalities in the Turkish–Kurdish conflict, that is with the elected Kurdish representatives – now organized in the Peace and Democracy Party, BDP, the successor to the banned DTP – and with the man whom many Kurds regard as their natural leader, the PKK leader Abdullah Öcalan, weakened its hand in resolving this core conflict in modern Turkey. In September 2010, the government finally entered into indirect talks with Öcalan, prompting hopes that a solution was forthcoming. Despite the progress in matters of education and media, and the appointment of a new generation of more service-oriented, often more religious but less nationalist and less statist governors, however, the issue of Kurdish rights continued as a key arena where guardian state manipulation and nationalist fervour combined to create a potentially explosive situation. In the final analysis, however, it was also clear that the Justice and Development government's policies have legitimized and normalized Kurdish identity beyond a point of no return.

### Engaging with the world

If Turkey's domestic politics after the 2007 elections remained agitated, its foreign policy took a steadier, more successful and more visible course. Soon, however, the AKP government would have to face the complexities of Turkey's neighbourhood and explain itself to an increasingly worried international public. One man was behind this shift in policy: Ahmet Davutoğlu. He had been the architect of the AKP government's foreign policy since his nomination as chief adviser to Prime Minister Erdoğan in 2002 and as ambassador in 2003. In May 2009, he became the foreign minister and put into practice the doctrine for Turkey's engagement with the world in the new millennium. Called 'Strategic Depth', it was based on the idea of a new geography of good neighbourly relations and economic interaction, in which Turkey played a central part, rather than being peripheral to other regions such as Europe or the Middle East. A reconstituted Ottoman space, wherein Turkey would act with the responsibility of the former imperial power, was at the heart of this world vision. This new 'Pax Ottomanica' or Ottoman Commonwealth was to be realized by achieving 'zero conflict with all neighbours' through the resolution of protracted disputes.

Davutoğlu's doctrine was also responding to the changing global power structure and acknowledged the emergence of new power centres in Asia and Latin America. His professional experience as professor of international relations at the Islamic University in Malaysia had made him take account of non-Western powers and non-Western modernities, which were challenging the hegemonic global role of the 'West'. Hence, at least in Davutoğlu's thinking, neither the European Union nor NATO and the USA could maintain the hegemony that they had enjoyed for much of the last five decades. With this worldview, Davutoğlu continued to observe the premise that first Turgut Özal and then Ismail Cem had postulated: if Turkey is to become a country that matters in the world, it first has to embrace its past as an imperial power and to engage with its immediate neighbourhood.

Turkey hence became active on several levels of foreign relations, from leading roles in international organizations to growing regional cooperation. This began with the government's commitment to the Organization of the Islamic Conference (OIC), the global body representing Muslim-majority countries, which was a mildly significant institution that was competing with the more influential Arab League. When the Turkish professor Ekmeleddin Ihsanoğlu was elected to its presidency in 2004, however, the OIC became an audible voice in the international debates about Islam. It also became a key partner in the UN programme 'Alliance of Civilizations', which the Turkish and Spanish governments launched in 2005 to counteract the 'clash of civilizations' theory popularized by Samuel Huntington and eagerly adopted by many European and American conservatives, and ironically by Islamists as well. After a sustained campaign of development cooperation and heavy lobbying, particularly in a number of African countries, Turkey was also elected to a non-permanent seat on the UN Security Council, which it employed well to influence world opinion after Israel's attack on the *Mavi Marmara* boat.

*Soft power and strategic depth* Davutoğlu's term indeed saw an impressive extension of Turkey's economic, political and cultural presence in the world. Opening embassies in Africa and Latin America, Turkey established official representation where the missionary schools of Fethullah Gülen had prepared the ground. The regions where Turkey's proactive foreign policy became most visible were – not surprisingly – the Balkans and the Middle East. Economic interaction with the Arab world, particularly with the immediate neighbours Syria, Jordan and Lebanon, increased significantly thanks to the introduction of visa-free travel and free trade. Even though they were small trading partners in comparison to the European Union, trade volumes increased also with Iran, Iraq, Libya and North African countries, often significantly. This transformation of relations was impressive indeed: where Turkey had been at the brink of war with Syria in 1998 over Hafiz al-Assad's embrace of the PKK, Syria now became a key focus of the government's new foreign policy. The local businessmen of Gaziantep and Hatay played a key role in furthering relations and opening Syrian markets to Turkish produce. In the years of the second AKP government, the fruits of this strategy became visible: reunited with its historic hinterland – cities like Antakya, Gaziantep and Urfa had been part of the province of

Aleppo before the emergence of nation-states – the Turkish–Syrian border region experienced a real boom in regional trade, as well as in the numbers of visitors. Only 20,000 Turkish passport holders had visited Syria in 1990, but close to a million did so in 2010.

In the Balkans, Turkey followed a differentiated strategy as a regional negotiator and problem solver, as well as guardian of the Muslim communities of the Balkans. In addition to a role in the local police force of Kosovo – Turkey was also one of the first countries to recognize Kosovar independence in October 2008 – Davutoğlu was particularly dedicated to the future of Bosnia-Herzegovina. He presided over a series of monthly trilateral meetings with Serbia, Croatia and Bosnia-Herzegovina to address issues between Bosnia and its neighbours. The appointment of the Bosnian ambassador to Serbia – long rejected by Belgrade – as well as the apology of the Serbian parliament for the massacres of Srebrenica in March 2010 were to a large extent the result of Davutoğlu's shuttle diplomacy between Balkan capitals. As the Turkish foreign policy became more pronounced in the region, however, critical voices over Turkey's 'real aims' increased: was Turkey back to lure the Balkans away from Europe and bring them back in the Ottoman fold? Many also wondered why Davutoğlu seemed not to understand that the Ottoman-Islamic reference is not a positive one for virtually all Christian and some Muslim communities in the Balkans.

In economic terms, Turkey's role in the Balkans was less important than that of its competitor for regional leadership, Greece. Investments were concentrated especially in transport infrastructure (airports in Macedonia and Kosovo). Even if the trade volume with all Balkan countries rose almost six times between 2000 and 2010, from US$3 billion to US$18 billion (trade with the more advanced economies of Greece, Bulgaria and Romania excluded), the Balkan markets were too small to excite Turkish investors, and their total share in Turkey's exports remained at 7 per cent, compared to roughly 40 per cent for Turkish exports to the EU. The Balkans for Davutoğlu, as well as for a significant portion of the Turkish public, were important for emotional, cultural and historical reasons, and because of the existing ties between Bosniak, Macedonian, Kosovar and Bulgarian Turkish immigrant communities in Turkey and their countries of origin.

Cultural diplomacy was hence particularly central: from the operation of Turkish cultural centres and the reconstruction of Ottoman mosques and monuments, carried out by the Turkish Development

Cooperation Agency (TIKA), to the construction of new mosques particularly in Kosovo and Macedonia under the aegis of the Directorate
of Religious Affairs (Diyanet), Turkey became a visible presence. The
Diyanet and Turkish Islamic organizations like the Fethullah Gülen
movement or religious brotherhoods and foundations such as the
Association for the Furthering of Science (*Ilim Yayma Cemiyeti*) had
become active in many Balkan countries in the early 2000s, when
pro-American governments in the region were urged to cut ties with
Saudi and other Arab foundations suspected of jihadist tendencies and
links to al-Qaeda. Under the new foreign policy, Turkey's influence in
Islamic matters rose considerably, with annual regional conferences
of the Muslim leaders of the Balkans held by the Turkish Diyanet. In
these meetings, the president of the Diyanet acts in all but name as
the patron of the almost ten million Muslims in the Balkans, hence
competing with the religious leader of Balkan's largest Muslim community, the Bosniak Reis-ul Ulema Mustafa Efendi Cerić.

Relations with Russia deepened further as trade relations and energy
cooperation – especially gas pipelines between the two countries and
the Caucasus and Turkey – developed. Russia was Turkey's foremost
single trade partner, with a trade volume of well over US$20 billion,
surpassed only by the combination of all twenty-seven European Union
countries. Another important step was the suspension of visas between
Turkey and Russia in 2010, which significantly extended the geographical reach of countries that Turkish passport holders could visit. By
by the end of 2010, Turkey had scrapped visa regimes with almost all
of its eastern neighbours. Considering that citizens of Turkey have
to go through often humiliating processes of visa applications and
rejections, if they wish to travel to the European Union, this emerging
space of visa-free travel in Russia, its eastern neighbours, much of the
Arab world and Asian countries massively expanded opportunities for
Turks to engage with the world on a personal level. This new space
could also be read as an indicator of the new global maps with which
Davutoğlu was operating: this was a geography in which the European
Union and the United States have lost their central location.

Finally, another aspect of 'soft power' – popular culture – became
both a major export for Turkey and a remarkable success story in terms
of disseminating a positive image. TV series marked the country's
emergence as a pole of attraction in many Balkan countries – including
Bulgaria and Greece with their non-Turkish or non-Muslim majorities

– as well as throughout the Arab world and Central Asia. In Kosovo and Macedonia, series on the mafia and on political conspiracies, such as *Valley of the Wolves*, became major crowd-pullers, with tens of thousands of Albanians and Turks greeting their stars when they visited Prizren and Priština. In the Arab world, Turkish TV series turned into important popular culture phenomena, gluing millions to the screens and sparking controversy between different segments of society.

The TV serial *Nour* turned into a public obsession in the entire Arab world from Morocco to the Gulf and the Levant when it was screened on a Saudi network and with colloquial Syrian voice-overs. Based on the love story and eventual marriage of a rich and good-looking Istanbulite and his hard-working employee, Nour, the series dealt with issues of extramarital sex and projected a model of equal gender relations, which struck a chord with Arab (and Balkan) audiences. Responses were mixed: on the one hand were the critical voices of the Islamic authorities, who went so far as to suggest that these films were the work of the devil. On the other, streets in most Arab cities emptied during the screening of the serials. And in terms of the tourism market, the tens of thousands of fans travelling to Istanbul to visit the sumptuous seaside villas on the Bosporus where the series was shot made a tangible difference. Above all, however, the series made Turkey a more visible and more positive presence in the mind of its viewers. For many Arabs, as well as Bulgarians and Greeks, the image of the Turks from the history textbooks – whether as slayer of Christians or godless destroyers of Islam (a reference to the abolition of the Caliphate) – was complemented by the promise of an exciting mix between the old and the new, between tradition and modernity, and between Eastern and Western cultural affinities.

Thanks to the popular culture influence, Turkey became a country that especially, but not exclusively, Muslim people in the post-Ottoman space identified with and felt sympathetic to. It should be noted that there are limits to the impact of popular culture on high politics: in Greece, for instance, viewing figures for Turkish TV series are among the highest for any TV programme, yet the vast majority of Greeks continue to see Turkey as the most substantial threat to national security. Then again, in many other countries, particularly those with a Muslim population, Turkey swiftly became what its leaders would probably like it to be, even if they might not say it out loud: a leader of the Muslim world. When the Turkish national football team beat Croatia and only narrowly missed reaching the finals of Euro 2008, for instance, Turkish flags were waved in Bosnia and Kosovo, in Azerbaijan and in Arab countries. Very significantly, the same happened in Germany and France among members of the immigrant communities, surprising many onlookers. Davutoğlu's foreign policy, delivered with a smiling face and a sympathetic attitude, built on this popular goodwill. Yet his 'zero conflict policy with neighbours' would soon be severely tested.

*The limits of strategy: Israel, Iran and Armenia* The strategy of 'zero conflict' could not have been anything but a lofty normative principle, considering the nature of conflicts in Turkey's neighbourhood. The course of relations with Israel, Iran and Armenia soon highlighted the constraints on Turkey's emerging regional power. The most significant departure from established relations came with regard to Israel, an important ally since the early Özal years and the First Gulf War, and a strategic partner since the Madrid peace talks in 1991 and the visit to Jerusalem of Prime Minister Tansu Çiller in 1994. This partnership was dominated by the goals of military and security cooperation, with a particular focus on intelligence cooperation in Turkey's war against the PKK. Representatives of the security and intelligence communities were hence the leading actors in this relationship, which was regarded with little sympathy by the general public and met with emphatic protest in Islamist circles. Particularly in the eyes of the 'unreconstructed' Islamists of the Felicity Party – with anti-Semitism very much part of its ideological worldview – the alliance with Israel was nothing short of treasonous. The AKP government, however, had taken a rather more pragmatic line and supported a boost of economic relations, which saw the bilateral trade volume rise to over US$3 billion, and hence eclipse Turkey's trade with the three Arab neighbours in the Levant, Syria, Jordan and Lebanon. Despite his criticism of Israel's Palestinian policy, Prime Minster Erdoğan was considering a major role for Turkey in a future peace process, and was involved in secret talks between Syria and Israel. The Turkish government invited Israel's president, Shimon Peres, in 2007, despite Israel's assault on Lebanon a year earlier. Peres was the first Israeli representative to address the Turkish Grand National Assembly amid well-meant applause from the floor.

The AKP's benign pragmatism suffered a severe blow, however, when Israel attacked the Gaza Strip at the end of 2008, ostensibly in order to fight Hamas positions, but in fact killing more than a thousand mostly civilian Palestinians. The Israeli assault not only frustrated any Turkish role in negotiating a Palestinian settlement, it caused deep indignation in Turkish policy circles. The government felt compelled to make a choice between the Arab world and Israel. This frustration found expression during the World Economic Forum Meeting in Davos in January 2009, when the Turkish prime minister, angered by his host telling him to finish his presentation, uttered the words 'one minute'. He then hurled at President Shimon Peres the reproach 'You know well how to kill people' and accused him of 'crimes against humanity'. 'One minute' became a familiar quotation in Turkey, capturing both Erdoğan's short temper and the changing mood towards Israel. Both governments nevertheless tried to play things down. Yet the downward spiral seemed to have become irreversible, as both Erdoğan, who turned relations with Israel into his prime foreign policy issue, and Prime Minister Binyamin Netanyahu, who now headed an extreme nationalist government in Jerusalem, opted for a language of escalation and a policy of media-based humiliation.

A year later, Israeli Foreign Minister Ayalon publicly humiliated the Turkish envoy to Tel Aviv for the anti-Israel stance in an episode of *Valley of the Wolves*, and another provocative TV drama dealing with the Gaza war on Turkish state TV. Eventually, Ayalon was forced to apologize, but the efforts to save the bilateral relations increasingly rang hollow. While Turkish TV series sparked sympathy elsewhere, in this case they had come to mark the rapid deterioration in relations. Another symbol would mark their temporary suspension: the former ferry *Mavi Marmara*. Purchased by the relief organization IHH, close to the staunchly Islamist Felicity Party, the vessel was part of a concerted effort to bring humanitarian aid to Gaza in May 2010. Gaza had been under a severe Israeli blockade, which had deprived the population of basic provisions and had been criticized repeatedly by members of the international community. On board the flotilla of boats, which approached the Israeli coast on 31 May, were hundreds of activists from different countries and representatives of international pro-Palestinian organizations. There was also a small group of militant Islamist activists, who used force to defend themselves when Israeli forces stormed the ship late at night, while it was navigating in international waters. In the ensuing brawl, Israeli soldiers killed nine Turkish activists.

This storming of the *Mavi Marmara* was a calculated risk taken by the Netanyahu government. It would prove to be a nearly mortal blow to the Turkish–Israeli partnership. In its aftermath, the rhetoric between Ankara and Tel Aviv was belligerent, with Turkey using its seat on the UN Security Council to press for an international inquiry. Despite the high rhetoric, however, Turkish government representatives did not resort to anti-Semitic language – at least not in the visible arena of international and national politics – and insisted that it was not taking a position against the Israeli people or against the Israeli state, but only against the Netanyahu government. Observers suggested that Erdoğan might have overplayed his hand with Israel – some also sensing a shift away from the pro-Israeli bias of the USA and much of Europe – others saw the position of Israel endangered by a thuggish president and a radicalizing domestic political scene. Continuing bilateral trade, family relations between the Turkey-based Jewish community and Israel as well as intensive behind-the-scenes diplomacy on the part of the United States ensured that the conflict did not escalate any further.

What emerged clearly from the episode was that Turkey's strategic interests were now better served by a low-profile relationship with Israel. And this was certainly true with regard to the Arab world and other Muslim-majority countries. It was also true with regard to Iran: in a quest to ensure good relations with its eastern neighbour, and in order to harness the potentially massive Iranian market for Turkish goods, Turkey repeatedly defied US and European requests to support an embargo against Iran. Together with Brazil, Davutoğlu tried to cut a deal with Iranian president Mahmud Ahmadinejad that would have allowed for curtailment of Iran's nuclear ambitions. While this initiative did not receive the support of the international community, and hence was inconclusive, it did raise eyebrows in European capitals and Washington.

The deterioration of Turkish–Israeli relations also brought to the fore one of the key points of cooperation between the two countries: the support of the pro-Israel lobby in the United States for the Turkish denial of the Armenian genocide. In Washington at least, Turkey was alone in its defence against Armenian lobby groups. An initiative by Turkey to improve relations with Armenia and eventually open the borders between the two countries was Davutoğlu's double coup: it was in line with his 'zero conflict policy with neighbours', but also aimed at driving a wedge between the Armenian republic – dependent on good relations with Turkey for its economic and political survival – and the Armenian diaspora over the issue of genocide recognition. There was stiff opposition, especially from the more nationalist segments of the Armenian diaspora and the Armenian Revolutionary Federation (*Tashnaksutyun*), which was aware of the thinking behind the rapprochement. More significantly, Turkey's neighbour and ally Azerbaijan interfered to prevent Turkey from reaching any agreement with Armenia, lest it legitimize the occupation of Azeri territory in Karabagh. In October 2009, the Turkish and Armenian foreign ministers nevertheless signed two protocols amid great international publicity and the prodding of high-level dignitaries such as Hillary Clinton, Sergey Lavrov and Bernard Kouchner, the foreign ministers of the United States, Russia and France. The protocols formulated a commitment to open the borders and stipulated the foundation of an ill-defined joint historical commission to address the issue of 1915 and related events. Before the protocols could be ratified, however, both governments gave in to external and internal pressures and backtracked on their declared goals. When Turkey announced that the opening of its borders would be conditional on progress on the Karabagh issue, the Turkish–Armenian rapprochement faltered.

When the Swedish parliament voted in favour of a motion recognizing the Armenian genocide in March 2010 – as the French and Swiss parliaments and the Foreign Affairs Committee of the US House of Representatives had done earlier – the charade of public anger, ambassadorial recall and threats of political consequences began once again. As in earlier cases, the anger and the sabre-rattling were of little consequence: the ambassador returned eventually and the world had moved one minimal small step closer to acknowledging the suffering of the Armenians in the final years of the Ottoman Empire. That the genocide issue was as much about foreign policy as about domestic politics would be brought home to the government – to the dismay of Davutoğlu and President Gül – at the end of 2008 and the beginning of 2009, when an 'apology campaign' persuaded 30,000 signatories from Turkey to apologize publicly for the denial of the suffering of the Armenian people in 1915. On 24 April 2010, thousands of Turks and Kurds – ninety-five years after the murders of 1915 and in defiance of the government – commemorated the genocide and its victims in Istanbul's Taksim Square. Even though the government disagreed with the action, it did ensure its peaceful realization.

It also opened another door: 19 September saw an Armenian apostolic mass celebrated in the Surp Khach (Holy Cross) Church on the island of Ahtamar. A highly symbolic place of memory for most Armenians all over the world, Ahtamar is located in the province of Van, which had been home to a large and prosperous Armenian community before its destruction in 1915. Criticism was levelled by nationalist diaspora organizations, which saw the event as part of a cynical public relations campaign, and the holy see of Etchmiadzin boycotted the mass over the lack of a cross. Yet the mass attracted several thousand Armenians and Turks and challenged a significant blockage of the mind: after ninety-five years of silence, denial and forgetting, the chant of Armenian liturgy and the sound of church bells were heard in one of the former heartlands of the Armenians of the Ottoman Empire. In Van, several hundred families opened their houses to accommodate the visitors, possibly starting a new era of openness in one of south-east Turkey's most hopeful cities. Around the same time, a decision of the European Court of Human Rights confirmed what many observers had expected anyway: Turkey had wronged Hrant Dink, not only by failing to protect his life, but by perverting the course of justice and failing to grant a proper investigation and due process. The government decided not to appeal against the decision, as the guilt was undeniable. Neither though did it take action to ensure that justice would be done.

*The limits of Europe* The most tormented aspect of Turkey's international relations in the second AKP government since 2007 was its engagement with Europe. On the surface, Turkey had been on the road to EU membership since the start of accession negotiations in October 2005 and the opening of six chapters of the European acquis, the body of EU law that needs to be adopted by every future member state. In reality however, only thirteen chapters out of a total of thirty-five were negotiated, while some of the most important chapters had been frozen: some were stalled in 2006 over the lack of progress on Cyprus. Turkey refused to recognize the government of Cyprus and to open its ports and airports to Cypriot vessels, with the justification that European promises about alleviating the economic and political isolation of Turkish Cypriots had not been honoured. French president Sarkozy blocked the crucial economy chapter in 2008 in order to prevent an irrevocable step towards Turkey's membership.

Even more chapters were frozen in 2009 at the behest of the Republic of Cyprus, which was now a full member intent on blocking Turkey's EU accession in order to get a better deal with regard to the future of the Turkish-Cypriot north.

Members of the European Commission and their counterparts in the Turkish government acted as if the accession process was on track, and in fact the technical negotiations over legal reform and adoption of standards did continue. In reality, however, the late effects of 9/11 and the 'clash of civilizations', as well as the rising role of Islamophobic populism and extreme right-wing politics in much of Europe, took their toll. By now, a large coalition of actors had emerged, from Christian Democrats, who believed that a Christian Europe (the more sophisticated advocates of this Euro-fundamentalist perspective spoke of a Judaeo-Christian Europe) could not accommodate a Muslim nation, to disaffected middle classes who saw their jobs and livelihoods threatened by Muslim immigrants. There were also racist groups, which hated Turks and Muslims simply for being Turks and Muslims, and they became increasingly audible in European talk shows and media debates. This shift of mood marked the emergence of a different Europe, a set of anxiously xenophobic countries, which Arjun Appadurai aptly labeled, in 2006, 'Pim Fortuyn's Europe', and which we may call today 'Geert Wilders's Europe'. For all of them, Turkey's membership quest became a symbol, against which they could project their fears of globalization, of Islam, Islamist terrorism and Muslim immigration, as well as of economic displacement. French president Nicolas Sarkozy and German chancellor Angela Merkel were the two personalities in European politics who relentlessly pushed for an arrangement falling short of full Turkish EU membership, and they had significant portions of the European publics behind them. One of the few countries which has been consistently supportive of Turkey's membership, irrespective of the party in government, was Great Britain, but to little avail.

Despite the European impasse and the ongoing disagreements with Israel, Armenia and the Armenian diaspora, however, the second term of the Justice and Development Party witnessed a further acceleration of growth and a globalization of the Turkish economy. According to the World Bank, Turkey was the world's fifteenth-largest economy in terms of the purchasing power parity of its gross domestic product in 2008. The transformation from a developing country into an increasingly industrialized economy continued, even if extreme regional imbalances and pockets of significant urban and rural poverty diminished the otherwise positive indicators. In the case of the global financial crisis of 2008, Turkey fared relatively well, owing to its re-regulated banking sector, the role of independent overseeing bodies and the autonomy of its central bank. As of early 2010, Turkey had exited recession, and in the third quarter it had attained miraculous growth rates of 12 per cent, rapidly offsetting the losses of the 2009 crisis. Probably the single most graphic indicator of Turkey's changing place in the world was the ascent of its national flag carrier, Turkish Airlines. Between 2002 and 2009, the number of international passengers at Turkey's airports almost doubled from 25 million to 45 million, as Turkish Airlines became Europe's fourth-largest carrier and expanded its network to Latin America and Africa, in addition to its dense network of destinations in Europe, the Balkans, the Middle East, Russia and Asia.

Turkey did not, as some feared or wished, make a paradigmatic shift away from NATO and the EU to an alliance with Russia, Iran and Syria. Yet AKP foreign policy, especially under Foreign Minister Davutoğlu, explored and found alternatives to the country's exclusively Western orientation and to the prospect of an EU membership that looked increasingly unlikely. Despite the neo-Ottoman overtones in Davutoğlu's policy, despite the high rhetoric in the case of Israel and despite the vision of Turkey's leadership of the Muslim world, however, this change was dictated more by pragmatic considerations and the subjection of Turkish foreign policy to democratic scrutiny than by ideology: the growth markets and economic centres of the world are shifting to Asia and Latin America, and this is where both Turkish businesses and government initiatives were starting to invest. Furthermore, constituencies from the south-east and eastern border regions of Turkey used to have little impact on the formation of foreign policy, which was considered very much an elite endeavour limited to the exclusive circles of the Foreign Ministry and, in times of military interventions, to the Chief of the General Staff. All this changed with the Justice and Development Party and its cadres, which contained significant numbers of Kurds, Turks and Arabs from the border regions with Syria, Iraq, Iran and Armenia. Their presence was a constant reminder for the government of the need to engage with the countries beyond the border in a sensible way and with a view on family ties and economic dependencies on both sides. Businessmen with interests in the region were pushing for better relations, visa-free travel and tax-free trade. The return of the eastern and south-eastern provinces into politics – after two decades of war – also refocused Turkey's attention on its neighbourhood in the east. And the xenophobic and Islamophobic turn in many European Union countries raised questions in Turkey over the desirability of a European future. After sixty years of membership of the Council of Europe and more than forty years of negotiation with first the European Community and then the European Union, membership was not at the top of Turkey's to-do list any more.

**The second** term of the Justice and Development government was not yet completed at the time of writing. Through the curtain of misinformation and manipulation, revelations and gagging orders, there emerged the image of a Turkey that was still unsettled and prone to manipulation, still under the spell of its authoritarian past and still shaped by the politics of denial, if less so than formerly. This was a Turkey caught between the determination to normalize and the lure of old conflicts and guardian state meddling: investigations into the army's responsibility for the political violence of the last three decades raised hopes that the guardians, their clandestine security operations and parallel power structures would finally be rooted out. Yet before long, the court proceedings risked being hijacked by the power struggle between the coalition of the military and the high judiciary on one side and the AKP and its supportive religious brotherhoods on the other. Legal reform continued, sometimes expanding freedoms, but often also taking away rights that had been granted only with the EU packages of the early years of AKP rule. The Police Law of June 2007, for instance, created the backdrop for an increase in cases of maltreatment and a shift to violent forms of policing, which resulted in several dozen men and women being killed in police custody. Government initiatives addressing Kurdish grievances alternated with attempts to isolate and close down pro-Kurdish parties and obstruct the work of elected Kurdish mayors. While the role of the armed forces was seriously questioned in public, tax fines on unsympathetic media corporations put the freedom of expression at risk, and so did a barrage of court cases against journalists, Kurdish politicians and anti-militarist activists, while the government shied away from taking a principled stand in favour of human rights and liberties. Particularly the military judiciary continued to condemn conscientious objectors to ostracization from public services and severely limited their life choices by inflicting on them what the European Court of Human Rights has called 'social death'. What was at stake for the generals was the privilege to shape Turkish identity through the bondage of compulsory military service.

Despite this ambiguous situation in terms of human rights and some authoritarian tendencies in the party and in Prime Minister Erdoğan's demeanour, however, a new form of politics and civil society activism emerged that seriously challenged the hegemony of the guardian state as well as the values of militarism and nationalism which it engendered. New social movements, from gay and transsexual organizations to Roma associations, and from anti-racist and anti-militarist groups to conscientious objectors, joined the more organized Alevis and Kurds in their struggle for rights and against discrimination. Yet amid the burgeoning political activism, amid rapid economic growth – slowed down only briefly by the global economic crisis, which led to a temporary contraction of almost 12 per cent – and increased international interaction, Turkey's political system remained volatile and resisted its transformation into a liberal democracy. With the anchor of European Union membership having suffered massively from the watering down of Turkey's membership prospects, such transformation proved ever harder to achieve.

The AKP government's developmental model of religious conservatism and social discipline combined with an entrepreneurial spirit nevertheless substantially altered the appearance of Turkey domestically and in the world sphere. The massive developmental push came at a price, however: as the country was catching up with Europe in terms of infrastructure, social housing and urban planning, natural resources were often treated irresponsibly. Several dams and hydroelectric power plants were being built in the country's most sensitive historically protected environmental areas, threatening heritage sites such as Hasankeyf, the Munzur river in the Alevi province of Tunceli/Dersim and the mountain torrents of the eastern Black Sea and the Hemşin region. While these projects of the State Water Works Agency pre-dated the government by several decades, widespread opposition and citizen mobilization against their realization failed to move the government towards a less developmentalist and more consensus-driven policy. In the cities, and particularly in Istanbul, aggressive rent-driven urban transformation and gentrification created pockets of extreme affluence and pushed out former residents.

Finally, as 2010 was drawing to a close, a series of potentially groundbreaking changes were about to happen that would, if followed through, erode the foundations of the anger that has held sway over Turkey for so long. A highly contested referendum on constitutional changes took place on the symbolic date of 12 September, on the thirtieth anniversary of the military coup. The package was opposed, if for different reasons, by the Republican People's Party as well as by the Nationalist Action Party and most groups on the left, while the Kurdish Peace and Democracy Party boycotted the vote. The No campaign was once again based on the premise that this time the secular republic would really be destroyed if the people voted yes. And vote yes they did. The constitutional reform package was accepted by 58 per cent of the electorate, albeit with significant regional differences. Many of the western coastal areas and Istanbul's old middle-class districts voted no, while many – but not all – in the Kurdish provinces joined the boycott.

Nevertheless, the constitutional changes suspended the infamous Article 15 of the 1980 constitution, which granted impunity to the perpetrators of the coup. They also reduced the closed-shop mentality of the high judiciary, by giving parliament the right to choose some of the judges of the Constitutional Court, and by extending the membership of the Supreme Board of Judges and Prosecutors – the oversight body – to prevent direct intervention from non-elected bodies in the judicial process. Cases such as the dismissal of the Van prosecutor Ferhat Sarıkaya, who had targeted as a suspect the commander of the armed forces in his indictment of a terrorist attack, are highly unlikely to happen henceforth. Towards the end of the year, hundreds of criminal complaints had reached the prosecutors, and the possibility had arisen that men like Kenan Evren, his officers and the thousands of torturers of the 1980s would eventually have to stand in the dock, thirty years after they had turned their country into a slaughterhouse. Hopeful observers believed that a deeply entrenched culture of impunity might be coming to an end, while critics saw the high courts falling under government control. There is little doubt that the judiciary in Turkey used to be an instrument of governance for the powers that be. Yet whether the new arrangements will help the emergence of an independent judiciary able to mete out justice remains to be seen.

Significantly, the Republican People's Party, which finally rid itself of
the divisive Deniz Baykal, began to take on a more conciliatory and less
ethno-nationalist approach with its new chairman, Kemal Kılıçdaroğlu.
After the party's referendum defeat, Kılıçdaroğlu signalled his readiness to support the government in preparing a new constitution
that would once and for all end the illiberal legacy of the 1980 coup.
Notwithstanding the poor chances of the former 'party of the state',
and apparently also of the 'guardian state' in transforming itself into
a modern social democrat party, this step suggested a departure from
the politics of categorical obstruction and militarization for which the
party has been known for the last decade. And not less importantly,
indirect talks began between the government and the imprisoned
leader of the PKK, Abdullah Öcalan, in September, while an extended
ceasefire by PKK combat units suggested that a peaceful solution of
the Kurdish conflict was now a serious possibility. Yet this exciting
moment of opportunity soon seemed to resemble the short periods
of respite before yet another cycle of manipulation and escalation, of
which the country has seen so many. The fact is, however, that Turkey
had never been closer to addressing the roots of many of its most
pressing problems than in the autumn of 2010.

## Turkey's possible futures

Taking a step back from the flurry of Turkey's perplexing everyday
politics, there emerges the image of a country that is torn by multiple
political crises and often consumed by its anger. Nevertheless, it
develops rapidly economically owing to the entrepreneurial spirit
of its industrialists, the hard work of its people and the unfettered
capitalist exploitation of its workers, facilitated by a largely deregu-
lated labour market. It is an image populated as much by angry
men and women from all walks of life and communities who are
galvanized into action by their own experiences of exclusion and
discrimination or by the prodding of others. I have discussed in detail
the role of manipulation in the making of this 'angry nation'. I have
particularly looked at the responsibility of the guardian state – the
coalition of military commanders, the high judiciary and parts of the
bureaucracy – which has governed the country through much of the
historical period examined in this book, under the pretext of saving
the republic first from communist and then from Islamist conquest.
The guardians ruled on grounds of state preservation rather than

legitimate political process, with which they meddled when they saw their hegemony in danger.

Crucially, though, the guardians were never powerful enough to subdue the electoral process, once it took its course. Throughout the period here discussed, the guardians succeeded when they could garner the support of influential social classes – parts of the intelligentsia and the middle classes as well as the Istanbul-based large industrialists – with which they formed the republican hegemonic block. The last few years of AKP rule, however, have witnessed a series of blows against the guardians and their socio-economic base. Today, the republican bloc has lost the support of the more dynamic segments of society, consisting of the Anatolian middle classes as well as Istanbul capital, western intellectuals and Anatolian conservatives. Most Kurds had not been part of the republican coalition anyway. The guardians are fast losing power and are now dependent on an increasingly ghettoizing xenophobic social base that regards men and women in the street as pious ignoramuses and tries to offset its loss of political and economic power and of social status with a cultural elitism that is as aggressive as it is shameless.

The question, hence, is not whether the republican state with its guardian alter ego will survive. In fact, it has already become not much more than an empty shell with some of the outwardly visible trappings of Kemalist modernity: paintings and monuments of Atatürk, annual republican balls and mass children's gymnastics reminiscent of Nazi Germany and the Soviet Union, the lip-service to Kemalist secularity that never was. The lament of Sey Rıza of Dersim, 'this is a shame, this is injustice, this is a murder', muttered before his execution in 1937, proved to be prophetic for most of Turkey's republican history. Yet since the summer of 2010, his statue has adorned one of the main squares of Dersim's provincial capital. In a symposium at Tunceli University in October 2010, scholars and activists discussed the genocide during sessions that were also attended by the governor of the province. Even if Turkish supremacism is still celebrated every day in primary schools, where children are forced to blurt out the formula 'Happy is he who calls himself a Turk', even if militarist thinking is still instilled into young brains in 'National Security' lessons, even if the racist inscriptions on hilltops in the Kurdish regions wither away only slowly but surely, and even though courts still tend to defend the state against its citizens and hence often the perpetrator against the victim and the powerful against the weak, the political tradition that has created modern Turkey, Unionism and Kemalist nationalism, is obsolescent. Soon, it will be a thing of the past.

The question is what kind of new hegemonic bloc will replace the Kemalist republican one. Dependent on the outcome of this transformation is the question in what form Turkey will continue to exist. Will the nominally secular tutelage regime of the republican guardian state, in which the military watched over the government and the government over its people, be replaced by a new tutelage arrangement, in which religious networks and Islamic brotherhoods pull the strings? A regime in which the AKP acts much like an Islamic version of the Republican People's Party and imposes its conservative social values and its religiously grounded fears of a sexually liberating society through an ever-expanding Diyanet and an oppressive machinery of Islamic moral disciplining? This would be a sorry mimicry, an Islamic tutelage scenario of kinds, but it would not be all too surprising. After all, as the Canadian historian Margaret MacMillan asked in 2009, with regard to the great transformations of the last century, '[h]ow often have we seen revolutionaries, committed to building new worlds, slip back unconsciously into the habits and ways of those they have replaced?' Significantly, for the checks and balances in a democratic system to work, one would normally need at least two parties representing different social groups and following different political visions of the future. Much hence depends on the future of the main opposition, the Republican People's Party. Until now, the party has been held in the tight grip of militarist cadres sympathetic to the deep state. One wonders whether the RPP will be able to emancipate itself from its authoritarian legacy and its racist ideological baggage. Will it choose to transform itself into a modern social democrat party with a firm commitment to Turkey's Europeanization, or will it continue to look at the world through the spectacles of 1920s Europe?

Such a constructive opposition of reformed republicans could help the realization of the second scenario, that of a consolidating liberal democracy. Yet will the Turkish state be able to transform itself into a liberal body, whose *raison d'être* is neither the creation of a docile – if Western- or Eastern-looking – people, nor its self-perpetuation through polarization, but the good life of its citizens? Where the high courts' most noble role is to defend the individual against the abuses of the state, and the weak against the powerful, and not vice versa? Such a scenario is not impossible, but how it will become reality without the strong backing of the European Union is anybody's guess. And finally, there is the worst-case scenario: we could also imagine the resurgence of an invigorated guardian state, which would aim to restore its power by increasing levels of manipulation and violence – e.g. by inciting Turks against Kurds and by provoking the Kurdish guerrillas to wage war in the urban centres of western Turkey.

Connected to the scenarios of 'neo-Islamic tutelage', 'liberal state' and 'guardian resurgence' are the scenarios of Turkey's future boundaries. The first possibility is the continuation of Turkey as a large country, whose population is made up of Turks and Kurds and other minorities. The second is the division into a larger Turkish state and a small independent Kurdistan in the east amid ethnic violence and massacres directed against Kurds in the country's west. The scenario of guardian resilience would almost certainly lead to a break-up of the country, as the spirit of its governance would have to be based on the provocation of large-scale inter-ethnic violence between Turks and Kurds. A Kurdish–Turkish settlement with the broadest individual and group rights would be possible both in the liberal state scenario and at least potentially also in the Islamic tutelage scenario, provided that the hitherto dominant secular Kurdish nationalist movement is eclipsed by Islamic Kurdish movements. This, however, is unlikely.

Which combination of scenarios will become reality is based on a number of factors that are beyond the control of actors in Turkey: these range, most importantly, from the attitude of the European Union and the United States towards Turkey, to US policy in the Middle East and Iran, but also to developments in Iraq and the future of Iraqi Kurdistan. Whether Turkey will become a European Union member and a confident European, whether it will seek to balance its European with its Middle Eastern and Asian perspectives, or whether Europe will become an increasingly distant neighbour also depend on whether the European Union will be able to manage the virulently anti-Turkish voices in its ranks and reaffirm convincingly its commitment to Turkey's European future. Failing this, the European Union will continue to play a limited role with regard to Turkey, ambiguous at best and destructive at worst. European navel-gazing, rejection of world politics, populism and Islamophobia in response to the unsettling effects of globalization and economic crisis will not help pro-European reforms.

Based on the trajectory of the last three decades and beyond, the more likely scenario seems to be a mix of the liberal state and elements of the neo-Islamic tutelage scenario, with all the inherent contradictions that it would bring. Interestingly, this is also the assumption of a leaked report sent from the US embassy in Ankara. It suggests that 'Turkey will remain a complicated blend of world-class "Western" institutions, competencies, and orientation, and Middle Eastern culture and religion' (US embassy, Ankara, 2010). If this 'muddling through' option tilts towards the liberal side – if, for instance, the current AKP efforts to establish a democratic constitution that breaks with the authoritarian legacy of the 1980 coup continue, and indirect talks with the PKK prove conclusive – Turkey might be able to transform itself into a state of its citizens, in which ethnic belonging and religious conviction do not matter as much as they do now. Even in this half-baked scenario, Turkey in the next ten to twenty years would become much richer than it is now, and catch up with and probably eclipse the Mediterranean success story of Spain's late but forceful development in the 1980s and 1990s. Turkey's middle classes, including a growing Kurdish bourgeoisie, would further expand and grow more self-confident, and they would be less sympathetic to radical ideologies and militarism. Most likely, they would also be less prone to political manipulation. Such a Turkey would be more diverse and welcoming towards its ethnic, linguistic and religious differences and more at ease with its own traumatic history. Maybe it would be a country where the perpetrators of crimes against humanity were held responsible for their deeds, and where the state apologized for its responsibility for the suffering of so many of its own citizens. This, however, is only one of the possible scenarios for Turkey, which today still remains under the spell of the anger generated during decades of guardian state politics, state preservation and nationalism, and during repeated episodes of ethnic cleansing and mass violence. Whichever scenario in the end materializes, however, will matter not only to Turkey but to Europe and the Middle East. It will shape the future of close to five million Turks and Kurds as well as many Muslim immigrant communities in the European Union, the Muslims in the Balkans and the men and women in the streets of Damascus and Gaza.

# Postscript

In late November 2010, only a few weeks before *Angry Nation* went into print, the website WikiLeaks released thousands of memos, reports and policy briefs sent from US American embassies all over the world to the State Department. Also dubbed 'Cablegate', the leaked documents provided a fascinating insight into the workings of world diplomacy and the behind-the-scenes politics conducted by the United States, its allies and its enemies. I have only been able to include a couple of highly insightful quotes from dispatches prepared by the US embassy in Ankara. I would like to draw attention, however, to an important question, which the leaked documents raise: how transparent is government and how much manipulation is acceptable in democratic societies? Can transparency be suspended to satisfy the needs for a loosely defined 'national security'? To what extent can liberal states justify support for terrorist organizations and the financing of ethnic and religious conflict abroad? These are questions of great significance for Turkey, whose ruling elites have used such methods repeatedly over the last decades, in fact more in the realm of domestic politics than in its international relations.

'Cablegate' also reminds us that the 'deep state' and the machinations of unelected 'guardians' are not unique to Turkey. The records made available by WikiLeaks reinforce the argument that a significant part at least of the foreign policy of the United States is carried out in covert fashion and involves operations and strategies that strike us as cynical and would probably be deemed unlawful, if brought to a US court. 'Cablegate' hence helps us to put the Turkish deep state into perspective: behind-the-scenes politics, intrigues, conspiracies, misinformation and cooperation with the 'enemies of our enemy' are part and parcel of the invisible dimension of government, which all but the most transparent states possess. What has been different in Turkey in the three decades examined in this book is that this 'invisible state' has eventually become so powerful and 'visible' that the

legitimate government has been severely weakened. The circumstance
that so many of these clandestine connections are being exposed in
Turkey today may be a chance. Whether the spell of manipulation will
be broken in Turkey and elsewhere and transparent government and
democratic control prevail, however, will be dependent on the success
of those who struggle against government cover-ups and 'deep state'
manipulation.

# Sources

## Interview partners

Nebahat Akkoç, chair of the women's organization KAMER, *Kadın Merkezi* (Women's Centre), Diyarbakır, 13 July 2009.

Cengiz Algan, activist at the anti-racist and anti-nationalist movement *Irkçılığa ve Milliyetçiliğe DurDe* (Say No to Racism and Nationalism), Istanbul, 8 July 2009.

Şahin Alpay, professor of political science at Bahçeşehir University, and columnist for the newspapers *Zaman* and *Today's Zaman*, Istanbul, 13 July 2009.

Mehmet Bekaroğlu, politician and former mayoral candidate for Istanbul of the Islamist Felicity Party, Ankara, 13 July 2009.

Şeyhmus Bey, employee of the municipality of Greater Diyarbakır, Diyarbakır, 1 August 1996.

Fatma Budak, former political activist, now feminist and counsellor at the Women's shelter foundation *Mor Çatı* (Purple Roof), Istanbul, 15 September 2009.

Osman Can, legal scholar and former rapporteur at the Constitutional Court, Ankara, 10 July 2009.

Abdullah Demirbaş, mayor of the Suriçi district of Diyarbakır for the pro-Kurdish DTP, Diyarbakır, 11 July 2009.

Ayşe Kadıoğlu, professor of political science at Sabanci University and public intellectual, Istanbul, 8 July 2009.

Karin Karakaşlı, writer and columnist, Istanbul, 9 July 2009.

Osman Kavala, businessman and curator of the cultural initiative *Anadolu Sanat* (Anatolian Art), Istanbul, 9 July 2009.

Buse Kılıçkaya, member of the queer rights organization *Pembe Hayat* (Pink Life), Ankara, 2 April 2009.

Suat Kınıklıoğlu, chair of the Foreign Affairs Committee of the Justice and Development Party, Ankara, 10 July 2009.

Frederic Misrahi, expert at the delegation of the European Union in Ankara, Ankara, 12 July 2009.

Tezer Öktem, former lecturer at the University of Istanbul, Istanbul, 10 February 2003.

Nora Onar, professor of international relations at Istanbul's Bahçeşehir University, Istanbul, 9 July 2009.

Sırrı Süreyya Önder, director of the film *Beynelmilel* (The International) and columnist for the newspaper *Habertürk*, Istanbul, 8 July 2009.

Mahmut Ortakaya, former chair of the Diyarbakır Medical Chamber, Diyarbakır, 11 July 2009.

Fatma Sayman, former political activist, now psychologist, Istanbul, 14 June 2009.

Ece Temelkuran, lawyer, author and investigative journalist at the newspaper *Habertürk*, Oxford, 15 June 2009.

Osman Ulagay, economist and journalist at the newspaper *Milliyet*, Istanbul, 9 July 2009.

## Further reading on Turkey

Ahmad, Feroz (1993) *The Making of Modern Turkey*, London: Routledge.

Anastasakis, Othon, Kalypso Aude Nicolaidis and Kerem Öktem (eds) (2009) *In the Long Shadow of Europe: Greeks and Turks in the era of postnationalism*, Leiden/Boston, MA: Martinus Nijhoff.

Bloxham, Donald (2005) *The Great Game of Genocide: Imperialism, nationalism and the destruction of the Ottoman Armenians*, Oxford: Oxford University Press.

Bozdogan, Sibel and Resat Kasaba (eds) (1997) *Rethinking Modernity and National Identity in Turkey*, Seattle/London: University of Washington Press.

Clark, Bruce (2006) *Twice a Stranger: How mass expulsion forged modern Greece and Turkey*, London: Granta.

De Bellaigue, Christopher (2009) *Rebel Land: Among Turkey's forgotten peoples*, London: Bloomsbury.

Finkel, Andrew (2011) *Turkey. What Everyone Needs to Know*, Oxford: Oxford University Press.

Kadıoğlu, Ayşe and Fuat Keyman (eds) (2010) *Symbiotic Antagonisms: Competing nationalisms in Turkey*, Utah: University of Utah Press.

Kandiyoti, Deniz and Ayşe Saktanber (eds) (2002) *Fragments of Culture: The everyday of modern Turkey*, London: I. B. Tauris.

Kasaba, Reşat (ed.) (2006) *The Cambridge History of Turkey: Turkey in the modern world*, Cambridge: Cambridge University Press.

Kedourie, Sylvia (ed.) (1999) *Turkey Before and After Atatürk: Internal and external affairs*, London: Frank Cass.

Ker-Lindsay, James (2011) *The Cyprus Problem. What Everyone Needs to Know*, Oxford: Oxford University Press.

Kerslake, Celia J., Kerem Öktem and Philip Robins (eds) (2010) *Turkey's Engagement with Modernity: Conflict and change in the twentieth century*, Basingstoke: Palgrave Macmillan.

Kieser, Hans-Lukas (ed.) (2006) *Turkey Beyond Nationalism: Towards postnationalist identities*, London: I. B. Tauris.

Mardin, Serif (2006) *Religion, Society, and Modernity in Turkey*, Syracuse, NY: Syracuse University Press.

McDowall, David (2004) *A Modern History of the Kurds*, London: I. B. Tauris.

Navaro-Yashin, Yael (2002) *Faces of the State: Secularism and public life in Turkey*, Princeton, NJ/Oxford: Princeton University Press.

Oran, Baskın (ed.) (2010) *Turkish Foreign Policy – Facts, Documents, and Comments*, Utah: Utah University Press.

Özyürek, Esra (2006) *Nostalgia for the Modern: State secularism and everyday politics in Turkey*, Durham, NC/London: Duke University Press.

Pamuk, Orhan (2005) *Istanbul: Memories of a city*, London: Faber and Faber.

Pope, Nicole and Hugh (2004) *Turkey Unveiled: A history of modern Turkey*, Woodstock: Overlook Press.

Robins, Philip (2002) *Suits and Uniforms. Turkish Foreign Policy Since the Cold War*, London: Hurst.

Temelkuran, Ece (2010) *Deep Mountain*, London: Verso.

Tuğal, Cihan (2009) *Passive Revolution. Absorbing the Islamic Challenge to Capitalism*, Stanford, CA: Stanford University Press.

Üngör, Uğur Ümit (2011) *Mass Violence and the Nation State in Eastern Turkey, 1913–1950*, Oxford: Oxford University Press.

Zürcher, Erik J. (2004) *Turkey: A modern history*, London: I. B. Tauris.

**Literature**

Adıvar, Halide Edib (2005) *Memoirs of Halidé Edib*, Piscataway, NJ: Gorgias Press.

Akçam, Taner (2004) *From Empire to Republic: Turkish nationalism and the Armenian genocide*, London: Zed Books.

Aker, Tamer, Ayşe Betul Celik, Dilek Kurban, Turgay Unalan and Deniz Yukseker (2006) *Coming to Terms with Forced Migration: Post-displacement restitution of citizenship rights in Turkey*, Istanbul: TESEV.

Aktar, Ayhan (2000) *Varlık Vergisi ve 'Türkleştirme' Politikaları*, Istanbul: İletişim Yayınevi.

— (2007) 'Debating the Armenian massacres in the last Ottoman parliament, November–December 1918', *History Workshop Journal*, 64: 241–70.

Altinay, Ayşe Gül (2005) *The Myth of the Military Nation. Militarism, Gender, and Education in Turkey*, New York: Palgrave Macmillan.

Altunisik, Meliha (2000) 'The Turkish–Israeli *rapprochement* in the post-Cold War era', *Middle Eastern Studies*, 36(2).

Anastasakis, Othon, Kalypso Nicolaidis and Kerem Öktem (eds) (2009) *In the Long Shadow of Europe: Greeks and Turks in the era of postnationalism*, Leiden/Boston, MA: Martinus Nijhoff.

Appadurai, Arjun (2006) *Fear of Small Numbers. An Essay on the Geography of Anger*, Durham, NC/London: Duke University Press.

Arıoba, Süreyya (2009) *The Istanbul Pogrom of 6/7 September 1955 and Its Impact on the Turkish Armenian Community*, Unpublished BA thesis, Oriental Institute, University of Oxford, 2009.

Ataman, Muhiddin (2002) 'Özal leadership and restructuring of Turkish ethnic policy in the 1980s', *Middle Eastern Studies*, 38(4): 123–42.

Ayata, Bilgin (2008) 'Mapping Euro-Kurdistan', *Middle Eastern Report*, 247: 18–24.

Ayata, Bilgin and Deniz Yükseker (2005) 'A belated awakening: national and international responses to the internal displacement of Kurds in Turkey', *New Perspectives on Turkey*, 32: 5–43.

Bali, Rıfat (2005) *The 'Varlık Vergisi' affair. A Study on Its Legacy*, Istanbul: Isis Press.

— (2008) *1934 Trakya Olayları*, Istanbul: Kitabevi Yayınları.

Bayraktar, Hatice (2006) 'The anti-Jewish pogrom in eastern Thrace in 1934: new evidence for the responsibility of the Turkish government', *Patterns of Prejudice*, 40(2).

Bechev, Dimitar and Kalypso Nicolaidis (2010) *Mediterranean Frontiers: Borders, conflict and memory in a transnational world*, London: Tauris Academic Studies.

Birand, Mehmed Ali (1991) *Shirts of Steel*, London: I. B. Tauris.

Bloxham, Donald (2005) *The Great Game of Genocide*, New York: Oxford University Press.

Bozdogan, Sibel (2001) *Modernism and Nation Building: Turkish architectural culture in the early republic*, Seattle: University of Washington Press.

Bozdogan, Sibel and Resat Kasaba (eds) (1997) *Rethinking Modernity and National Identity in Turkey*, Seattle/London: University of Washington Press.

Bruinessen, Martin van (1978) *Agha, Shaikh and State: On the social and political organization of Kurdistan*, Utrecht: Rijksuniversiteit.

— (1996) 'Turks, Kurds and the Alevi revival in Turkey', *Middle East Report*, 200, July–September 1996.

Brussels European Council (2004) *16/17 December 2004, Presidency Conclusions*, Council of the European Union, www.consilium.europa.eu/ueDocs/cms_Data/docs/pressData/en/ec/83201.pdf.

Çalışlar, Ipek (2006) *Latife Hanım*, Istanbul: Doğan Kitap.

Çetin, Fethiye (2008) *My Grandmother: A memoir*, London: Verso.

Chomsky, Noam (2004) *Hegemony or Survival*, London: Penguin.

Clark, Bruce (2006) *Twice a Stranger: How mass expulsion forged modern Greece and Turkey*, London: Granta.

Copenhagen European Council (2003) *12 and 13 December 2002, Presidency Conclusions*, Council of the European Union, www.consilium.europa.eu/ueDocs/cms_Data/docs/pressData/en/ec/73842.pdf.

Dadrian, Vahakn N. (1995) *The History of the Armenian Genocide: Ethnic conflict from the Balkans to Anatolia to the Caucasus*, Oxford: Berghahn Books.

Danforth, Nicholas (2008) 'Ideology and pragmatism in Turkish foreign policy: from Atatürk to the AKP', *Turkish Policy Quarterly*, 7(3): 83–95.

Davison, Roderic H. (1963) *Reform in the Ottoman Empire, 1856–1876*, Princeton, NJ: Princeton University Press.

Demetriou, Olga (2005) 'To cross or not to cross? Subjectivization and the absent state in Cyprus', *Journal of the Royal Anthropological Institute*, 13(4): 987–1005.

Demetriu, Thanos and Sotiris Vlahos (2009) *Ihanete uğramış ayaklanma*, Ankara: Arkadaş Yayınları.

Demirel, Tanel (2003) 'The Turkish military's decision to intervene: 12 September 1980', *Armed Forces & Society*, 29(253).

De Waal, Thomas (2010) *The Caucasus. An Introduction*, New York: Oxford University Press.

Dink, Hrant (2005) 'The water finds its crack: an Armenian in Turkey', *Open Democracy*, 13 December, www.opendemocracy.net/democracy-turkey/europe_turkey_armenia_3118.jsp.

Dressler, Markus (2002) *Die Alevitische Religion: Traditionslinien und Neubestimmungen*, Würzburg: Deutsche Morgenländische Gesellschaft.

Dündar, Fuat (2008) *Modern Türkiye'nin Şifresi. İttihat ve Terakki'nin Etnisite Mühendisliği (1913–1918)*, Istanbul: İletişim.

Ersanlı-Behar, Büşra (2003) *Iktidar ve tarih: Türkiye'de 'Resmi tarih' tezinin olusumu, 1929–1937*, Istanbul: AFA.

Eşsiz, Veysel (2009) 'The Mardin massacre and the village guard system in Turkey', *Open Democracy*, 28 May, www.opendemocracy.net/article/the-mardin-massacre-and-the-village-guard-system-in-turkey.

European Stability Initiative (2005) *Islamic Calvinists. Change and Conservatism in Central Anatolia*, Berlin/Istanbul.

— (2008) *Turkey's Dark Side. Party Closures, Conspiracies and the Future of Democracy*, Berlin/Istanbul.

Faroqhi, Souraiya (2004) *The Ottoman Empire and the World Around It*, London: I. B. Tauris.

Gambetti, Zeynep (2005) 'The conflictual (trans)formation of the public sphere in urban space: the case of Diyarbakir', *New Perspectives on Turkey*, 32: 43–71.

Garton Ash, Timothy (1990) *We the People: The revolution of '89 witnessed in Warsaw, Budapest, Berlin and Prague*, Cambridge: Granta.

— (1999) *History of the Present: Essays, sketches and dispatches from Europe in the 1990s*, London: Allen Lane, Penguin Press.

— (2009) *Facts are Subversive. Political Writings from a Decade without a Name*, London: Atlantic.

Genç Siviller (2009) *Sizin İçin Geldiklerinde Orada Olacağız*, www.gencsiviller.net/haber.php?haber_id=210.

Gocek, Fatma Muge (2011) *The Transformation of Turkey: Redefining state and society from the Ottoman empire to the modern era*, London, I. B. Tauris.

Göksu, Saime and Edward Timms (eds) (1999) *Romantic Communist: The life and work of Nazım Hikmet,* London: Hurst.

Gourevitch, Philip (1998) *We wish to inform you that tomorrow we will be killed with our families: Stories from Rwanda*, New York: Farrar, Straus and Giroux.

Güllapoğlu, Fatih (1991) *Tanksız Topsuz Harekat*, Istanbul: Tekin Yayınevi.

Gunter, Michael M. (2008) *The Kurds Ascending: The evolving solution to the Kurdish problem in Iraq and Turkey*, New York: Palgrave Macmillan.

Güven, Dilek (2005) *6–7 Eylül Olayları*, Istanbul: Yurt Yayınları.

Güvenç, Bozkurt (ed.) (1975) *Social Change in Izmir: A collection of five papers.* Ankara: Social Science Association.

Hale, William M. (2000) *Turkish Foreign Policy, 1774–2000*, London: Frank Cass.

Hamilton, Alastair, Maurits H. van den Boogert and Bart Westerweel (2005) *The Republic of Letters and the Levant*, Leiden/Boston, MA: Brill.

Hanioğlu, M. Şükrü (2001) *Preparation for a Revolution: The Young Turks, 1902–1908*, New York: Oxford University Press.

— (2008) *A Brief History of the Late Ottoman Empire*, Princeton, NJ: Princeton University Press.

Hann, Chris (1995) 'Subverting strong states: the dialectics of social engineering in Hungary and Turkey', *Daedalus*, 124(2): 133–53.

Hartley, L. P. (1985) *The Go-between*, London: Heinemann Educational.

Hiçyılmaz, Bülent (1984) 'Eşkiyayı Asmayıp da Besleyelim mi?', *Milliyet*, 4 October.

Hirschon, Renee (ed.) (2003) *Crossing the Aegean: An appraisal of the 1923 compulsory population exchange between Greece and Turkey*, New York/ Oxford: Berghahn.

Human Rights Watch (1994) *Turkey. Forced Displacement of Ethnic Kurds from Southeastern Turkey*, Helsinki: HRW.

İnsel, Ahmet (2009) 'This conduct was a crime against humanity: an evaluation of the initiative to apologize to the Armenians' (trans. Ayşe Ünaldı and Kenan Erçel), *Birikim*, 238, February.

Itzkowitz, Norman (1971) *Ottoman Empire and Islamic Tradition*, Chicago, IL: University of Chicago Press.

Kaplan, Sam (2006) *The Pedagogical State: Education and the politics of national culture in post-1980 Turkey*, Stanford, CA: Stanford University Press.

Ker-Lindsay, James (2000) 'Greek–Turkish rapprochement: the impact of "disaster diplomacy"?', *Cambridge Review of international Affairs*, 14(1): 215–32.

Ker-Lindsay, James and Hubert Faustmann (eds) (2009) *The Government and Politics of Cyprus*, Oxford: Peter Lang.

Kieser, Hans-Lukas (ed.) (2006) *Turkey beyond Nationalism: Towards post-nationalist identities*, London, I. B. Tauris.

Kieser, Hans-Lukas, Astrid Meier and Walter Stoffel (eds) (2008) *Revolution islamischen Rechts. Das Schweizerische ZGB in der Türkei*, Zurich: Chronos Verlag.

Kinzer, Stephen (2001) *Turkey between Two Worlds*, New York: Farrar, Straus and Giroux.

Köker, Osman (ed.) (2005) *Armenians in Turkey 100 years ago. With the Postcards from the Collection of Orlando Carlo Calumeno*, Istanbul: Bir Zamanlar Yayıncılık.

Korkut, Hüseyin (2007) *Ateş Manisa'ya da Düştü*, Istanbul: Imge Kitabevi.

Kurdish Human Rights Project (2002) *Internal Displacement*, London: KHRP.

Lewis, Geoffrey (1999) *The Turkish Language Reform: A catastrophic success*, Oxford: Oxford University Press.

MacMillan, Margaret (2009) *The Uses and Abuses of History*, London: Profile Books.

Maksudyan, Nazan (2005) *Türklüğü Ölçmek, Bilimkurgusal Antropoloji ve Türk Milliyetçiliğinin Irkçı Çehresi 1925–1939*, Istanbul: Metis Yayınları.

Mango, Andrew (2004) *Atatürk*, London: John Murray.

Marcus, Aliza (1996) 'Should I shoot you? An eyewitness account of an Alevi uprising in Gazi', *Middle East Report*, 199, April–June.

Mardin, Şerif (2000 [1962]) *The Genesis of Young Ottoman Thought. A Study in the Modernization of Turkish Political Ideas*, Princeton, NJ: Princeton University Press.

Mater, Nadire (2005) *Voices from the Front, Turkish Soldiers on the War with the Kurdish Guerrillas*, Basingstoke: Palgrave Macmillan.

Mazower, Mark (2004) *Salonica. City of Ghosts*, London: HarperCollins.

McCarthy, Justin (1996) *Death and Exile: The ethnic cleansing of Ottoman Muslims, 1821–1922*, Princeton, NJ: Darwin Press.

McCarthy, Justin, Esat Arslan, Cemalettin Taşkıran and Ömer Turan (2006) *The Armenian Rebellion at Van*, Salt Lake City: University of Utah Press.

McDowall, David (2000) *A Modern History of the Kurds*, London: I. B. Tauris.

Milliyet (1996) 'Çillerden şok eden sözler: Abdullah Çatlı şerefli', 27 November.

Milton, Giles (2009) *Paradise Lost. Smyrna 1922: The destruction of Islam's city of tolerance*, London: Sceptre.

Nicolaidis, Kalypso and Stephen Weatherill (2003) *Whose Europe?: National models and the constitution of the European Union*, Oxford: Oxuniprint.

Ökte, Faik (1948) *Varlık Vergisi Faciası*, Istanbul: Nebioğlu Kitapevi.

Öktem, Kerem (2006) 'Return of the Turkish "State of Exception"', *Middle East Report Online*, June.

— (2007) 'Harbinger of Turkey's second republic', *Middle East Report Online*.

— (2008a) 'Being Muslim at the margins: Alevis and the AKP', *Middle East Report*, 246, www.merip.org/mer/mer246/oktem.html.

— (2008b) 'Another struggle: sexual identity politics in unsettled Turkey', *Middle East Report Online*, September.

— (2008c) 'The nation's imprint: demographic engineering and the change of toponyms in republican Turkey', *European Journal of Turkish Studies*, November.

— (2008d) *The Patronising Embrace: Turkey's new Kurdish strategy*, Basle: Stiftung Forschungsstelle Schweiz-Türkei.

— (2009a) 'The Armenia–Turkey process: don't stop now', *Open Democracy*, October, www.opendemocracy.net/article/armenia/the-armenia-turkey-process-don-t-stop-now.

— (2009b) 'Turkey and Israel: ends and beginnings', *Open Democracy*, December, www.opendemocracy.net/kerem-oktem/turkey-and-israel-ends-and-beginnings.

— (2009c) 'Un cosmopolitanisme sans fierté', *La Pensée de Midi*, 29.

— (2010) 'Alles Stehende verdampft: Homosexuelle Bewegungen und Identitäten im Kontext patriarchaler Machstrukturen in der Türkei', in Elisabeth Holzleithner and Sabine Strasser, *Multikulturalismus queer gelesen. Zwangsverheiratung und gleichgeschlechtliche Ehe in pluralen Gesellschaften*, Frankfurt: Campus.

Olson, Robert (1989) *The Emergence of Kurdish Nationalism and the Sheikh Said Rebellion, 1880–1925*, Austin: University of Texas Press.

— (2000) 'The Kurdish rebellions of Sheikh Said (1925), Mt Ararat (1930), and Dersim (1937–8): their impact on the development of the Turkish air force and on Kurdish and Turkish nationalism', *Die Welt des Islams*, 40(1): 67–94.

Oran, Baskın (2005) *M.K. Adlı Çocuğun Tehcir Anıları – 1915 ve Sonrası*, Istanbul: Iletisim Publishers.

— (2006) *Kenan Evren'in yazılmamış Anıları*, Istanbul: Iletişm.

Özal, Turgut (1991) *Turkey in Europe and Europe in Turkey*, Nicosia: K. Rustem & Brother.

Ozkan, Gulcin (2005) 'Currency and financial crises in Turkey 2000–2001: bad fundamentals or bad luck?', *World Economy*, 28(4): 541–72.

Özkirimli, Umut and Spyros A. Sofos (2008) *Tormented by History: Nationalism in Greece and Turkey*, London: Hurst.

Pamuk, Orhan (2004) *Snow*, London: Faber and Faber.

Pamuk, Şevket (2004) 'The evolution of financial institutions in the Ottoman Empire, 1600–1914', *Financial History Review*, 11(1): 7–32.

Peirce, Leslie (1993) *The Imperial Harem: Women and sovereignty in the Ottoman Empire*, New York: Oxford University Press.

Perle, Richard (1999) 'A Turkish story, the first annual Robert Strausz-Hupé Lecture', *Foreign Policy Research Institute Wire*, 7(11), www.fpri.org/fpriwire/0711.199909.perle.turkishstory.html.

Poulton, Hugh (1997) *Top Hat, Grey Wolf and Crescent: Turkish nationalism and the Turkish Republic*, London: Hurst.

Pulur, Hasan (1997) *Milliyet*, 2 January.

Quataert, Donald, Çağlar Keyder and Eyüp Özveren (1993) 'Port cities of the eastern Mediterranean, 1800–1914', *Review*, special issue, Fall.

Radikal (2005) Headlines, 25 September.

Robins, Philip (1997) 'Foreign policy under Erbakan', *Survival*, 39(2): 82–100.

— (2002) *Suits and Uniforms. Turkish Foreign Policy Since the Cold War*, London: Hurst.

Rogan, Eugene (2009) *The Arabs. A History*, London: Allen Lane.

Seal, Jeremy (1996) *A Fez of the Heart: Travels around Turkey in search of a hat*, London: Picador.

Sever, Metin and Cem Dizdar (1993), *Cumhuriyet Tartışmaları*, Ankara: Başak, cited in Sedat Laciner (2009), 'Turgut Özal period in Turkish foreign policy: Özalism', *USAK Yearbook of International Politics and Law*, 2: 153–205.

Shafak, Elif (2005) *Flea Palace*, London: Marion Boyars.

— (2007) *The Bastard of Istanbul*, London: Viking.

Shaw, Stanford J. (2000) *From Empire to Republic: The Turkish war of national liberation, 1918–1923*, Ankara: Türk Tarih Kurumu Basimevı.

Suny, Ronald Grigor, Fatma Muge Gocek and Norman M. Naimark (eds) (2011) *A Question of Genocide. Armenians and Turks at the End of the Ottoman Empire*, Oxford: Oxford University Press.

T. C. Başbakanlık (1981) *T. C. Devlet Başkanı Orgeneral Kenan Evren'in Söylev ve Demeçleri*, Ankara: Başbakanlık Basımevi.

Tachau, Frank and Metin Heper (1983) 'The state, politics, and the military in Turkey', *Comparative Politics*, 16(1): 17–33.

Traboulsi, Fawwaz (2007) *A Modern History of Lebanon*, London: Pluto Press.

US Embassy Ankara (2004) 'Turkish PM goes to Washington. How strong a leader in the face of strong challenges?' 20 January, http://wikileaks.ch/cable/2004/01/04ANKARA348.html.

— (2010) 'What lies beneath Ankara's new foreign policy?' 20 January, http://wikileaks.ch/cable/2010/01/10ANKARA87.html

Veremis, Thanos M. (2007) *Greeks and Turks in War and Peace*, Athens: Athens News.

Volkan, Vamik D. and Norman Itzkowitz (1984) *The Immortal Atatürk: A psychobiography*, Chicago, IL: University of Chicago Press.

Vryonis, Speros (2005) *The Mechanism of Catastrophe: The Turkish pogrom of September 6–7, 1955, and the destruction of the Greek community of Istanbul*, New York: greekworks.com.

Watts, Nicole F. (2004) 'Turkey's tentative opening to Kurdishness', *Middle East Report Online*, June.

White, Paul J. (2006) *Primitive Rebels or Revolutionary Modernizers? The Kurdish Nationalist Movement in Turkey*, London: Zed Books.

Yavuz, Hakan and John L. Esposito (eds) (2003) *Turkish Islam and the Secular State. The Gülen Movement*, Syracuse, NY: Syracuse University Press.

Zeldin, Theodore, (1973) *A History of French Passions. Politics and Anger*, vol. 2, Oxford: Oxford University Press.

Žižek, Slavoj (2008) *Violence. Six Sideways Reflections*, London: Profile Books.

Zürcher, Erik-Jan (2009) 'The late Ottoman Empire as laboratory of demographic engineering', *Il mestiere di storico*, 1: 7–18.

— (2010) *The Young Turk Legacy and Nation Building: From the Ottoman Empire to Atatürk's Turkey*, London: I. B. Tauris.

# Index

of, 70; foreign policy of, 77; liberal
views of, 74; 'new man' project, 72
Özbilgin, Mustafa Yücel, 150
Özkök, Hilmi, 124

Palestinian training camps, 49
Pamuk, Orhan, 147; *Istanbul:
memories of a city*, 10; *Snow*, 158
Papadopoulos, Tassos, 137, 138
Papandreou, Giorgios, 114
Peace and Democracy Party (*Barış ve
Demokrasi Partisi* – BDP), 169, 184
penal code: adopted from Italy, 29;
Article 301, 146, 147; reform of, 135
(revocations of, 143)
People's Houses (*Halkevleri*), 30
People's Labour Party (*Halkın Emek
Partisi* – HEP), 93
People's Liberation Army of Turkey
(*Türkiye Halk Kurtuluş Ordusu*),
48, 50, 53
People's Liberation Front, 49, 50
Peres, Shimon: Erdoğan's attack on,
176; invited to Turkey, 175
Perinçek, Doğu, 149
Perle, Richard, 59
Petroleum Pipeline Corporation,
89–90
Pittard, Eugene, 31
pogroms: against Greeks and non-
Muslims in Istanbul (1955), 44–5,
145, 148; against Kurds, 161, 169
*see also* Kurds
police custody, deaths in, 182
Police Law (2007), 182
polygamy, 29
Populist Party (*Halkçı Parti*), 66
poverty: of Kurds, 93; urban, 70
Presidency of Religious Affairs, 30
prisons, 58–60
privatization, 116–17, 118
protectionism, 69

Qaeda, al-, 134
Qur'an, Turkish translation of, 30

radicalization of political groups,
8, 47; of Islamist groups, 131;

of Kurdish nationalists, 65; of
rightwing groups, 48
*Radikal* newspaper, 149
railways, building of, 17
rape, 36
referendum (1982), 61
religion, 33–5
Republican Peasants and Nation
Party (*Cumhuriyetçi Köylü Millet
Partisi* – CKMP), 47
Republican People's Party
(*Cumhuriyet Halk Partisi* – RPP), 7,
9, 27, 29, 30, 38, 40, 41, 46, 47, 51,
85, 117, 120, 123, 153, 154, 155, 158,
164, 165, 168, 184, 185, 187
Revolution of 1908, 22
Revolutionary Culture Hearths of
the East (*Doğu Devrimci Kültür
Ocakları*), 47
Revolutionary Path (*Devrimci Yol*), 53
Revolutionary Workers' Unions
(*Devrimci İşçi Dernekleri
Federasyonu*), 48
Rıza, Sey, 186
roads, building of, 17, 43
Roma associations, 183
Romania, 17
Russia, 19, 25, 70, 81, 94; trading
relations with, 173

Sabahaddin, Prince, 22
Sabancı family, 69
Sağlar, Fikri, 96
Şahin, Leyla, headscarf case, 136
Said Piran, Sheikh, 35
Said-i-Nursi, Bediüzzaman, 128
Sakık, Şemdin, 109
Samast, Ogün, 150, 151
Santoro, Andrea, killing of, 150, 151
Sarıkaya, Ferhat, 142; dismissal of, 184
Sarkozy, Nicolas, 180; EU
intervention of, 140, 179
'Say No to Racism and Nationalism'
campaign (DurDe), 132, 151
Saylan, Türkan, 163
Sayman, Fatma, 51
Schabowski, Günther, 56
schools: Gülen schools, 80; military